EurographicSeminars

Tutorials and Perspectives in Computer Graphics

Edited by W. T. Hewitt, R. Gnatz, and D. A. Duce

D. B. Arnold R. A. Day D. A. Duce C. Fuhrhop
J. R. Gallop R. Maybury D. C. Sutcliffe (Eds.)

Graphics and Communications

Proceedings of an International Workshop
Breuberg, FRG, October 15–17, 1990

With 84 Figures and 7 Tables

Springer-Verlag
Berlin Heidelberg New York
London Paris Tokyo
Hong Kong Barcelona
Budapest

EurographicSeminars

Edited by W. T. Hewitt, R. Gnatz, and D. A. Duce
for EUROGRAPHICS -
The European Association for Computer Graphics
P. O. Box 16, CH-1288 Aire-la-Ville, Switzerland

Volume Editors

David B. Arnold
School of Information Systems
University of East Anglia
Norwich NR4 7TJ, UK

Robert A. Day, David A. Duce, Julian R. Gallop,
Robert Maybury, and Dale C. Sutcliffe
Informatics Department
Rutherford Appleton Laboratory
Chilton, Didcot, Oxon OX11 0QX, UK

Christian Fuhrhop
GMD-FOKUS
Hardenbergplatz 2, W-1000 Berlin 12, FRG

ISBN 3-540-54001-6 Springer-Verlag Berlin Heidelberg New York
ISBN 0-387-54001-6 Springer-Verlag New York Berlin Heidelberg

Library of Congress Cataloging-in-Publication Data
Graphics and communications: proceedings of an international workshop, Breuberg, FRG, October 15–17, 1990 / D. B. Arnold (eds.) ... [et al.].
p. cm. - (Eurographic seminars)
Proceedings of an International Workshop on Graphics and Communications.
Includes bibliographical references.
ISBN 0-387-54001-6
1. Computer graphics - Congresses. 2. Computer networks - Congresses. I. Arnold, David B. II. International Workshop on Graphics and Communications (1990: Breuberg, Hessen, Germany) III. Series. T385.G6964 1991 006.6-dc20 91-28024 CIP

Typesetting: Camera ready by author

45/3140-543210 - Printed on acid-free paper

Preface

Hotel Burgterrasse, high above the village of Breuberg in the state of Hessen in Germany, was the location for an international Workshop on Graphics and Communications, which took place from 15 to 17 October, 1990. The Workshop was organised within the Esprit II research project 2463, ARGOSI (Applications Related Graphics and OSI Standards Integration). The Workshop was included in the Eurographics workshop programme for 1990.

The ARGOSI project essentially arose from the observation that international standards in the graphics and networking areas were, generally speaking, being developed in isolation and insufficient attention was being paid to the needs of applications whose requirements spanned several standards. The importance of the integration of graphics and networking has been growing over recent years, with the growth of interest in multi-media systems to support cooperative working, and the use of computer graphics techniques in the visualization of the results of scientific and engineering computations. The latter frequently involve high speed links between workstations and supercomputers.

The organizing committee for the workshop:

Co-Chairmen: D.B. Arnold, F. Dilonardo
Programme Committee: A. Ducrot, J. Rix, G. Pfaff, J.-J. Bardyn, R. Fairbairns, E. Pelucchi, M. Loupis, R.A. Day, G.J. Reynolds, P. Egloff, F. Dilonardo, L. Moltedo

was drawn from the partners in the ARGOSI project. We wish to express our thanks to them for their contribution, and especially we express our thanks to the participants and authors, for making a highly successful workshop.

Particular thanks are due to David Duce, Bob Day and Lilian Valentine of Rutherford Appleton Laboratory, who handled much of the organisation, and to Stefan Noll of FhG-AGD, who handled the local arrangements.The staff of the Hotel Burgterrasse provided an excellent environment for a workshop and the prevailing climatic conditions (mist and low cloud) ensured effective isolation from the real world of the valley below and detraction from the window as the 'area of maximum interest in any meeting'!

D.B. Arnold
R.A. Day
D.A. Duce
C. Fuhrhop
J.R. Gallop
R. Maybury
D.C. Sutcliffe

Table of Contents

Part I

Workshop Report and Conclusions

Chapter 1

Introduction

1.1 Background

The ARGOSI project (Applications Related Graphics and OSI Standards Integration) was proposed in response to the first call for proposals under the second European Strategic Programme for Research and Development in Information Technology (ESPRIT II). The project began in March 1989 with a project duration of 3 years. It has involved twelve organizations:

Prime Contractor	Thomson-CSF	France
Partners	INRIA	France
	RAL	UK
	Hitec	Greece
	Tecsiel	Italy
	COSI	Italy
	GMD-FOKUS	Germany
Associated Partners	University of East Anglia	UK
	Laser-Scan	UK
	GESI	Italy
	FhG-AGD	Germany
	GTS-GRAL	Germany

The project's aims are to:

(1) advance the state of the art in the transfer and use of graphical information across international networks;

(2) improve the quality and applicability of Standards in this area.

As part of the research it was proposed that a number of workshops would be run, bringing together experts from the graphics and networking areas, in order to examine relevant issues about the interactions between the two. This book is the proceedings of the first Workshop which was held in Breuberg, Germany on 15–17 October 1990. For more details of the ARGOSI project the reader is referred to the paper by Day *et al.* included in Part II of this book.

The Workshop was attended by 29 invited participants from 9 countries. A complete list is included at the end of the book.

1.2 Structure

The Workshop was run in eight sessions over the three day period with papers presented in the first six sessions followed by a session of parallel small group discussions of some of the questions resulting from the presentations. The Workshop concluded with a plenary session to which the small groups reported their discussions. Following the reports, which are included in the next three chapters, the plenary session discussed future progression of the work. The results of this discussion are included in Chapter 5.

The papers were presented in the order in which they are included in Part II of this book. The first session was an introduction to the Workshop, the ARGOSI project and the overlap between graphics and networks.

The second session focussed on the current uses of networking and graphics and included presentations on the ODA Standard for interchanging compound documents, a distributed application involving use of two 64Kbit/sec channels and a description of the work on classification of graphics applications undertaken in the ARGOSI project. Unfortunately it has not been possible to include a paper of the talk given by K. Klement. A paper by C.T. Little on the requirements placed on graphics and networking by applications in meteorology is also included in this session. The paper was submitted to the Workshop but the author was unfortunately unable to attend to present his findings due to an unavoidable clash of dates.

Four sessions of papers were presented on the second day. The two sessions in the morning concentrated on access to large volumes of remotely stored graphics with six presentations covering a number of topics. In the first session the standards requirements for MIS systems for road transport management, the BERKOM broadband interconnect trial and the PIC metafile format were presented. The second session looked at the various aspects of the CGM Standard's applicability in networked applications with presentations describing CGM's relation to the FTAM Standard and to the concept of Application Profiles, and the use of access to subunits within CGMs.

A number of presentations on the afternoon of the second day focussed on the theme of distributed interactive graphics. The afternoon began with a paper describing current Standards efforts in Image Interchange. Four of the papers which followed over the two sessions looked at aspects of the relationship between ISO work in graphics and networking and the X system. There were also extra papers presented on the STEP product interchange Standard and practical issues in using CGMs in a heterogeneous environment.

The sessions of presentations concluded with one describing some of the new problems to be faced in implementing networked multi-media applications.

1.3 Discussions

Following the final presentation the group spent some time analyzing themes which appeared to have recurred in the discussions following each paper. Six major topics were identified.

1.3.1 Impact of Multi-media

A range of related issues arose from considering future directions which multi-media applications, including voice and video as well as generative graphics, would take. Given the difficulties encountered in merging the use of current networks and graphics there was a strong feeling that further extension to other media would be complex and that in addition there would be new problems in synchronization of the various streams of information. Synchronization would require new network services and there was concern over how such applications would migrate into OSI environments.

1.3.2 Relationship of X Windows to Standards

Given the number of papers in which various aspects of the relationship between X Windows and its different components and ISO Standards were discussed, it was clear that this was an area of concern to participants. Of particular concern was that, given the fixed functionality of the X protocol and the consequent need to use the extension mechanism to accommodate additional functionality in support of graphics Standards (e.g. PEX), the end result would be a large number of extensions (maybe one or more for each Standard) and consequently enlarged servers with less guarantee of any particular X server providing the full functionality. Another important concern was that a system with fixed functionality would become obsolete in the foreseeable future. If this was a real expectation, it becomes a question as to whether it would be worth the efforts needed to define and improve the interworking of X and other Standards. Given the effort required, perhaps the area would be best ignored in the expectation that a new readily extensible protocol would be defined in the medium term, rather better integrated with other ISO efforts. It was felt that, in no small part, many of the difficulties arose due to the way the X definition partially addressed so many different aspects of the OSI and graphics reference models.

1.3.3 Improvements to the CGM

A group of topics for discussion was identified as potentially requiring revisions to improve the CGM Standard. These topics covered such things as requirements for network access to metafiles including random access to individual pictures or even segments. This implied the need to limit the context sensitivity of the metafile which is defined as an ordered (and hence context sensitive) sequence of elements.

There were also a number of issues related to the encoding of metafiles which had arisen in the presentations. Finally, the use of a heterogeneous environment, incorporating different implementations of CGM generators and interpreters, has consequences for the range of implementation latitudes that can be allowed while still generating a successfully networked application.

1.3.4 The Role of Application Profiles

In many areas of standardization, the concept of Application Profiles, which refine the definition of a Standard by tightening areas of implementation latitude, specifying minimum and maximum requirements etc., is utilized. It was clear to participants at the Workshop that such Profiles were being proposed for a variety of purposes including:

- improving the definition of ''faulty'' Standards;
- satisfying the requirements of interoperability for particular application areas;
- defining escapes and other entities.

In view of this variety of purposes the Workshop decided that some further investigation to define appropriate use of the Profiles concept was necessary.

Other concerns in the area related to the ISP mechanism in ISO/IEC JTC1, which was reported as allowing a Profile relating to any Standard to become officially recognized by ISO without reference to the committee which originated the Standard.

1.3.5 Image Interchange Standards

Although only one paper had been presented specifically on this topic, the influence of possible Standards in this area on the implementation of multi-media and other networked applications was clear. The Workshop therefore felt that topics such as the definition of Image Interchange Format objects and the mechanisms by which they could be moved across OSI networks merited further discussion. There was also debate about whether this was an area to which the ARGOSI project should make a specific contribution.

1.3.6 ARGOSI Classification Taxonomy

A number of application areas which had been described had suggested possible alternative metrics or refinements to metrics within the ARGOSI Classification scheme for graphics applications requirements.

The first of these was whether the taxonomy's concentration on the requirements over one link was the most appropriate aspect to examine or whether analysis of individual transaction types within the application would be a better approach. There were discussions about the most appropriate metrics to specify the requirements of applications in the area of acceptable error rates (currently part of the quality of service metric). Finally the selection criteria metric might require revision in the light of the requirements for distributed access to data in STEP format over OSI networks.

1.4 Working Groups

Following identification of the various topics listed in 1.3 the Workshop debated which would be appropriate for further discussion at the Workshop in the limited time available for small group work. The topics arising on the ARGOSI classification metrics were felt appropriate to refer back to the ARGOSI project for further discussion in that forum. Of the other five topics the Image Interchange Format was left for future discussions, whilst it was interesting that, when asked which were the topics on which they wished to work, none of the participants felt that the relationship between X Windows and other Standards was top priority. (This was not felt to be the case for the interaction between X Windows and OSI — here it was felt that those participants of the Workshop qualified to progress this topic were already doing so together in other groups.) Whether or not this feeling answers the question as to whether the X Windows System's interaction with Standards should indeed be ignored and a new, better integrated system definition awaited, is left to the interpretation of the reader! Suffice it to say that the topic remains on the list of questions to be further explored.

The Workshop split into three groups examining the remaining questions. The reports of these three groups are included in Chapters 2, 3 and 4 of this book.

Chapter 2

Improvements to the CGM

2.1 Participants

S. Carson
R.A. Day (Rapporteur)
D. Fellner
C. Fuhrhop (Chair)
F. Kappe
P. Kokkinidis
S. Liapakis
E. Pelucchi
M. Re
P. Tabastot
N. Vezirgiannis

2.2 Introduction

The motivation for the discussions reported in this Chapter was the perceived need for access to CGMs across networks, and over OSI networks in particular. The discussion was divided into the following topics:

(1) the appropriateness or otherwise of the encodings defined in ISO 8632 in an OSI environment;

(2) the restrictions that need to be placed on context-sensitive information appearing in a CGM that will be subject to partial transfer over an OSI network;

(3) issues raised over the requirements on CGM generation and interpretation software for successful interworking in a heterogeneous environment.

2.3 CGM Encodings

The three encodings specified in Parts 2-4 of ISO 8632 were discussed, with a view to assessing their usefulness as transfer syntaxes when CGMs are moved over OSI networks. For the purposes of the discussion a functional distinction was made between the 'clear text' encoding and the 'binary' and 'character' encodings — the latter two were seen as intended to fulfill similar requirements with respect to networks, whereas the first was seen to have a different purpose less related to networks.

2.3.1 The Clear Text Encoding

The practical uses of this encoding were discussed. It was considered that there were two classes of use:

- as an aid to debugging when generator and/or interpreter software is under development, and when interworking problems occur between two implementations;
- as a low-cost means of editing CGMs, via use of a conventional text editor rather than a purpose-built editing tool.

It was felt that both of these requirements could better be accomplished by the use of conversion tools which would convert a CGM generated in either the binary or character encodings to a convenient human-readable form. An issue was raised as to whether such a conversion tool would be able to re-encode a CGM edited in clear text form into a character encoding, coded as efficiently as the original. It was felt that in all but isolated cases this would be achievable.

In summary, it was felt that the use of clear text encoding should be regarded as undesirable, in that it adds (or more accurately retains) complexity in ISO 8632, without providing a significant increase in functionality. It was suggested that this encoding should now be relegated to being a non-normative Annex to ISO 8632 rather than being accorded the same status as the other two encodings. However, it was felt that this could not be a high-priority concern at this stage.

2.3.2 The Binary and Character Encodings

It was noted that the other two encodings specified in ISO 8632 are both inherently suitable for transfer of CGMs across OSI networks, and in some sense are competitive. The advantages usually quoted for the character encoding are:

- it can be used over networks that can only carry 7-bit characters;
- it leads to a more compact encoding, and hence more efficient use of network bandwidth.

It was felt that the first of these advantages is no longer relevant to today's networks, and is certainly irrelevant to OSI networks. Claims are sometimes made that it is difficult, using character encoding, to generate an efficiently encoded metafile automatically, but the discussion group felt that, although this can be the case, it was normally possible to achieve significant compaction compared to use of the binary encoding.

It was also noted that the MAP/TOP CGM profiles specify that CGMs should use the binary encoding. The rationale for this is that the implementation burden of writing generators and interpreters for the character encoding is significantly greater than that for the binary encoding. This burden was felt by MAP/TOP to outweigh the compaction achievable from the character encoding.

The need for retaining both encodings was examined. It was felt that the binary encoding would always be needed as the simplest to generate and interpret. It was also felt that it would be difficult to abolish the character encoding due to its use outside CGM, as this encoding was developed by ISO/IEC JTC1/SC2 as a common encoding format for many graphical applications. It was noted that, in particular, this encoding is used within Videotex systems. Thus the issue of the desirability of retaining a character encoding in CGM probably has a wider context than just this Standard.

2.3.3 The Use of FTAM Document Types to Transfer CGMs

The ARGOSI project has developed a set of FTAM Document Types to assist in the structured transfer of CGMs using ISO FTAM (ISO 8571). This work has been submitted to ISO/IEC JTC1/SC21 WG5, and currently two Document Types are proposed:

- FTAM-6, to be used to transfer either clear text or character encoded CGMs;
- FTAM-7, to be used to transfer binary encoded CGMs.

The paper given to the Workshop by Re gives the background to this work. (*Editorial Note*: subsequent to the Workshop discussions within ISO/IEC JTC1/SC21 WG5 have resulted in the merging of these two Document Types into a single, parameterized Document Type applicable to either binary or character encoded CGMs. Somewhat confusingly, this has been designated Document Type FTAM-6! The designations current at the time of the Workshop have been used in the rest of this Chapter.)

The discussion group examined problems that will potentially occur with the use of these Document Types.

If a character encoded CGM is transferred using the FTAM-6 Document Type currently under development, the transfer syntax will be a sequence of ASN.1 *IA5String* primitives. At the receiving end these IA5 strings will be translated by the host system into the local character representation. This will lead to a problem, if the latter is not also IA5 (e.g. if it is EBCDIC), as a CGM so stored will have the codes represented as characters, but identified by numeric value, arbitrarily altered. The CGM would then become uninterpretable. This problem would also exist if a CGM was transferred as an unstructured file using the FTAM-1 Document Type.

It was felt that this problem had its origins in the fact that what is historically described as a *character* encoding should really be regarded as an *octet* encoding, as it is the numeric values of the characters that are important. It was suggested that the FTAM-7 Document Type, currently also under development, and which uses a transfer syntax of a sequence of ASN.1 *OctetString* primitives should be used accordingly. It was also suggested that an education exercise was needed to clarify this issue for implementors, preferably by having the misnomer *character* replaced by a more suitable description such as *octet*.

In discussions held by the members of the ARGOSI project immediately after the Workshop, it became clear that a similar potential difficulty is present if a clear text encoded CGM is transferred using the FTAM-6 Document Type. If the CGM contains elements that cause character switching then the numeric values of certain strings of characters in the CGM will be used as indices. Therefore these numeric values must be preserved over the transfer.

None of the Document Types available and proposed for CGM use contain any means by which different parts of a CGM can be transferred in different string transfer syntaxes. Therefore the only options are either that the CGM is transferred as a sequence of *OctetStrings*, in which case the 'clear text' may be converted wrongly to another character set representation if the target system does not use the same encoding as the source system, or that *IA5Strings* are used, in which case the character-switching mechanism is broken. Again the problem would also occur with the unstructured transfer of a CGM using FTAM-1 (or FTAM-3).

It was felt to be imperative that a transferred CGM be guaranteed correct upon receipt. The only feasible ways of ensuring this were believed to be:

- to force the FTAM to examine the *element list* in the CGM Metafile Descriptor before transfer, and to refuse the transfer if this indicated that the problem would occur;
- to develop a CGM Profile that disallowed character-switching, to ensure the Profile identification was tagged in the Metafile Descriptor, and then to force the FTAM to check this before transfer.

In both cases it was felt that these conditions could never be guaranteed. It was therefore tentatively concluded that the clear-text encoding can never be a safe encoding for transfer over OSI Networks, and that the need for the FTAM-6 Document Type should be re-evaluated.

2.3.4 Development of an ASN.1 Description and Encoding

The Working Group considered the advantages and disadvantages of the development of a description of a CGM in ASN.1 (ISO 8824), and the use of ASN.1 Basic Encoding Rules (ISO 8825) to encode it.

The advantages of having such a description available were seen to be:

- ASN.1 is becoming the *lingua franca* of the OSI community, and is increasingly being adopted for other Standards work;
- the use of ASN.1 abstract and transfer syntaxes within FTAM is more natural and would allow an FTAM implementation (which already has code to generate and interpret ASN.1) access to the structure of a CGM without needing to contain code to interpret CGMs;
- there are an increasing number of general tools to handle ASN.1 (such as compiler generators) which could be used to build specific tools to handle CGMs.

The Group questionned whether ASN.1 is a powerful enough language to describe the syntax of all possible CGMs. It was felt that this would only become clear from experimentation. It was suggested that an approach might be to start with only a partial description of a CGM in ASN.1, picking out the 'landmarks' of the CGM such as the elements marking the beginning and ending of pictures within the file. Such a description might be useful enough for FTAM purposes from the outset, and could be built upon in successive refinements as the need to describe finer structural detail became apparent.

2.4 Context Sensitive Information within CGMs

The Group considered the particular issue of context sensitivity of segments within a CGM (i.e. as defined by Amendment 1 to ISO 8632). Given a need to transfer individual segments of a CGM (as a logical development of the need to transfer individual pictures), these must be capable of context-free use. The paper given to the Workshop by Ducrot identified the issues involved.

The question of whether segment independence should be tackled as a Profile issue or via changes to the Standard was discussed. It was felt that if an attempt were made to tackle the problem within the Standard, there was a very real possibility that fundamental changes to the concept of the CGM would need to be introduced. It was felt that there is work now starting to define the concept of collections of small, context-independent graphical objects rather than monolithic blocks of information. If and when this work comes to fruition, it may lead to the replacement of the CGM with a facility more amenable to structured access.

In the interim, it was felt that useful work could be done by the use of Profiles. Such Profiles should be considered as 'style guides', to be used by CGM generators, and which would mandate that the appropriate contextual information (e.g. attributes to be bound to the elements within a segment) were present.

It was noted that some of the difficulties encountered were due to the need to capture within a CGM information at different logical levels to meet the needs of other Standards e.g. GKS. There might be a case for use of a Profile to forbid this. Nevertheless, it was felt that there would still be a need for reasonably straightforward mappings between CGM and GKS and CGI to remain possible.

The Group also discussed a potential need for a Profile to define Escapes to allow the delimiting of 'groups of objects', to supplement the use of segments. There was, however, a feeling that the introduction of Escapes, albeit publicly defined, was to be discouraged in principle.

2.5 Interworking of CGM Generators and Interpreters

The paper given to the Workshop by Arnold *et al* suggested that CGM is fundamentally a good interchange format, albeit that there were interworking problems between generators and interpreters.

The question of whether a PICS (Protocol Implementation Conformance Statement) would be of use in reducing these problems was discussed. Although ISO 8632 addresses only the format of the CGM, and not its interpretation, it was felt that it was to an interpreter that the PICS would principally apply.

It was noted that in the OSI world the use of the PICS had proved successful for capturing the static information relating to an implementation's claimed conformance, although other techniques are needed to check conformance of dynamic behaviour. Superficially it would seem that the static nature of a CGM should lend itself well to the PICS technique.

It was felt that a PICS for CGM would essentially be a checklist, asking the implementer of an interpreter to specify which options have been chosen. As there is little that is mandatory in a CGM, the OSI approach of a PICS to check conformance to mandatory behaviour and facilities would be limited. However, it should be considered whether the completion of a PICS should be made mandatory for any implementer producing software claiming to generate and interpret metafiles conforming to ISO 8632.

It was noted that the construction of a suitable PICS proforma will not be a trivial task, due to the large number of options available in the CGM Standard. For example, the PICS will need to tie down information such as whether an interpreter draws a rectangle edge as the locus of the supplied set of points or as the 'inside' of the set.

It was concluded that an attempt to construct a PICS proforma would be worthwhile. It was also noted that if ISO TR 10000 was going to be used as a guideline for producing a CGM Profile in ISP format, there would be a requirement for an associated PICS.

Besides the use of a PICS, the Group also considered briefly the use of information placed in the CGM Metafile Descriptor to assist with interworking. It was noted that the CALS Profile for CGM already specifies the inclusion of a Profile identifier in the Metafile Descriptor, and this was felt to be a minimum requirement. It was felt that there was scope for extension of this to include information such as:

- what ESCAPEs, if any are present;
- the maximum number of points in any POLYLINE etc;
- assumptions made by the generator over items such as edges, continuation of linestyles etc.

It was felt that this was very much a matter for further study, both to describe the information that should be included, and to define an encoding mechanism.

Some specific recommendations were proposed by the Working Group to the Workshop closing plenary session. These were integrated into the recommendations of the Workshop as described in Chapter 5.

Chapter 3

The Role of Application Profiles

3.1 Participants

D.B. Arnold
D.A. Duce (Secretary)
A. Ducrot
P. Egloff
A.M. Mumford
D.C. Sutcliffe (Chair)

3.2 What is the Role of an Application Profile?

The Working Group started by considering three questions:

(1) If standards are properly defined, what is the purpose of Application Profiles?

(2) Should Profiles be directed towards satisfying user/application requirements or be directed towards what technology can readily support?

(3) Are the mechanisms for producing International Standardized Profiles adequate?

The discussion centred on the role of an Application Profile.

Within the SC21 networking community, Profiles were found to be necessary in order to achieve interworking between different implementations of Standards. Within SC24, the notion of Profiles is built into the CGI Standard, and Profiles for CGM are emerging from the CALS and MAP/TOP initiatives.

The paper given to the Workshop by Mumford lists a number of things that an Application Profile may do and these were taken as a starting point for discussion. The paper by Reynolds and Arnold on CGI Profiles for X includes a related discussion on the potential purposes of profiles. The first of these in Mumford's paper is:

- complete the semantics to 'plug the holes' in the Standard.

Two subdivisions were identified:

(1) errors;

(2) reducing implementation dependencies.

The conclusions reached were:

(1) *Errors*: Profiles should NOT be used for correcting errors in Standards. There are other ISO/IEC procedures for doing this (for example the defects procedure) and these should be used.

(2) *Reducing implementation dependencies*: there are many places in the graphics standards, where behaviour or values are left as implementation dependent. It may be that to satisfy the requirements of a particular class of applications, a particular behaviour or set of values is required.

It was agreed that this was a sensible role for an Application Profile. However it was noted that where Registration procedures exist for defining new values of entities (eg linetypes), these should be used, not Application Profiles. The Application Profile should then refer to the registered items.

The second function identified in Mumford's paper was:

- specification of maximum and minimum resource requirements.

An example of this would be the statement that polylines with at least 1024 points should be supported. Resource requirements in this sense are motivated by the needs of applications and there was agreement that this was a good usage for Application Profiles.

The third function discussed was:

- specification of performance characteristics.

In general the existing graphics standards do not address issues of performance. For example, there are no specifications of response times for particular commands in particular circumstances. It was pointed out that performance characteristics are highly dependent on the overall system in use and it might be inappropriate to attach these to individual components. The general view was that performance characteristics might be one of the kinds of entity that could be defined by an Application Profile, but there were reservations about the feasibility, desirability and appropriateness of this.

The fourth function was:

- specifying groupings of separately Registered linetypes etc.

The Registration procedures allow additional linetypes, marker types etc. to be defined. One possible usage for an Application Profile is to say that for a particular class of applications, particular values of linetypes, marker types, hatch styles etc. (which are defined through the normal Registration mechanism) should be used. The idea of using Application Profiles for specifying groups of entities was seen as a good usage of the mechanism.

A general statement was made about Application Profiles at this point.

An implementation which conforms to an Application Profile should also conform to the underlying base Standard(s) to which the Profile refers.

In the light of this statement, the use of Application Profiles for specifying defaults was discussed.

- specifying defaults.

In the existing graphics standards, the behaviour or meaning of certain entities may be dependent upon a default state or components of a state. An example would be the representation with which a polyline in GKS would be displayed if no values have been explicitly set for polyline attributes and bundle representations. Two cases are distinguished in current work on CGI Profiles as reported in Reynolds *et al.*:

(1) Implementation dependent defaults. If a Standard specifies that a default value is implementation dependent, an Application Profile can specify a particular value to be used as default.

(2) Defaults defined in a Standard. If a Standard defines a particular default value, and an application requires a different default, it would be a violation of the conformance principle given above, for an Application Profile to specify a different default state. However, it would be appropriate for the Application Profile to specify that certain functions should be invoked, with particular parameter values, to change the default state, before further processing takes place.

There was discussion as to whether an Application Profile might encompass several Standards, or specify provisions for a single Standard. An example might be usage of CGM for transferring data for a particular class of applications across a network, where restrictions might need to be applied to both CGM and networking standards. There was sympathy for the view that a Profile might encompass several Standards and the need for this was clearly seen. It was pointed out that one way to accomplish this would be through a linked set of Application Profiles for a set of Standards. This led into a discussion of how many Application Profiles are expected to be standardized. No clear answer emerged to this question, except for the statement that there is a need for a set of Application Profiles to span a range of application areas.

The next usage of Profiles considered was taken from Mumford's paper:

- specifying the behaviour of the required software, eg CGM interpreter/generator.

There were seen to be some dangers in this. The CGM standard carefully avoids talking about the behaviour of metafile interpreters and generators. CGM has a notion of a picture at a particular level of abstraction, in which some of the information required to render the picture on a display is bound in, and some has to be supplied outside the metafile. Specification of the behaviour of interpreters is often seen as a way of providing the additional information, for example the bundle representations to be used for displaying the picture.

It was felt that such uses of Application Profiles are wrong, in that they are counter to the intention and philosophy of the Standard to which they refer. In the case of CGM, the issue is really about the environment in which the content of a metafile is to be understood. Amendment 1 to CGM allows some environmental characteristics, for example, bundle representations, to be transmitted with a picture representation as part of the picture descriptor. It was recognized that the Amendment 1 structure might not be perfect in this respect, for example, in its treatment of colour tables.

The view was that provisions for environmental control should be introduced through changes to base Standards, rather than through Application Profiles. Modification of the base Standard is more likely to preserve the conceptual integrity of the Standard, whilst the Application Profile approach, through the limitations in the ways it can act, is likely to result in a pragmatic solution which distorts the conceptual basis of the Standard.

- Define useful subsets of the Standard.

It was agreed that this is a valid use for Application Profiles.

3.3 Mechanisms for ISPs

Concerns were expressed that existing mechanisms, to standardize Application Profiles that relate to graphics standards, may not result in a coherent set of Application Profiles for the graphics standards. There was agreement on the need to study these mechanisms, along with the role of Application Profiles in graphics, and, if necessary, argue for changes to the mechanisms.

There is a need to produce a framework and ground rules for Application Profiles in the graphics area and it was felt that this was something that the ARGOSI project could pursue.

3.4 Requirements for Application Profiles

There was agreement that Application Profiles should be driven by applications rather than technology. The key issue is what functionality, value ranges etc, are appropriate to particular classes of applications. All Application Profiles should contain a definition of the constituency addressed. The ARGOSI classification taxonomy was seen as providing some useful input to identify potential constituencies.

There was seen to be a need for quick mechanisms for producing Application Profiles. It was thought that there might be some merit in having a structured set of Profiles, which build upon each other in some way, though it was noted as reported in Reynolds *et al.* that the approach taken in CGI, of building upon a foundation profile, can lead to redundant functionality in particular profiles.

There was seen to be an interesting open question in whether a proforma could be defined for Application Profiles for graphics standards. If this were possible, producing a new Profile would be a matter of filling in value ranges and other parameters. Again, this was seen as a topic meriting study.

3.5 Conclusions

The recommendations coming out of the discussion were summarized and presented to the closing Plenary session. The following conclusions were reached.

General

- An implementation conforming to an Application Profile should also conform to the base Standard(s).
- The focus is on users and applications rather than what technology can provide. The constituency of a Profile needs to be clearly defined in terms of users and applications.

What is the role of a Profile?

An Application Profile is NOT:

- A method for patching up Standards and correcting errors.
- A back door method of standardization for adding new functionality to existing Standards, or defining new Standards.
- A mechanism for changing the provisions of existing Standards.
- A way of by-passing existing Registration mechanisms, eg the Register of Graphical Items.

An Application Profile IS a mechanism for:

- Giving "application specific" meanings to implementation dependencies and defaults.
- Subsetting the provisions of a Standard.
- Specifying minimum and maximum resource requirements.
- Specifying groupings of Registered items.

An Application Profile MAY BE (these require further discussion):

- A mechanism for specifying performance requirements.
- A way for defining an environment in which a Standard operates.

Some specific actions were proposed by the Working Group and these were subsequently agreed by the Workshop closing plenary session and are included in the recommendations in Chapter 5.

Chapter 4

Impact of Multi-media

4.1 Participants

R. Brennan (Chair)
J. Gallop (Secretary)
D. Lewis
R. Maybury
J. Mortelmans
M. Planes

4.2 Introduction

The Working Group arose out of several papers given to the Workshop, namely those by Lewis, Brennan and Egloff.

4.3 Examples of Requirements for Distributed Hypermedia

Several examples of requirements were discussed.

(1) A single user accesses a hypermedia object over a network. A number of problems need to be solved. The component parts of the object may reside at different places in the network. Browsing needs to take account of connectivity between the component parts and the variety of media. Synchronization needs to be solved.

In Europe, the RAVI group are working in this area. Standardization is beginning in the Multi-media Hypermedia Experts Group (MHEG) of ISO/IEC JTC1/SC2 and CCITT. Groups involved in this Workshop need to be aware of these hypermedia groups.

Hypermedia on videodisc presents some of the same problems and RAVI and MHEG are including this in their work.

The tradeoffs between hypermedia on videodisc and hypermedia over networks need to be understood. The frequency of updates is clearly an important factor.

(2) A group of people connected via a network engage in a network conference or a network based cooperative working system. A network conference is typically a session where the multi-media manifestation for all participants is temporarily under the control of one of the participants. A network based cooperative working session allows a number of participants to solve a common problem by interacting with an information base and its hypermedia view. In either case problems of session control need to be solved: who holds the conch? How is it passed? Does anyone need to hold it? These problems are added to the problems of single user access to hypermedia.

Most of the Working Group's time was devoted to the consequences of (2).

4.4 Examples of Existing Work

The paper given by Lewis to the Workshop, "Multipoint Protocol Aspects of Audiovisual Teleconference via 1or 2 64KBits/sec channels", described work on audiovisual teleconferencing under the ESPRIT Projects MIAC and MIAS.

In the Working Group, he asserted that this work shows that real-time video is possible over 64Kbit/sec, although with limitations that need to be understood. In addition to compression within a single frame, the compression techniques take advantage of similarities between one frame and the next. It is expected that, in conferencing, the moving picture is a view of the speaker who is filmed against a constant background and does not move too quickly. Fast movements can be accommodated, but there is a visual effect of catching up; if the entire frame changes, about 3 seconds is needed before the frame is completely transmitted.

4.5 Perceived Limitations of OSI for Distributed Multi-media Applications

It is common at present for distributed multi-media applications not to use OSI networking. The Working Group discussed the reasons why this was the case. It is important to understand how fundamental the reasons really are.

(1) There is no mechanism in present OSI work for the routing of multicast/multipeer messages, appropriate for broadcasting or setting up and joining a group engaged in a conference or cooperative working session.

An ANSI committee ASC X3S3.3 is working on this and has received several proposals. A process of assimilation and assessment is taking place.

(2) One strategy for controlling a conference session is to pass a token. Several algorithms are possible and there is no agreed best method. In general there is a lack of good algorithms and protocol specifications to handle connections with many participants.

(3) Speed has a number of aspects here. It is claimed that OSI standards impose increasing overheads as the network bandwidth increases, but there is disagreement about the bandwidth at which they become significant. One factor is the end to end time for acknowledgement, which we discuss later.

As the bandwidth increases, more demanding applications are implemented, applications that would be inconceivable at lower speeds. Some of these applications have strict timing constraints. Broadband is an example of a higher bandwidth communications technology over which protocols other than OSI are planned. Clearly applications of OSI on lower bandwidth networks could run over broadband with improved performance. However broadband is also used for voice and video (isochronous services) and realtime constraints must be observed. This means that voice data must be enclosed in small packets (less than 50 octets) which imposes additional load on the OSI networking service.

(4) Synchronization is essential, for example between video and voice, but is difficult in OSI. Supposing there are two streams of information to be synchronized, should they be carried over a single network connection or should each be carried over its own network connection? If the former, synchronization problems may be easier to solve. However in general, the streams may arrive from different points on the network and so require different network connections. This pushes the problem of synchronization to a higher OSI layer. Work on this is taking place in MACF (Multiple Association Controlling Function) in ISO/IEC JTC1/SC21/WG6. However there is a limit to what can be done in OSI, since OSI standardizes the connection, not the interpretation of the data.

(5) Current OSI usage is dominated by connection-oriented protocols. This is perceived by some to be an obstacle when attempting to support demanding applications, such as distributed multi-media. The argument is that handshaking and other features of connection-oriented protocols impose unacceptable overheads and that connection-less protocols can be used when more reliable networks become widely available. However it is believed by others that alternative implementation decisions can be made in a connection-oriented context, that these alternative decisions could considerably reduce the overheads and that these alternatives have not been investigated. This area requires further study and prototyping, which could be performed with a more straightforward but still quantitatively demanding OSI application such as a highly interactive X11 client.

    A study of lightweight protocols would also be instructive for this application.

(6) In some situations (see Lewis's paper), the normal advantages of OSI do not add value because (a) inherently the packets are unique and sequence independent; (b) the channel is over a point to point connection with no intervening network. However there is no reason why the participants in a multi-media conference should not already be connected by a dedicated line, especially if they belong to different organizations and use different computing infrastructure.

4.6 Modularity

Egloff's paper introduced the idea of modularity in the BERKOM Reference Model, using a set of common data structures and profiles which can be called upon to build new applications in a coherent way. Lewis's paper exploited modularity in a different sense. The individual facilities in MIAS, which are mapped onto virtual pipes, are drawn from existing standards where possible; moving picture and fax are examples of this.

4.7 Computer Graphics and Distributed Multi-media

Multi-media is often associated with video, but computer-produced graphics are also an essential element of multi-media. In principle, the computer graphics could be rendered to an image before transmission, but commonly in computer graphics this is wasteful and commits to a particular device resolution. It appears that multi-media should include streams with computer graphics content.

Some multi-media projects incorporate graphics, including RAVI and MHEG. MIAS does not, but the mechanisms it employs to combine different information streams could in principle be used to accept a computer graphics stream.

It does appear that the groups working on distributed graphics and those working on distributed multi-media are only partially aware of each other's work. More knowledge of each other's work would be fruitful and this Workshop has made some useful introductions.

Two courses of action could be recommended:

(1) that the requirements for standard computer graphics within a distributed multi-media context be analyzed and that a study of suitable solutions be made. The work of RAVI and MHEG should be drawn upon.

(2) that the solutions for distributed graphics within ARGOSI be extended to cover distributed multi-media in consultation with the multi-media experts.

The former was passed to the Workshop closing plenary session together with other specific actions where they were agreed and are included in the recommendations in Chapter 5.

Chapter 5

Summary and Conclusions

The Workshop concluded with a final session, following the presentation of the Working Group reports. The three sets of recommendations were integrated and, where appropriate, augmented to generate a set of recommendations for the Workshop. In view of the links between the Role of Application Profiles Working Group and the Improvements to CGM Working Group, these were considered first, beginning with the former.

It was agreed that Profiles were an important topic and that it was timely to pursue further study in this area. This was illustrated by some of the current proposals for Profiles which did not fall within the criteria derived by the Working Group. The following actions were recommended.

- Define a framework and a set of ground rules for Profiles for use with Computer Graphics Standards.
- Review current proposals for Profiles in the light of this work.
- Study whether Profiles can be expressed through proformae.
- Gain a familiarization with the International Standardized Profile (ISP) mechanism (pursuing any changes that might arise) and explore its use for Profiles for Computer Graphics Standards.

  This also includes consideration of the use of PICS (Protocol Implementation Conformance Statement) for implementations of Computer Graphics Standards.

While the use of PICS (in the last action above) does not seem appropriate from the name, PICS have received wider usage than the name implies in the OSI community and their usage was believed to be possible for Computer Graphics Standards.

The Improvements to the CGM Working Group had naturally not spent time considering the role of Profiles and had used current proposals as a guideline. The ground rules emerging from the Role of Application Profiles Working Group were agreed and the actions arising from the Improvements to the CGM Working Group were modified accordingly. As a result the following actions were recommended:

- Submit a CGM defect report recommending a change of name of the *character* encoding to be *octet* encoding confusion. (Note the need for creating greater understanding of the distinction through education.) The proposed FTAM Document Type was flawed as a result of misunderstanding in this area and should be corrected.
- Produce an ASN.1 encoding for the CGM and explore the most appropriate way of standardizing this. Consider whether a partial ASN.1 encoding to express the CGM structure and using an existing encoding for the content would be useful.
- Produce a CGM profile to constrain the use and ordering of certain CGM elements to allow independent access to segments within CGMs conforming to the profile.
- Study what elements should appear in metafile and picture descriptors in a CGM.

The actions arising from the Impact of Multi-media Working Group bore less relation to those of the other two Working Groups than the actions of those Working Groups did to each other, but this was to be expected from the topics for consideration. The actions also did not need to be amended owing to other actions, with the result that the following recommendations were made:

- Study the use of connection-oriented protocols in multi-media.
- Explore the use of lightweight protocols in multi-media.
- Consider the position of computer graphics within multi-media; study the needs and architecture of multi-media applications and explore the abstractions necessary to include computer graphics in multi-media. (Note that there is a need for a multi-media paradigm for new applications, a sort of multi-media reference model.)

The Workshop was considered a success by all the participants and there was a common desire to disseminate the results of the Workshop to others interested in the area of graphics and communications. The meeting recommended a further set of actions to effect this:

- Produce proceedings of the Workshop including the presented papers, the discussion arising, the results of the Working Group discussions and the agreed recommended actions. Explore means of publishing the report in book form.
- Produce a summary report of the Workshop for submission to appropriate journals in the fields of graphics and networking.
- Produce a submission for the forthcoming ACM SIGCOMM/SIGGRAPH Workshop on Graphics and Networking (in Boulder, Colorado, January 1991) reporting the results of this Workshop.

Part II

Position Papers

Chapter 6

P2463: The ARGOSI Project for ISO/IEC Graphics and Networking Standards

R.A. Day, D.A. Duce, J.R. Gallop, R. Maybury, D.C. Sutcliffe

1 Introduction

Project 2463, ARGOSI — Applications Related Graphics and OSI Standards Integration, started on 1 March 1989 and is of 3 years duration. Eleven organizations are involved in the project:

Prime Contractor	Thomson-CSF	France
Partners	INRIA	France
	RAL	UK
	Hitec	Greece
	Tecsiel	Italy
	COSI	Italy
	GMD-FOKUS	Germany
Associated Partners	Laser-Scan	UK
	FhG-AGD	Germany
	GESI	Italy
	University of East Anglia	UK

The project arose from the recognition that within ISO/IEC, as elsewhere, standards for computer graphics and standards for Open Systems Interconnection have been largely developed in isolation and little serious attention has been paid to issues of integration. The objectives of the project are twofold:

- Advance the state of the art in the transfer of graphical information across international networks.
- Improve quality and applicability of standards in this area.

The project is expected to make an impact under a number of headings:

(1) *Knowledge*: when the project started, there was little understanding of the requirements which graphics place on networking in terms of the particular networking services required to transfer graphical information across networks. Such requirements arise, for example, because of the structure inherent in graphical information and the need to access subunits within an overall structure.

(2) *Standardization*: international standardization activities are seen as a key mechanism for achieving coherence and interoperability in an otherwise fragmented area. The contribution of the ARGOSI project to standardization activities will be to identify requirements for future graphics and networking standards and make appropriate inputs to the standardization committees concerned. The organizations involved in the project have a long tradition of contributing independently to graphics and networking standardization. ARGOSI provides the opportunity for these organizations to work together in the standards-making process and so to form the nucleus around which a more coordinated and coherent European input can be made to the international process.

(3) *Industry*: From an industry standpoint the project sets out to demonstrate what can be achieved in distributed graphics using existing international public data networks (PSPDNs). This will point the way to what can be expected as better international PSPDNs become available in the future and to the requirements for such facilities from applications. To demonstrate the state of the art, an application demonstrator is being constructed. This is described later in this paper.

(4) *Commercial*: the project will develop software tools for graphics and networking services which will form the basis directly, or indirectly, of commercial products. The prototype demonstrator will also generate knowledge and experience of how to (and equally importantly, how not to) build distributed graphics applications using ISO/IEC standards.

The remainder of the paper describes what has been achieved so far in the project, concentrating on the prototype demonstrator and related activities.

2 Methodology

As the project title implies, the project is driven by applications and their requirements in terms of graphics and networking services. Effort in the project is being devoted to classifying applications according to these requirements. This work is briefly described in the next section.

A Study of Services task is looking at how the requirements emerging from the Classification activities can be satisfied by existing ISO/IEC graphics and networking standards and to what extent new standards or amendments to existing standards are necessary. The results of this activity will be fed into the appropriate Standards bodies and committees as they arise. The work to date is described in section 6.

To demonstrate what is possible now with existing or emerging graphics and networking standards and international networking facilities, an application demonstrator is being developed. Before the demonstrator could be defined, it was necessary to ascertain what bandwidth could be delivered between partners' sites by PSPDNs. This work is described in section 4. The demonstrator is described in section 5.

Finally, the project will assess the success of integration achieved and will identify those areas where future standarization activities are required.

3 Classification of Applications

The principal aim of this part of the project is to investigate requirements for graphics and networking services in combination and to present this information as a taxonomy of applications in terms of these requirements. To establish such a classification scheme it is essential to derive an understanding of how current applications use graphics and networking services in combination, together with an understanding of how requirements will evolve in the future. Requirements can never be totally divorced from technology and so it is also necessary to have an understanding of how the underlying technology will evolve, leading to speculation on how existing applications can use improved technology and what new applications become possible because of improved performance and other characteristics.

The method of data collection adopted has been:

(1) *Interviews*: visits to organizations developing applications which use graphics and networking, either now or in the future. Technical people in these organizations have been interviewed. A questionnaire was constructed to guide the interviews.

(2) *Postal survey*: to gather information from a broader spectrum, a postal questionnaire was constructed and sent to a wide range of organizations, worldwide.

Replies to the postal survey have now been received, and detailed work on the construction of a taxonomy of applications has taken place.

From the replies to the postal survey received, some trends could be seen.

(1) There is less experience of graphics and networking than expected. From the point of view of the classification work this is a disappointment. However, from the point of view of the impact of the project, there is an opportunity to develop practical experience of the combination of graphics and networking standards before these come into widespread use, and to correct any defects found.

(2) Replies to the networking part of the questionnaire seem to apply to an organization as a whole rather than to the applications at that organization which use a combination of graphics and networking services. This points both to the lack of experience of graphics and networking in combination and also to the penetration of networking services into the general level of computing infrastructure that is assumed to be available.

(3) Following on from the last point, it was interesting to note that local area networking is now widespread and important.

The histogram in Figure 1 shows the distribution of responses to the questionnaire by application area.

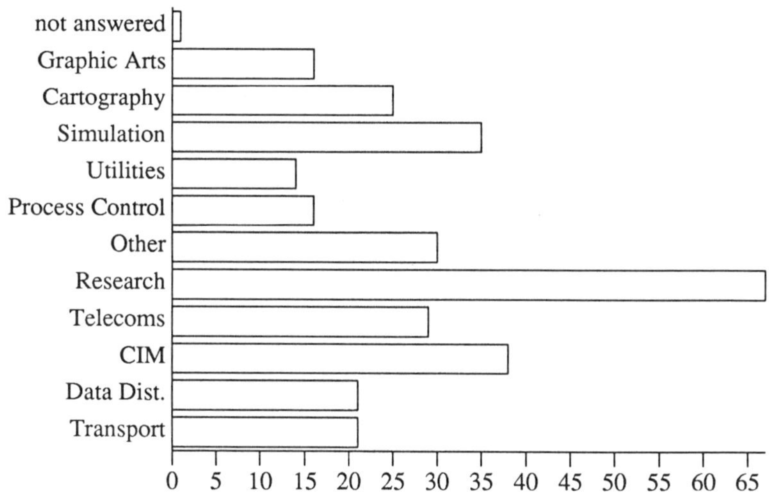

Figure 1. Distribution of responses by application area

Figure 2 shows the distribution of graphics systems used. It is interesting to note the high level of usage of GKS (the Graphical Kernel System ISO 7942 — the first ISO standard for computer graphics, published in 1985) and X11 (a *de facto* windowing system standard). What is unclear from the responses is whether X11 is used directly by applications or is a layer beneath a graphics system. Further studies are being carried out to clarify such issues.

A series of questions was asked concerning the number and size of graphics primitives used by each application area. Figure 3 shows part of the results for the maximum size of the fill area (polygon) primitive by application area (for a subset of the application areas). Note that larger polygons are used in cartographic applications and some very large polygons are used in simulation applications.

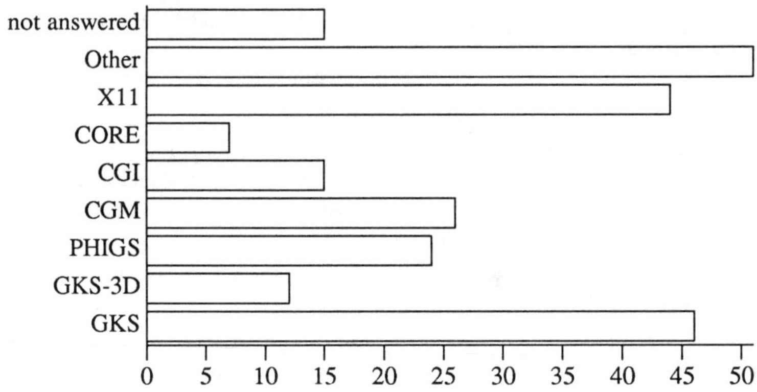

Figure 2. Usage of graphics systems

Organizations were asked why graphics and networking standards are *not* used. The results are shown in Figures 4 and 5 respectively.

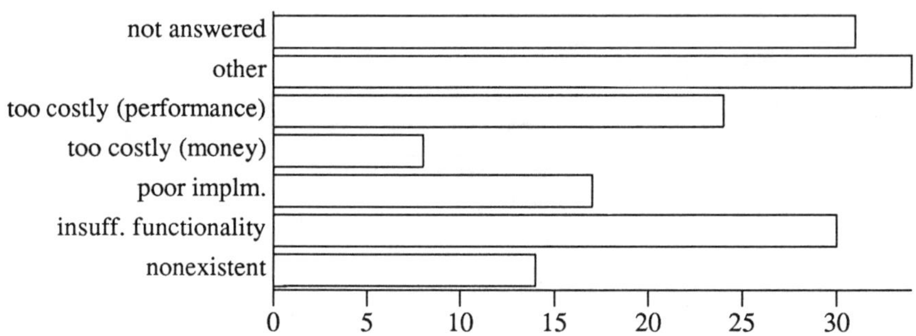

Figure 4. Reasons why graphics standards are not used

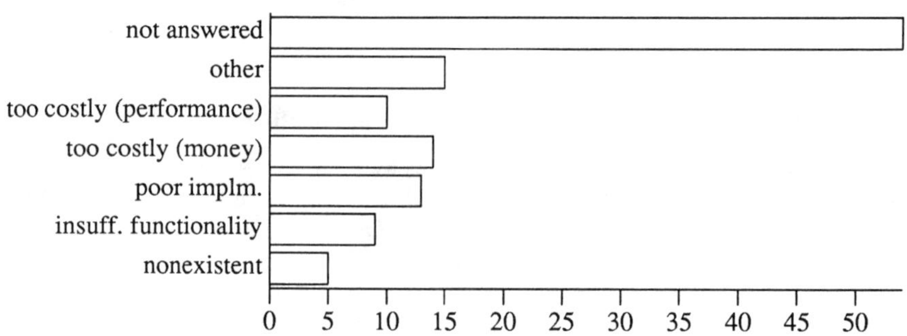

Figure 5. Reasons why networking standards are not used

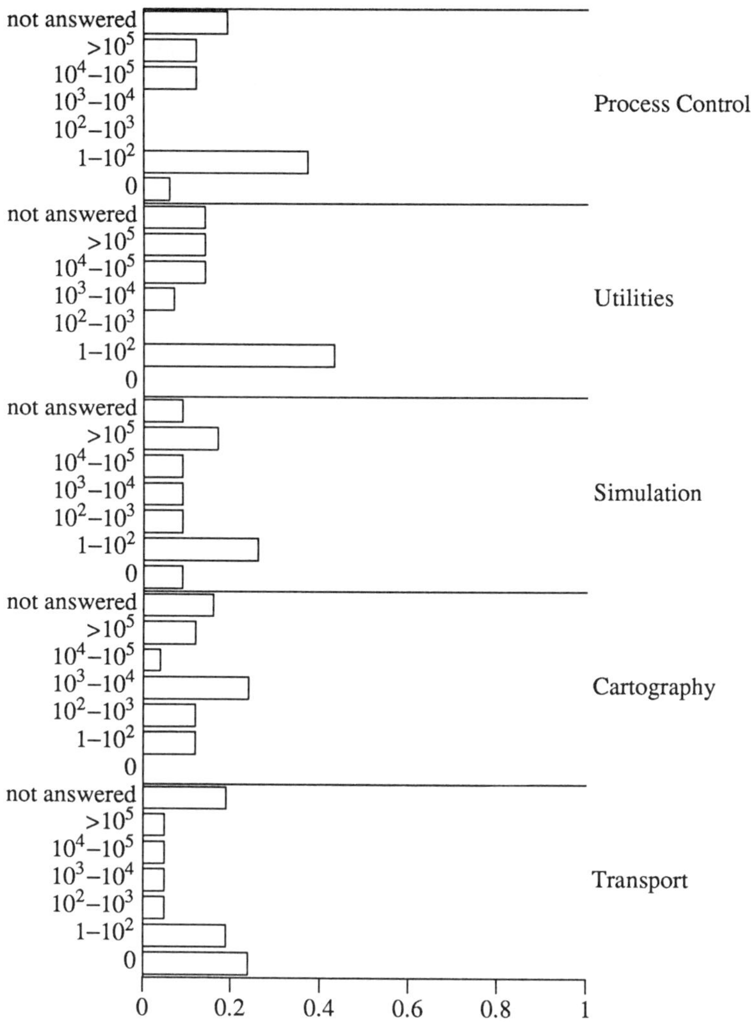

Figure 3. Maximum number of points in fill areas

From the number of 'not answered' replies to the questions, there appear to be more organizations using networking standards than graphics standards. This may reflect the fact that some form of standard is necessary before networking can take place. It is interesting to note that insufficient functionality rather than cost is the main reason given for not using graphics standards, whereas for networking standards, cost in monetary terms is the major impediment.

Interviews covered a range of application areas. Organizations in the countries represented in the project were interviewed. Meteorology will be taken as an example.

Several organizations working in this area were interviewed. Weather forecasting is inherently distributed. Raw data is received by forecasting centres from remote sites and forecasts are disseminated to a wide range of geographically distributed sites, both national and international. The data disseminated consists in the general case of satellite images or background maps with graphics overlays (eg contour maps) to present the forecast. CGM (Metafile for the storage and transfer of picture description information, ISO 8632) is starting to be used for representing such graphical data. One of the main problems in this application area is that data volumes are very large (for example satellite images and complex contours) and since the graphics standards do not in general make statements about the data volumes an implementation must support, many implementations are not able to handle the data volumes involved.

At the present time, much of the dissemination of forecast data is done by fax machines, but the advent of PSPDNs is heralding a move towards dissemination by transfer of CGMs or parts of CGMs. A CGM represents a sequence of pictures and there is a requirement from this application area to be able to transfer individual pictures in a CGM as well as a complete CGM.

Within the UK, attention has also focussed on the requirements for remote working, for example between a workstation and local compute server, or workstation and remote supercomputer, or document preparation system and remote library of stored graphics.

There are different networking characteristics and availabilities associated with different kinds of network. For example local area networks have bandwidths of 10Mbit/s to 100Mbit/s and wide area networks 1Kbit/s to 1Mbit/s. The theory of OSI solutions is that they should be applicable to all types of networking, in that the architecture inherent in OSI solutions is scalable.

By use of the interview and postal data a preliminary taxonomy for the classification of distributed applications according to their graphics requirements has been constructed. This focusses on a categorisation of a single network link between two co-operating parts of a distributed graphical application. This is the place where the integration of graphics with OSI services has significance. At present such links are treated in isolation (ie each is categorised separately with no attempt being made to consider interactions between links); a more complete categorization is a subject for future study.

The methodology adopted was to produce a set of *metrics*, each of which has a small number of values. In this way, with n metrics, a n-dimensional matrix can be constructed, and an individual application's link can be placed in a single 'cell' within the matrix, depending on the values of the metrics taken by the link. It should also be possible to assign appropriate combinations of graphics and OSI standards to each cell, and hence to advise on which standards are applicable to the part of the application categorised into that cell. If a set of standards cannot be assigned to a cell, this is an indication that a new standard may be needed.

The metrics currently defined are as follows.

- *semantic content* — a description of the graphics data flowing across the link, and categorised in terms of the ISO/IEC draft Reference Model for Computer Graphics;
- *dimensionality* — a categorization that can refer to both Euclidean or non-Euclidean geometry, and may also include time represented as an extra dimension;
- *data source* — a description of whether the data to be accessed is a complete, previously-defined body of structured information, or whether the information flowing across the link is being used to construct or alter a picture;
- *session control* — a description of which end of the link has control over the selection of data;
- *selection criteria* — a description of whether the graphical data is selected as a complete and pre-determined structure, a subset of this, or a structure that needs to be created dynamically from other data;
- *quality of service* — a description of the parameters that might affect the choice of networking facilities eg data volume, transaction time, acceptable error rate.

Further work is planned on the validation and refinement of this taxonomy over the coming months.

The classification work has so far made three definitive inputs to the remainder of the project. The first was to identify an application for the prototype demonstrator. The application chosen is an information system for European transportation road freight operators (lorry drivers!). The application is representative of a number of the areas considered and will use CGM and FTAM (File Transfer Access and Management — ISO 8571) as the basis for the graphics and networking services required.

The work has also identified the need for a standard way in which to map CGM onto FTAM. This point is returned to later. Finally the work has shown up a strong interest in using X windows over OSI networks and work has been initiated in collaboration with other interest groups to define a mapping of X onto OSI.

Prior to deciding on the prototype demonstrator, experiments were carried out to ascertain what performance could be expected by a demonstrator from existing international PSPDNs. This work is briefly described in the next section.

4 PSPDN Connectivity

The wish to demonstrate the prototype application in as general a context as possible, means that is should be possible to demonstrate it across international boundaries (to demonstrate the 'European' nature of the work) and between as many partner sites as possible (to demonstrate the 'Open Systems' nature of the work). These aims dictate the use of publicly available facilities - the usage of private, leased lines (for example) would be infeasible within the resources of the project. It is also an aim of the demonstrator to show that publicly available facilities *can* be used to offer useful services in conjunction with ISO graphics and networking standards. One result of the demonstration work should be to identify the weaknesses of currently available facilities and to make recommendations as to how these can be overcome. To do this 'real' service conditions must be experienced.

The connectivity work established what X.25 facilities could reasonably be made available at each site and carried out a series of experiments to estimate the bandwidth available between sites and estimate the reliability of connections. Attention was also paid to previous connectivity studies, most notably the COSINE studies of performance and reliability of PSPDNs (COSINE Study 6.2.2).

It was decided that the quantities to be measured as a means of gauging suitability of the connection should be kept simple, viz:

- throughput obtained, both to user and total (at the network level);
- call setup times for services;
- success rate for initiated test sessions;
- detailed statistics for services that failed (reason for call clearance etc).

A number of test methodologies were considered, based on which application-level software was to be used to conduct the tests. It was decided that the limited effort available dictated the use of the only software common and available to all sites — X.29. It was decided that testing would be done by listing a large file (approximately 150 Kbyte) over a terminal session set up via X.29. This would provide reasonable throughput and call failure statistics, but would not, however, yield call setup time statistics, due to the interactive nature of the sessions involved.

Figure 6 illustrates PSPDN connections available at the sites of each partner participating in the study. At the time the tests were carried out, Hitec were still awaiting a connection to Hellaspac, the Greek PSPDN. This is now in place. RAL used a connection to PSS routed through JANET for the experiments, but a direct connection has subsequently been installed (shown as a dotted line in the Figure).

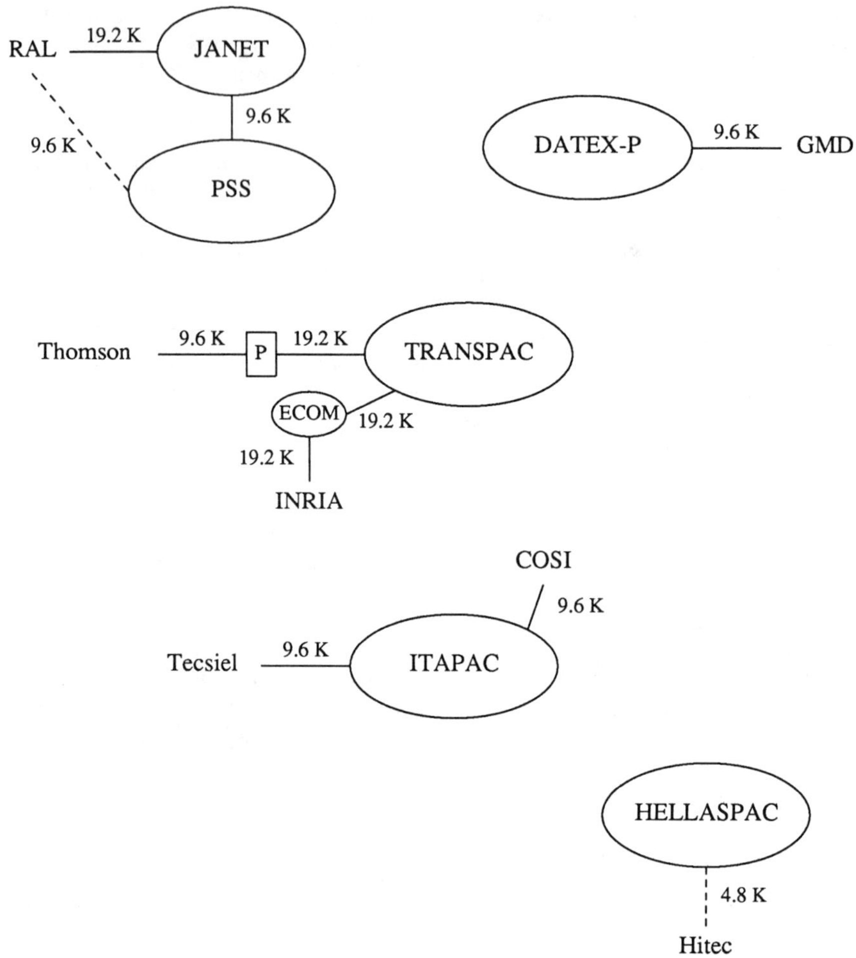

Figure 6. PSPDN connections available at participating partners' sites

An example of the results obtained for bandwidth (for data into and out of Thomson-CSF) is shown in Figure 7. The figures are the means obtained over typically 10 measurements made during normal working hours. Unsurprisingly good throughput was obtained to INRIA. Throughput to GMD-FOKUS in Berlin was also good, but the Italian sites (COSI and Tecsiel) were less good.

Reliability results were encouraging. Network congestion was the most frequent problem, most noticeablely at INRIA for incoming calls and at Tecsiel for outgoing calls.

The results of the experiments show that a general estimate of 3Kbits/s is reasonable for the throughput to be expected between the Partner sites. This is in broad agreement with the COSINE file transfer study - the figures are slightly worse, possibly due to the inclusion of ITAPAC sites in the present study. The best throughput figures were between TRANSPAC and DATEX-P. Figures to and from PSS were acceptable. There did seem to be evidence of problems with international connections to ITAPAC, with Tecsiel (Pisa) faring better than COSI (Milan) overall.

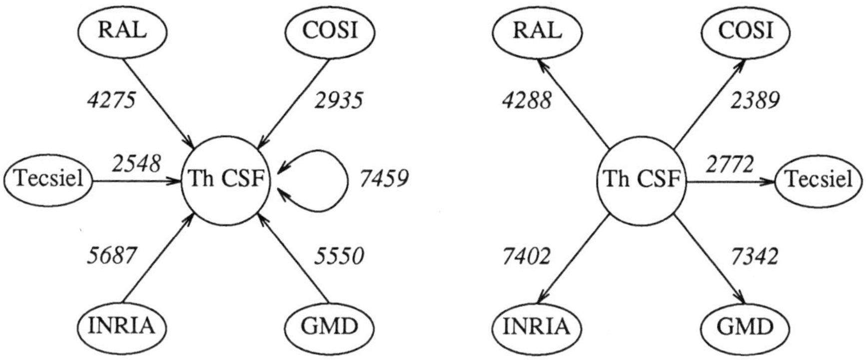

Figure 7. Bandwidth observed into and out of Thomson-CSF

5 The Application Demonstrator

The application demonstrator will take the form of a Geographical Information System. The aim will be to model a system whereby land-based freight operators may obtain information on likely transport difficulties due to adverse weather, roadworks etc in any European country. This information will be distributed via wide-area networks, with the assumption that it is effectively publicly available.

The overall architecture of the application at the display point is shown in Figure 8. The basic model is one whereby static information (road maps) will be stored at the display point. There will be a database of 'difficulties' associated with a particular country, held at one site in that country. The user software will interrogate the database to obtain the relevant information and overlay this graphically on the appropriate map. Thus a relatively small amount of information will need to be transferred in a transaction. By using the correct remote service, no application code is needed to serve the difficulty data.

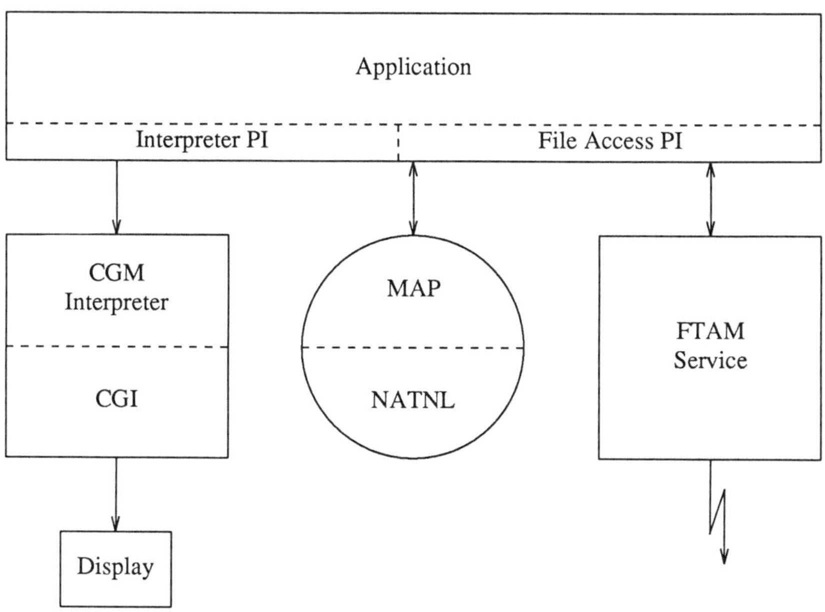

Figure 8. Architecture of the application demonstrator

It is intended that the data will be transferred as a Computer Graphics Metafile (CGM), or more precisely, that it will be abstracted from a CGM held in the 'difficulties' database. To do this, the CGM structure will need to be mapped onto an FTAM representation, and FTAM will be used for the data transfer. It has been shown that the desired performance requirements for queries can be satisfied with the bandwidth of 3Kbit/s which PSPDNs can currently provide between partner sites.

At the time of writing, the graphics architecture for displaying information had not been finalized. It is anticipated that this will use *inter alia* a subset of the emerging CGI standard (Interfacing techniques for dialogues with graphical devices — ISO DIS 9636).

A programming interface to FTAM is being developed, based on the MAP 3.0 API. A number of FTAM implementations are being utilised, including Marben, Tecsiel and ISODE. It is intended that demonstrations will be carried out using heterogeneous hardware and software platforms to illustrate the interoperability accruing from the use of standards.

The FTAM implementations being used need to be enhanced to support access to subunits of a CGM and this is discussed in the next section.

6 Study of Services

The Study of Services workpackage has defined a mapping of CGM onto FTAM. There are mechanisms within ISO/IEC for standardizing such mappings, which are known as FTAM Document Types, and the work being done here is being fed into this process.

Graphics metafiles provide a mechanism for storing graphical information for purposes such as transfer to another system for display, storing partly developed pictures for later modification and storing pictures for incorporation into documents.

ISO 8632 'Metafile for the storage and transfer of picture description information' provides a format for capturing 2D static pictures. The format consists of an ordered set of elements, which have a hierarchical structure as shown in Figure 9.

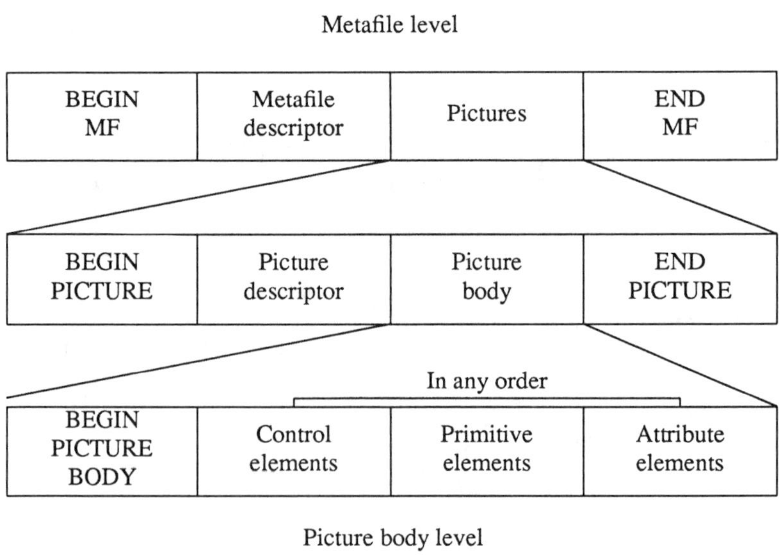

Figure 9. CGM structure

ISO 8632 is a multipart standard. Part 1 specifies the CGM elements, their parameters and the structure of a metafile (constraints on the permitted sequencing of elements). Parts 2 to 4 define these different encodings to represent the abstract syntax of the CGM elements, character encoding, binary encoding and clear text encoding. These have different characteristics relative to ease of generation and interpretation, size of the resulting metafile and ease of transmission between systems.

Several Amendments to CGM are being processed within ISO/IEC. Amendment 1 is of current relevance to this project in that it provides a picture segmentation mechanism. This provides a way to reduce the volume of information required to represent a picture by allowing units which occur repeatedly to be stored only once and invoked by name.

FTAM provides facilities for remote access to a filestore (see Figure 10).

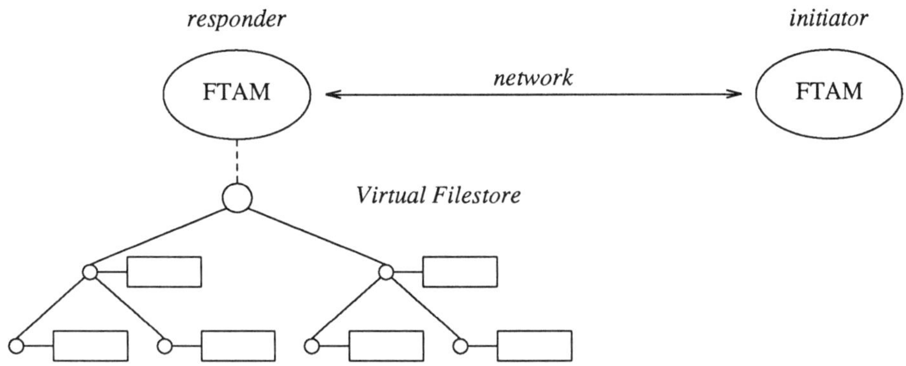

Figure 10. FTAM operation

The ways in which real filestores are implemented vary considerably between real existing systems. Different systems have a wide range of styles for describing the storage of data and the means by which it can be accessed. A common model for describing files and their attributes is needed before services, protocols and procedures for file transfer, access and management can be used in an OSI environment. Such a model is provided by the FTAM *virtual filestore*.

FTAM defines a virtual file as 'an unambiguously named collection of structured information having a common set of attributes'. The basic access units of a file and their relationships are described by the file access structure. This is a tree structure that describes the file in terms of the units which can be accessed separately (FADUs — File Access Data Units). A FADU is the minimal access unit and is a subtree of the hierarchical file; the actual data units are associated with the nodes of the tree, and can be identified by their relative node name. This is illustrated in Figure 11.

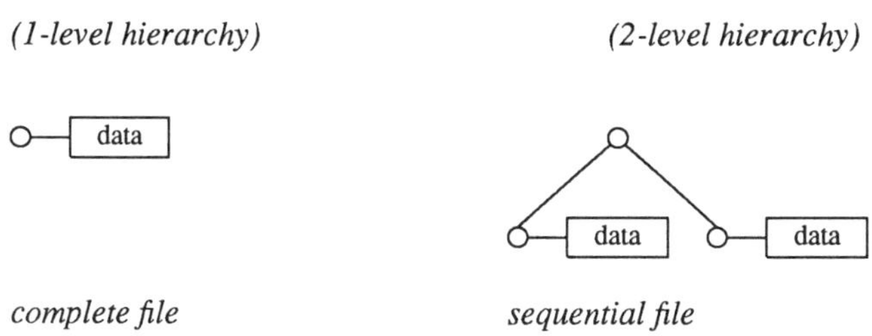

Figure 11. Examples of FTAM virtual filestores

FTAM introduces the idea of a *constraint set*, a set of restrictions and refinements of the general file model, tailored to the needs of a particular class of applications. A *Document Type* defines *inter alia* constraints on the file structure, the data types forming the data units and how the record structure of a real file maps onto the FTAM virtual filestore.

Two CGM Document Types have been defined within the project, corresponding to the three standardized encodings of CGM (one Document Type for the 'binary' encoding and one to be used with either the 'clear text' or 'character' encodings), in the spirit of other FTAM Document Types. The mapping of the CGM structure onto FTAM is illustrated in Figure 12. This structure will allow remote CGMs to be treated by an application in a similar way to local CGMs (ie with knowledge of the structure). Individual pictures within a metafile may be transferred, thus allowing efficient use of bandwidth.

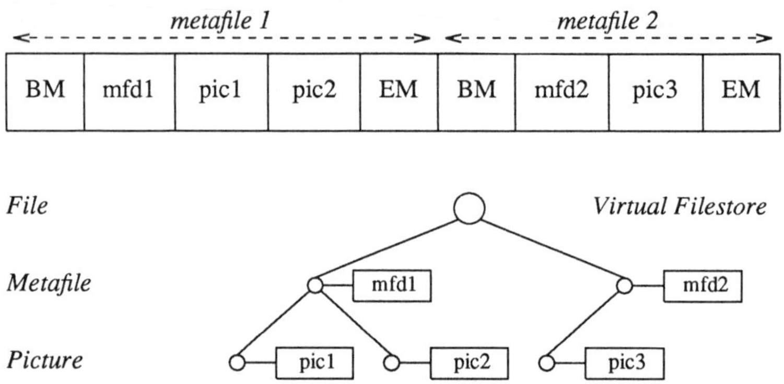

Figure 12. Mapping of CGM onto FTAM Virtual Filestore

The draft CGM Document Type being presented to ISO does not include support of CGM Amendment 1, but the structure can be extended to support segments by adding further levels of hierarchy. This will be explored in the context of the prototype application. However, to do so sensibly, requires additional constraints to be placed on the element sequencing defined in CGM in order to eliminate potential side effects of some elements and other dependencies. These constraints are to be investigated and it is envisaged that an Application Profile for CGM will be developed, which embodies these constraints, to allow more structured access to a CGM by FTAM.

The second piece of work that has been undertaken in this task is the development of a mapping of the X Window System over an OSI stack. ANSI, the US national standards body, has been working for some time on the creation of a national standard based on this windowing system. It is their intention to submit the national standard to ISO/IEC for 'fast track' standardization. To do this requires the development of an internationally acceptable mapping of X Windows over an OSI network; at present mappings only exist for TCP/IP and DECnet networks.

X Windows provides a windowing system based on the client/server model, and this model can be extended across a network. This is illustrated in Figure 13.

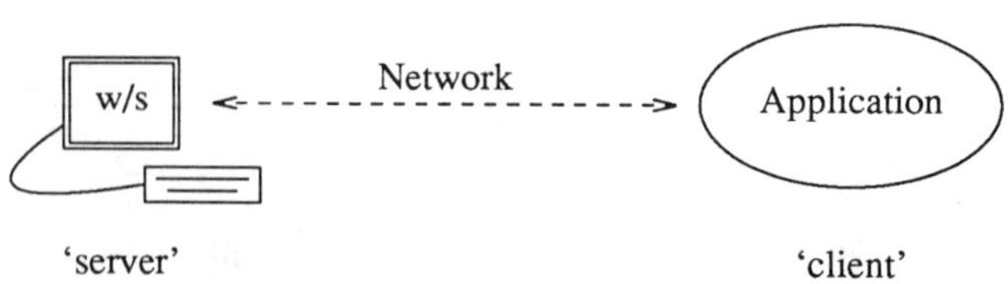

Figure 13. Client/server architecture of X Windows

The specification of X Windows asks only for a 'reliable byte stream' to be provided to do this. This is usually interpreted as a mapping at the Transport Service level. If an attempt is made to map X Windows over a full OSI stack an immediate problem is encountered in that the full stack provides more data-management services than are required by X Windows. Many of these services are either not required, or are already provided by the X Windows *byte stream protocol*. The extent of this overlap is shown in Figure 14.

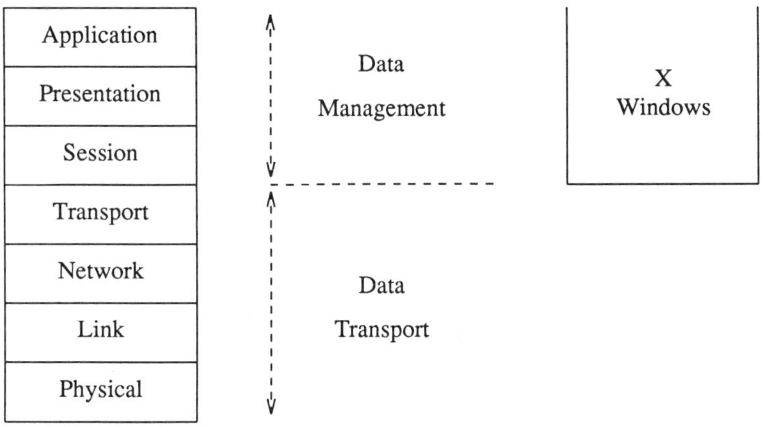

Figure 14. Mapping of X Windows onto an OSI stack

A number of developers have already attempted a mapping of X Windows over the full OSI stack, and over a partial stack extending up to the Transport Layer. Performance measurements have been made of such implementations. The general conclusion is that a mapping over a high-quality ISO Transport Service implementation gives equivalent performance to a mapping over TCP/IP. This is unsurprising, albeit reassuring. However, mappings over a full OSI stack are found to suffer a performance degradation of one-half to two-thirds of the performance of the TCP/IP equivalent. Some of this degradation can be accounted for by implementation inefficiencies (the measurements have been made largely using prototype versions of the supporting stack), but there has also been found to be a penalty in the mere fact that fully-functional Session and Presentation Services are in use.

These experiments have led to the conclusion within the community that a *lightweight* full-stack implementation is required, supplying *only* those services that X Windows needs. Such an implementation must be efficient whilst retaining conformance to OSI standards, and hence an ability to interwork. The first step is to produce a mapping definition that is carefully constructed to allow a lightweight implementation, but which is aligned to work in progress now within ANSI and later within ISO/IEC so that interworking between implementations is possible.

Such a mapping is being progressed through the auspices of EWOS by various interested parties, mainly although not exclusively in the UK. The project is supplying the effort to edit this document, which is scheduled for publication early in 1991 as an EWOS 'Technical Guide'. In this form the mapping will be able to be used as an intercept of any forthcoming ISO/IEC standard. When the latter emerges for 'fast track' it is anticipated that ARGOSI will have a role to play in harmonising European responses to the draft put forward for standardization.

7 Standards

Many of the participants in the ARGOSI project have a personal involvement in standardization work and it will be clear that many of the ARGOSI activities have a contribution to make to standardization. These activities are coordinated by the standardization workpackage. The most significant achievement to date from the project as a whole is the submission of the CGM/FTAM Document Type to ISO/IEC through the Italian national standards body.

Within the graphics area, ARGOSI provides support for the document editor of the CGI standard, and without this support the standard would not have progressed to Draft International Standard status during 1989.

8 Conclusions

Graphics and networking are enabling technologies finding use in an increasing number of application areas, from weather forecasting to remote consultancy in the medical domain. Standardization is a key issue in graphics and networking in order to promote coherence within the market place and avoid fragmentation. The ARGOSI project is demonstrating that integration and harmonization between different areas of standardization activities is also of key importance and through the construction of a prototype application demonstration is endeavouring to show the practical benefits such harmonization can bring.

For more information, please contact one of the authors of this paper, or the Project Manager:

J-J Bardyn
Thomson-CSF
Division Cimsa Sintra
160 boulevard de Valmy
92700 Colombes
FRANCE

Chapter 7

Graphics, Networking and Distributed Computing

George S. Carson

1 Introduction

This paper presents an overview of some important issues relating to implementing distributed systems incorporating computer graphics. It is based on 15 years of experience designing and implementing both large and small scale distributed systems for the US government. These systems typically:

- incorporate multiple computers;
- use graphical workstations that implement critical user interfaces for dedicated operators;
- use a variety of standard and non-standard bus, local area network (LAN) and wide area (WAN) technologies;
- operate in a hard real-time environment;
- incorporate significant amounts of custom software and hardware.

The paper takes a broad requirements-based perspective, not just limited to current and planned OSI and graphics standards. The focus is on what is needed to implement the highest-quality user interfaces in environments where user acceptance is crucial.

2 Fundamental Concepts

2.1 Definitions

This section defines fundamental terms used elsewhere in this paper. We have chosen informal definitions rather than formal ones from the OSI Reference Model and other sources [13].

By *computer graphics* we mean the creation of, manipulation of, and interaction with pictorial representations of objects, data, and/or concepts using computers. This is a deliberately broad definition that casts many text and office applications into the context of computer graphics. Given that these applications today are typically implemented on graphics workstations, it is the appropriate definition.

A *network* is an interconnected collection of autonomous entities. If we specialize to the case of computers, a *computer network* is an interconnected collection of autonomous computers. A *distributed system* is a network with a high degree of cohesiveness and transparency. A *protocol* is a set of rules and formats governing the communication behaviour among entities [13].

2.2 Motivation for Distribution

There are several well-known reasons that most systems today are distributed. These include [9]:

- improved performance;
- increased availability;
- resource sharing;
- incremental growth;
- improved control.

Each of these advantages carries corresponding and compensating disadvantages that require careful engineering in most situations to overcome. For example, resource sharing cannot be achieved without a degree of homogeneity in information exchange formats and special protocols for controlling access to shared resources.

2.3 Modelling Distributed Systems

For specification, design, and implementation purposes, distributed systems are usually modelled as a collection of communicating processes [4,8,9]. For our purposes, a *process* is defined as an entity with well-defined input, outputs, internal state, and behaviour that relates its outputs and state to its inputs. Processes communicate to:

- synchronize (achieve shared knowledge of system state);
- exchange information.

At the gross level, information exchanges by communicating processes can simply be called *messages*. Very often, special paradigms are adopted for inter-process communication and communication protocols are defined to support the adopted paradigm. Section 3.1 discusses some of these in more detail.

2.4 A Brief History of Distributed Graphics

It is instructive to note that, while the computer graphics market is very diverse, main-stream computer graphics systems have usually distributed graphical functionality in some way. This distribution has evolved through several stages:

- graphical displays for mainframe computers (beginning with the Sketchpad system);
- graphics terminals (such as the Tektronix 4014);
- raster graphics personal computers and workstations;
- ''windowing protocol'' terminals (such as X windows terminals)

Changes in distribution have been caused by economic factors, the availability of new technologies, increasing performance demands, and marketing factors.

3 Communication Concepts

3.1 Paradigms for Inter-Process Communications

The most common paradigms used for inter-process communication are illustrated in Figure 1.

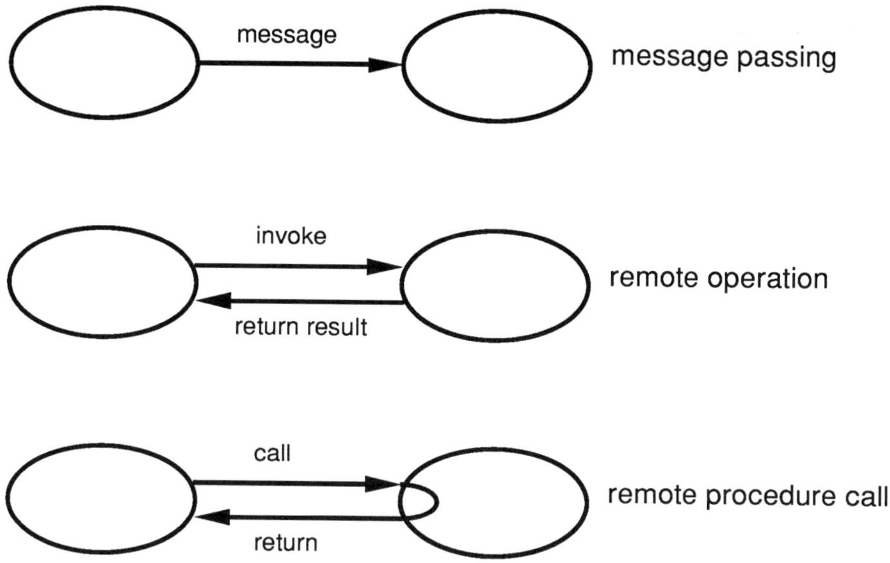

Figure 1. Common communication paradigms

Message passing – Processes communicate by exchanging messages. No additional formal structure on message exchange is imposed by the communication system, but the applications themselves adopt a protocol for understanding the messages. Communication protocols can be thought of as using message exchange to implement their functions [4].

Remote operations – Adds structure to communication among processes by viewing interchanges as a client invoking (remote) operations on a server. Results and errors can be returned to the client or the operation can be rejected [5].

Remote procedure call – Uses the subroutine or procedure call as the metaphor for exchanges between processes. The metaphor of procedure call can be extended in many different ways to incorporate synchronization and other properties in a single mechanism [7,11].

For the latter two paradigms to apply, communication should be transaction-oriented. That is a request for service and its reply are exchanged between active system elements (clients) and passive system elements (servers). For this reason, we often say that such a system follows a *client-server* model. Not all communications are best implemented with these paradigms, especially bulk data and low-latency transfers.

3.2 Communication Considerations

There are several characteristics of communication systems and standards that must be considered when choosing techniques to support the distribution of computer graphics functionality. The most important of these are:

Available services – Communications services of interest to computer graphics range from the simple (easily implemented, low cost) to the complex (more difficult to implement, higher cost) in roughly the following order:

(1) simple unreliable (datagram) transfer;

(2) reliable (connection-oriented) transfer services;

(3) transaction oriented services:

   (a) remote operations,

   (b) remote procedure call,

   (c) transaction processing;

(4) file transfer services;

(5) virtual terminal services.

Bandwidth – Communication bandwidth measures the amount of data that can be passed through a given system (or a portion of it, such as a single connection) per unit of time. It is usually measured in bits per second. Bandwidth is heavily dependent on supporting communication media and protocols, and becomes more expensive as the distance between the endpoints increases. Bandwidth varies with time in real systems and is thus statistically distributed. Therefore, it is only meaningful to discuss the bandwidth on this basis. The average and 90th percentile cases are often used measures of bandwidth.

Service delay – Service delay measures the amount of time between a request for service and its completion. Each of the communications services listed above has one or more associated delays. Delay is often measured in milliseconds (msec). One especially important delay is the end-to-end transfer time for a message of a given size, measured from the time it is presented for transfer by the originating process until it is delivered to the destination process. Service delays are statistically distributed in real systems, so it is only meaningful to discuss the delay for some percentile of all service requests. The 90th percentile is an often used measure.

Connection establishment delay – One important service delay is the time needed to establish a "connection" between two communicating entities. This can often be several seconds, even in simple systems.

The choice of strategy in a given system must be engineered based on many competing factors, including these:

– *Functional and Performance*

  capacity
  quality and accuracy
  manning
  availability
  security
  transition
  expandability
  reconfigurability
  organizational impact

– *Risk*

  schedule
  technology

– *Cost*

  software
  hardware
  operations
  integration
  cost effectiveness

It should be obvious that no single communication strategy or computer graphics technology can accommodate the needs of all – or even a majority of – systems.

3.3 Terminal Concepts

Among the earliest user interaction devices were keyboard/printers that resembled teletypes or typewriters in operation. As technology advanced, these were generalized to create the alphanumeric terminal, where a CRT screen replaced the paper in the printer. These terminals had instruction sets where coded character sets corresponded to actions taken by the terminal. Although it was reasonable (for a while) to continue this line of evolution by adding graphical instructions of increasing complexity, several flaws in this approach emerged:

- coded character sets intermixed semantically different information, such as glyphs and locations;
- fixed instruction sets proved inadequate for input, other than "string" input from keyboards;
- as terminals were separated from host computers over longer "wires", response times became intolerable.

Although terminals have proved useful in very cost-sensitive applications (such as videotext systems) where low-quality interfaces suffice, they have been found inadequate for general purpose graphics use. All attempts thus far to generalize the terminal concept – for example, by defining virtual terminals – have suffered from the same defects as the original concept and have not become commercially successful. This has fuelled the growth of the intelligent workstation market.

4 Human Factors Considerations

4.1 Response Times

In interactive systems there are several critical response times that must be met for a high-quality user interface. These response times provide a hard real-time limit against which candidate systems must be judged. A large number of response times have been experimentally determined and are in good agreement with those predicted from models of human performance [3].

The first important time deals with the characteristics of human movement in such tasks as tracking moving targets and freehand drawing. Human movement is executed in a series of preplanned microsteps of 70 msec each. The feedback loop from perception to action takes about 250 msec [3].

A second important response time is derived from the time that a perception of immediate causality degrades in a human. This is important if a user is to achieve a sense of "psychological closure" between actions and their consequences. The perception of immediate causality begins to degrade at 50 msec and ends about 100 msec [3].

Studies have shown that tolerable response times relate to user's expectations [10], and that consistency is more important than absolute response time [2]. The availability of personal computers and workstations – such as the Apple Macintosh computer – with "local" high-performance interfaces has raised the expectations of a significant number of users. Studies have also found that users are more productive with a somewhat slower system having a lower response-time variance than a somewhat faster (on the average) system with a wider variance.

4.2 Good Interfaces

There is a considerable body of evidence that demonstrates that there is no one best "user interface" for all applications. Successful systems have used a wide variety of interaction styles and techniques including these (overlapping) categories [1]:

- command line dialogues;
- natural language interfaces;
- menu systems;
- form filling dialogues;
- iconic interfaces;
- window systems;
- direct manipulation interfaces;
- graphical interaction.

Experience has also shown that a good bit of fine-tuning and experimentation is necessary to construct a good interface.

The above facts imply that:

- no single category of communications services best supports all interfaces;
- it must be easy to change a user interface, and to relocate processing to improve response times.

4.3 Inter-Referential I/O

Human factors experts studying modern graphical user interfaces have developed the concept of inter-referential I/O to explain an important feature of such systems [12]. *Inter-referential I/O* is defined as the ability for one part of the user-computer dialogue to refer to another. A simple example is a mouse pointing to (and selecting) an object. There are examples in all 4 obvious classes of relations: input-input (undo and re-do), input-output (graphical "pick input"), output-input (error messages), and output-output (interactive browsers). Considerations of inter-referential I/O leads to structuring interfaces as a hierarchy of objects.

Modern computer graphics interfaces incorporate complex inter-referential interactions, requiring quick (50-100 msec) changes in input and/or output based on user or system actions. The inter-referential coupling required can be of arbitrary complexity. Figure 2 shows two simple examples. In the first, an "icon" is inverted showing its selection based on a mouse-down. In the second, some amount of edited text is highlighted to show its selection.

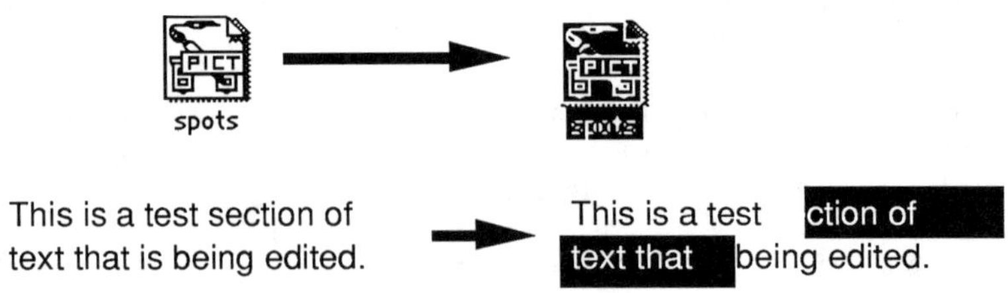

Figure 2. Inter-referential I/O examples

Implementing general inter-referential I/O means that either the user interface is provided locally, or that inter-referential actions can be defined remotely and "downloaded" to the "graphical workstation". The reason for this is that consistent 50-100 msec end-to-end responses in a distributed environment usually cannot be guaranteed. The former approach is taken in many distributed Macintosh applications (such as the Applelink and America On-line electronic mail systems). The latter approach is adopted in the Sun NeWS system.

5 System Considerations

5.1 System Bottlenecks

Performance problems arising in distributed systems can come from many sources. These include:

Operating system – A vast body of experience has shown that a true real-time operating system is required to support (distributed) graphics applications. Although non real-time systems – such as Unix – can be extended, the results are sub-optimal. Significant overheads (tens of milliseconds of delay) is often encountered in passing data between communications software/hardware and software processes.

Communications systems – Some overhead due to communications is inevitable. The most significant overhead sources are: connection establishment delay, round-trip (''mash-to-flash'') delays and throughput limitations. Due to the finite speed of light, there are significant and unavoidable delays in wide-area communications systems. For example, it takes about 500 msec to pass data through a link incorporating a communications satellite in geosynchronous orbit.

Graphical processing – The overhead due to round-trip delays necessary to process input or output is often significant in interactive applications (see Section 4.3). The bandwidth required to transfer ''elaborated'' graphical data often determines where elaboration – such as rendition – occurs. Even in non-interactive applications, the transfer of significant amounts of raster data can strain available bandwidth.

5.2 Categorizing Graphics Applications

Computer graphics ''applications'' may be divided into three major categories each of which has different communications requirements. These categories are:

Interactive – These are applications where computer graphics provides the user's primary interface to the system. Graphical input devices are usually used, and there are significant and time-critical inter-referential interactions.

Non-interactive – These applications involve the transfer of graphical data. Such data may be contained in one of several common forms:

- graphical metafiles;
- graphics in documents (such as office documents);
- graphics in messages (such as electronic mail);
- output device interfaces (printing).

Pseudo-interactive – These are applications where computer graphics technology does not provide the primary form of interaction. Such applications include (multi-media) conferencing systems (where display delays are expected and tolerable), cooperative work (where data may be displayed, reviewed, and turned around on a long time scale), and some data access systems, where a user reviews, but does not interact with, remote data.

Note that a single system may have functionality that spans all three areas. An example would be a cooperative document editing and publication system.

5.3 Using Communication Concepts in Computer Graphic Systems and Standards

First, there are several areas where computer graphics systems and standards incorporate concepts that are strongly ''communications-related'' in their nature. These include:

- identification (naming);
- locating named objects (directory services);
- resource management;
- file management;
- transaction management;
- synchronization;
- object representation and encoding;
- security.

There are two somewhat conflicting approaches to this area. First, it is only natural to believe that graphics standards/systems should not reinvent communications concepts. Second, graphics standards/systems cannot in general require OSI services to operate, since both cnetralized and distributed implementations should be possible.

Considering these two approaches, we conclude that graphics systems and standards should adapt/adopt accepted (standard) concepts from other areas (including communications) where possible; and there should be simple mappings (that can be standardized in profiles) between communication concepts specialized in graphics standards and OSI concepts.

Adding the above strategy can:

- eliminate needless duplication of effort;
- maximize the reuse of modular software and hardware components;
- insure system correctness;
- minimize the burden of mapping between graphics and communications approaches.

6 Conclusions

The above technical considerations and our experience in building actual, working distributed systems has led us to the following conclusions. Note that these apply to the class of systems in which we are involved, and must be generalized with care:

(1) The best user interfaces are built using local, dedicated processing. Even a local network cannot be reliably interspersed in an interactive graphical application.

(2) The concept of a fixed instruction set terminal – virtual or otherwise – has long-since outlived its usefulness.

(3) The proper distributed interface is at the IPC and database levels, not within the user interface. Remote access protocols (such as those to SQL database servers) and remote operations protocols are a useful paradigm here.

(4) OSI is useful in computer graphics systems for:

   - file transfer;
   - support for the IPC intrastructure;
   - connections for distribution in specialized situations.

7 References

1. Baecker, Ronald M. and William A.S. Buxton, *Readings in Human-Computer Interaction: A Multidisciplinary Approach,* Morgan Kaufmann, San Francisco 1987
2. Boehm, B., et al, "Interactive Problem Solving – An Experimental Study of Lockout Effects", *Proc SJCC,* 1971, pp 205-210
3. Card, Stuart K., Thomas P. Moran, and Allen Newell, *The Psychology of Human-Computer Interaction,* Lawrence Erlbaum and Associates, Inc. 1983
4. Carson, George S., Message-based Distributed Computing, *Proc. IEEE Real-time Systems Symposium,* Los Angeles, CA, December 1982, pp 170-183
5. CCITT Recommendation X.410, *Message Handling Systems: Remote Operations and Reliable Transfer Server* 1984
6. Cheriton, David R., *The Thoth System: Multi-process Structuring and Portability,* Elsevier, New York 1982
7. *Courier: The Remote Procedure Call Protocol,* Xerox System Integration Standard, Xerox Corporation, Stamford, CT 1981
8. Hoare, C.A.R., *Communicating Sequential Processes,* Prentice-Hall, London 1985
9. Lampson, B.W., M. Paul, and H.J. Siegert, *Distributed Systems: Architecture and Implementation, An Advanced Course,* Springer-Verlag, Berlin 1981
10. Miller, R.B., "Response Time in Man-Computer Conversational Transactions", *Proc 1968 FJCC,* pp 267-277
11. Nelson, B.J., *Remote Procedure Call,* Ph.D. Thesis, Carnegie-Mellon University 1981
12. Norman, Donald A. and Stephen W. Draper, *User Centered System Design,* Lawrence Erlbaum and Associates, Inc 1986
13. Tanenbaum, Andrew S., *Computer Networks,* Second Edition, Prentice-Hall, Englewood Cliffs, New Jersey 1988

Chapter 8

Office Document Architecture (ODA). The Standard for Compound Document Interchange

Peter J. Robinson

8.1 Abstract

In this paper I present a short history and outline the key functional aspects of the "Office Document Architecture (ODA) and Interchange Format" standard for compound document interchange ratified in 1988 by the CCITT, ECMA and ISO. The paper then develops in more detail the graphical aspects of ODA describing the standards used for the representation of the two graphical contents types currently defined in the standard. The paper then discusses the ODA document application profiles (DAPs) being developed by various national and international bodies and identifies the DAPs for interchange of compound documents containing graphics. The paper finally presents the work undertaken by the ESPRIT PODA (ESPRIT 1024) and PODA 2 (ESPRIT 2374) projects to develop and demonstrate interchange of compound documents containing text and graphics using ODA software.

8.2 The ODA Standard, History and Overview

The Office or Open Document Architecture and Interchange Format, ODA, is the new compound document interchange standard for use with Open Systems Interconnection, OSI. Compound documents are those comprised of several different types of content, normally text, graphics and image. ODA was initially published in 1985 by the European Computer Manufacturers Association as the standard, ECMA-101 [1]. Subsequently ODA was adopted by the International Standards Organisation (ISO) and the International Telegraph and Telephone Consultative Committee (CCITT) as basis for their developments to produce a standard document architecture for compound documents. ODA was to be applicable to all forms of communication services involving electronic document interchange. ODA was formally ratified in 1988 as an International Standard, ISO IS 8613 [2] and as the T.410 series of CCITT Recommendations [3]. Also in 1988 ECMA ratified a revised version of its ECMA-101 which brought the original standard into line with that of the CCITT and ISO. All three standards are essentially identical. The only major technical difference being that the ISO standard defines two encoding formats whereas the CCITT Recommendation and the ECMA standard define one.

The ODA standard enables compound documents containing character text, raster graphics (facsimile) images and geometric graphics to be encoded and interchanged electronically. In addition ODA has been specified to enable the interchange of electronic documents so that they can be imaged or printed by the receiver as the originator intended or can be edited by the recipient according to constraints or rules specified by the originator. ODA achieves these capabilities by specifying an abstract architecture representing information contained in a document. The encoded form of this information, for use over communication systems, is called the ODA Interchange Format or ODIF. ODIF uses the ASN.1 [4] abstract syntax notation and encoding scheme [5] used by many OSI protocols, e.g. the CCITT X.400 electronic mail standard [6].

ODA divides the information content of a document into three primary categories. These are:

- logical information;
- layout information;
- content.

The organisation of the information into these categories and the rules concerning its interpretation is termed the document architecture.

The logical information is information that is independent of the page layout. An example of such information is the subdivision of content into chapters, sections, paragraphs, titled figures, footnotes etc. The structuring of the information is in terms of hierarchy and order. For example a chapter may be defined to be comprised of a sequence of sections and section defined to be comprised of a sequence of paragraphs. ODA does not define or name specific logical organisations, or, to use the ODA term "logical structures". ODA provides the capability to define logical structure. The terms used for the hierarchic components of the logical structure are root, compound and basic logical objects. Basic logical objects are the lowest level components and contain content. The actual logical structures are designed by the document designer.

The layout information is concerned with positioning and other image related properties. Similar to the logical structure the layout information is called the "layout structure". Layout structures are comprised of a hierarchy of positioning components called page sets, pages, frames and blocks, blocks being the lowest level positioning components and which ultimately contain the content. Again as with the logical structure, layout structures are defined by the document designer, they are not dictated by the standard.

Content is information which predominantly represents human perceivable marks used to convey meaning, for example, characters or geometric shapes. I have used the term 'predominantly' since some of the information classed as content does not represent a visible mark. Examples of this type of content are the control function codes used by character encoding schemes and geometric control elements used in graphics. The current ODA standard specifies three distinct type of content. These are: character, geometric graphics and raster graphics. In the following section I discuss the two graphics content types in more detail. The rules and definitions pertaining to a content type are said to define a content architecture, for example, the raster graphics content architecture.

In the ODA architecture both the logical and layout structure contain, or more correctly refer to, the same content. This architecture enables either a logical view or a layout view to be taken of the information which is normally the bulk of the document, the content. The architecture also enables processes to be performed on a single ODA document in the most efficient manner. For example a printing process need only be concerned with the layout structures and the content to construct an image of each page. An editing process searching for each third paragraph in a section starting with a particular word would use only the logical structure and the content.

ODA defines three basic types of document dependent upon the information structures that can be present and the corresponding operations that can be performed on them. These are:

- processable documents;
- formatted documents;
- formatted processable documents.

Processable documents have logical structure and content. Formatted documents have layout structure and content. Formatted processable documents have both logical and layout structures as well as content. Processable documents are suitable for editing or searching operations. Formatted documents are suitable for printing and formatted processable documents are suitable for both. In addition the standard defines how, according to the "Layout Process", processable documents can be converted into formatted documents by application of the different attribute sets defined by the standard. For brevity I will only expand on the presentation style attributes.

Presentation style attributes specify characteristics which guide the format and appearance of document content. In the general case presentation style attributes apply to both logical and layout structures. However for the purposes of this paper I will only describe logical presentation style attributes. ODA defines the meaning of logical presentation style attributes in terms of layout structures and transformations to the logical content to give laid out content. This definition takes the form of a process specification, the so called content layout process.

The final components of the ODA architecture I will mention are termed generic structures. These are sets of rules, within an interchanged document, which when processed by a recipient's ODA conforming system, impose consistency as defined by the originator. ODA supports both logical and layout generic structures, thus enabling control over these two different aspects of a document to exercised.

In this section I have only mentioned the key architectural aspects of ODA. Those concerned with presentation styles will be used in the later sections of this paper. The standard is more complex than this brief outline implies and consequently it has a richer functionality than I have indicated.

8.3 Graphic Content Types

In the previous sections of this paper I described the basic principles and facilities of ODA, in particular how the content of a document is represented using a number of content types, each having its own specific content architecture. I now discuss the Raster Graphic and Geometric Graphic content architectures.

8.3.1 Raster Graphics Content Architecture

The raster graphics content architecture specifies a representation of pictorial information by representing a rectangular picture using dots. These dots are termed picture elements or "pels", and the rectangular arrangement of the pels representing the picture an "array of pels".

The raster graphics content architecture is based on CCITT Recommendations T.4 and T.6, "Coding schemes and control functions for Group 3 and 4 facsimile apparatus" [7]. A bitmap encoding scheme is also included which is different from the Group 3 and 4 facsimile encoding schemes.

The current ODA raster graphics content architecture is restricted to monochrome images, that is images comprised of two tones, normally black and white. Work is being undertaken by ISO to include multi-coloured images. This will be the subject of an addendum to the standard and is currently progressing through the ratification process.

The raster graphics content architecture supports formatted and formatted processable forms for raster content. The first of these can be used in formatted form documents. The latter can be used in formatted, processable and formatted processable form documents. These three forms are provided for in the raster graphics content architecture by:

- a "final" form in which the spacing of pels can take a limited number of values;
- a "fixed dimension" form in which the spacing of pels can take any positive rational value;
- a "scalable" form in which the spacing of pels is determined by the layout process so as to maximise the dimensions of the image within an available area.

The first of these is specifically for use with the ODA formatted form whereas the remaining two are applicable to the processable and formatted processable forms.

The fixed dimension form is designed for use with the logical structure. This form specifies that the raster graphics content can be included in a document having any page layout but that the raster graphics must have certain fixed dimensions.

This is an important feature of ODA raster graphics as it enables the document originator to indicate his intention that he is unconcerned with the layout of the content but that certain raster images must be presented with a fixed size.

The third form, the scalable form, is also for use with the logical structure. In this case it places no constraints on the dimensions of the resultant raster graphics image as specified. This form is the most flexible representation and as such, pictorial images can be included in any document irrespective of their page layout, the layout process adjusting the dimensions of the raster content.

The full set of raster graphics presentation attributes are listed below, they are:

- Pel path;
- Line progression;
- Clipping;
- Pel transmission density;
- Initial offset;
- Pel spacing;
- Spacing ratio
- Image dimensions.

I will describe "Clipping" in more detail as an example of the meaning and use of these attributes. The "clipping" presentation attribute is used to specify a subregion of the pel array used as the raster image. Pels outside the rectangular region defined by this attribute are not imaged. If this attribute is not specified then all pels of the pel array are used.

This attribute could be used to incorporate into a document a region of an existing raster picture without having to process the raster to select the region required. The complete raster can be incorporated into the document and by using the clipping attribute only the required region will be considered as part of the document.

The raster graphics content architecture recognises four distinct encoding schemes for the content. These are:

- the bitmap encoding;
- T.6 encoding;
- T.4 one dimensional encoding;
- T.4 two dimensional encoding.

In the bitmap encoding scheme an array of pels is represented as a bitmap. That is a two dimensional array of bits, each bit having the value of zero or one, zero representing the background tone and one the foreground tone. The bitmap encoding scheme is similar to that employed by current high resolution bit mapped graphics workstations.

The pel array is encoded such that the attribute "number of pels per line" is the number of columns of the array. Each row of the pel array is encoded as a sequence of eight bit values. Hence for certain pel arrays the last eight bit value of each sequence can contain between 1 and 7 padding bits. The padding bits are defined to be not part of the image and are ignored.

The T.4 and T.6 encoding schemes provide for both compressed and uncompressed forms of the content. The T.6 encoding scheme has been recommended by the CCITT for the efficient interchange of group 4 facsimile and hence is ideally suited to use within ODA as a format that is efficient for transmission.

8.3.2 Geometric Graphics Content Architecture

The geometric graphics content architecture enables ODA documents to include diagrams, figures etc. made from geometric elements such as lines, circles, arcs, pattern filled areas etc. This graphic capability is essential for ODA to be suitable for interchange of technical documentation such as reports, manuals etc.

A primary objective of the geometric graphics content architecture during its development was that it should be compatible with existing standards and application packages. This objective applies to content architectures in general and is likely to be adhered to for the new content architectures already being considered as extensions to ODA. In case of the geometric graphics content architecture this meant the use of an existing standard for graphics interchange rather than developing one exclusive to the ODA standard.

The geometric graphic content architecture is based on the ISO standard 8632 - Computer Graphics Metafile (CGM) [8]. This standard became a full International Standard in September 1986. CGM was chosen as it is suitable for the storage, retrieval and interchange of picture description information. These objectives are similar to those of ODA. The geometric graphics content architecture consists of:

- an ordered set of elements which structure the information in the content portions;
- presentation properties which are applicable to basic logical and layout structure components.

The geometric graphics content architecture can only describe a single geometric graphics picture completely contained within the dimensions of a block or contained within a single logical object.

An important property of each content architecture is the definition of how the elements of the content are to be positioned relative to the lowest level layout objects, blocks, in the layout structure.

In the case of the geometric graphics content architecture the geometric elements comprising the content of a picture are positioned according to the rules of the CGM standard in their own coordinate system, termed the virtual device coordinate space.

When CGM is used with the ODA standard, the content architecture defines how the coordinate system of the content portions (the CGM metafile elements) relates to that defined by the ODA layout structure. The geometric graphics content architecture defines a coordinate system local to each block of geometric graphics content and relates this to the virtual device coordinate space of the content, thereby specifying how geometric elements are to be positioned within blocks. Blocks are positioned within frames and frames within pages using the normal ODA positioning attributes. CGM has an element termed the Virtual Device Coordinate Extent (VDC Extent). The VDC Extent specifies the region of interest of a picture within a potentially infinite virtual space. The VDC Extent element has two parameters indicating the first and second corners within the virtual device space to be used as the region of interest; essentially this region defines the elements to be imaged in the picture.

In the geometric graphics content architecture the presentation style attribute "picture orientation" is used to specify how the region of the VDC Extent is mapped on to the block containing the content by mapping the first corner to a nominated corner of the block and the second corner to the opposite corner. By this mechanism not only is the picture related to and constrained by the block but also the directions of up, down, left and right are specified.

The geometric graphics presentation style attributes specify the initial conditions for formatting and imaging logical and layout objects referring to geometric graphics content. The geometric graphics content architecture presentation style attributes correspond to CGM elements that can also be present in the content. The justification for their inclusion as properties of the logical and layout structures is that for a document containing a number of pictures with a common style the properties need only be specified once. The geometric graphics presentation style attributes correspond to those elements of CGM which initialise values.

In order that a particular picture may define its own characteristics, and to allow for the inclusion within an ODA document of any picture constructed according to the CGM standard, any characteristics defined explicitly by CGM elements within a picture will override values specified by logical or layout objects which reference them. This reflects a generally applicable principle of ODA concerning explicit lower level attribute specifications overriding higher level specifications.

In the geometric graphics content architecture twelve presentation attributes are defined. These are:

- geometric graphics announcer;
- line rendition;
- marker rendition;
- text rendition;
- filled area rendition;
- edge rendition;
- colour representation;
- transparency specification;
- transformation specification;
- region of interest specification;
- picture orientation;
- picture dimensions.

8.4 ODA Document Application Profiles

As the preceding sections suggest, the ODA standard is necessarily complex in order to provide for its general applicability to all classes of compound documents. Recognising this, the ODA standard specifies how to form subsets of the total set of features for use by implementations servicing different levels of user requirements. These subsets are termed document application profiles, abbreviated to, DAPs.

Special technical considerations are required for the use of ODA for interworking between products designed independently of ODA. Whilst the products use their own realisation for features such as page headings and footnotes, ODA has a powerful and generalised architecture for describing the properties underlying those features. The ODA standard does not itself standardize particular constructions such as sections, paragraphs or footnotes. In order to have adequate flexibility, the definition of a DAP allows for the arbitrary creation of such constructions.

Thus, to match current equipment to the architecture of the standard the concept of document "constraint sets" has been developed. A constraint set is the term used to specify how the user-perceived features are encoded in ODA using attribute values. The constraint set concept is incorporated in the ISO/CCITT rules for the definition of application profiles for the use of ODA. A major part of the development of an application profile is the definition of appropriate constraint sets. The four profiles described below include constraint set definitions providing for all the document architecture features as well as composite constructions such as graphic images formed from overlaid character text, raster images, geometric images together with titles and a numbering scheme.

On a worldwide basis, a family of standard application profiles for the use of ODA is being developed within the CCITT and by a collaboration of the regional OSI workshops in a group known as PAGODA ("Profile Alignment Group for ODA"). PAGODA profiles will be ratified by ISO as International Standard Profiles (ISPs). The first ratified profile is CCITT's "Processable Mode 1" (PM1) and CCITT PM2 and PM3 and the corresponding ISO ISPs are to be ratified in 1990.

Within Europe, the application profiles under preparation within the European Workshop for Open Systems (EWOS) were ratified as European norms by the European standards bodies CEN and CENELEC in October, 1989. These are to be fully consistent with the CCITT/PAGODA profiles.

The following application profiles are being defined on an international basis for the use of ODA. The names quoted here are recognised internationally but are formally those applicable within the work programme of the European Workshop for Open Systems.

8.4.1 Q111

Application profile Q111 is functionally identical to the CCITT Recommendation for "Processable Mode 1" (PM1), CCITT T.502. This application profile provides for use of character text only, and is designed to be suitable for use between generally available PC word processing packages. Formal ratification of the specification of CCITT T.502 was completed by the CCITT in November 1988. Formal ratification as a European ENV was completed in October 1989. It is being ratified by PAGODA through the ISO ISP process as "Core-11".

8.4.2 Q112

Application profile Q112 has been derived from the experience of the European research project, known as the PODA project. The application profile supports character text, raster and geometric graphics, and is suitable for use between software systems derived from adding graphics functions to vendors' advanced word processors. Q112 is a strict superset of Q111 in the sense that apart from application profile identifiers Q111 data streams are also Q112 data streams. Formal ratification as a European ENV was completed in October, 1989. Q112 will be maintained fully compatible with the application profile being ratified by CCITT as "Processable Mode 2" (PM2) and by PAGODA through the ISO ISP process as "Core-26.

8.4.3 Q113

Application profile Q113 is to be derived from the ODA Implementors Agreement of the NIST OSI Workshop; this is a stable agreement. It is this application profile which is incorporated into the TOP Version 3.0 specification and is being incorporated into the US GOSIP-2 Recommendations. The application profile supports character text, raster and geometric graphics, and is suitable for use between desktop publishing systems. Q113 will be a strict superset of Q112. It will be fully compatible with the application profile being ratified by CCITT as "Processable Mode 3" (PM3) and by PAGODA through the ISO ISP process as "Core-36".

8.4.4 Q121

Application profile Q121 is a layout independent application profile intended for use in messaging systems, to support the interchange of simple character text messages; it provides for the support of aspects such as paragraphs and varying indentations. Formal ratification as a European ENV was completed in October, 1989. In this case, equivalent profiles are not being developed by the CCITT or by the PAGODA process.

8.5 ODA Compound Document Interworking Over X.400

The initial demonstrations of ODA interworking were undertaken at the Hanover CeBIT exhibitions in 1987, 1988 and 1989. These demonstrations focused on establishing the feasibility of ODA interchange between different vendors equipment without modification to underlying products.

Each of the companies taking part in the demonstrations provided conversion software between its proprietary format and ODIF, the ODA Interchange Format. Documents could be sent, in ODIF, from any one of the document processors to any other, where it could in turn be edited and if desired, forwarded again.

The hardware, operating systems and word processors used by each of the partners at the CeBIT demonstrations have provided a variety of different systems, including:

- Unix based systems, proprietary operating system and IBM compatible MS-DOS system;
- a wide variety of different proprietary word processors;
- print servers..

The most recent demonstration, at CeBIT '89 included ten organisations:

- ICL
- Bull
- Olivetti
- Siemens
- Nixdorf
- IBM
- British Telecom
- Oce
- National Computing Centre
- University College London

The interworking facilities demonstrated included:

- ODA used for character text level of interchange
- ODA used for full compound document interchange (text, graphics and image)
- ODA interchange on magnetic media
- ODA as a print format
- ODA conformance testing
- a full ODA editor.

The document features that were represented in the application profile demonstrated at CeBIT are representative of those likely to be found in documents ranging from simple memos to highly structured reports. The features that can be represented include:

Logical features

Sections with optional automatic section numbers
Titles
Paragraphs
Footnotes
Footnote references (automatic and user defined)

Layout features

Page formats
Synchronised columns
Snaking columns
Page numbering
Line spacing

Text Layout control

Single column text
Margins
Tabulation stops
Alignment (justified, centred etc.)
Word wrapped within margins
Non-breaking spaces
Forced page breaks
Soft hyphens

Text Rendition

Bold
Underline
Subscript and superscript

Character Set

The graphic character set supported is a subset of the Teletex subrepertoire of ISO 6937/2
Note: It is intended to focus also on ISO 8859 in future demonstrations
Raster Images
Content with a coding derived from the use of Group 3 and 4 Facsimile standards

Geometric Images

Content with a coding derived from a subset of the Computer Graphics Metafile standard (CGM ISO 8632)

The ODA standard is specifically designed to be independent of any particular communications protocol. However, it is anticipated that in many office systems ODA will be used in conjunction with the X.400 mail standard. Correspondingly, at CeBIT 88 and 89, X.400 was used to communicate ODA documents between machines.

The CeBIT demonstrations were organised by the PODA project, which is a major research project within the ESPRIT programme. PODA is ESPRIT project 1024, Piloting of the Office Document Architecture (PODA). The PODA project started in 1986 and its successor PODA 2 (ESPRIT Project 2374) will run until mid 1991. The prime contractor for PODA was Siemens; PODA 2 is being led by ICL.

The overall objective of the PODA 2 project is: "To advance the application of the ODA Standard to multi-media document handling in the context of multi-vendor systems and to support the rapid development of ODA based products that will benefit the whole Community. The result will be the practical exploitation, extension, refinement and promotion of ODA".

8.6 Overall System Design

The system created by the PODA project for demonstrating the interchange of documents using ODA is presented in the overall system diagram of figure 1.

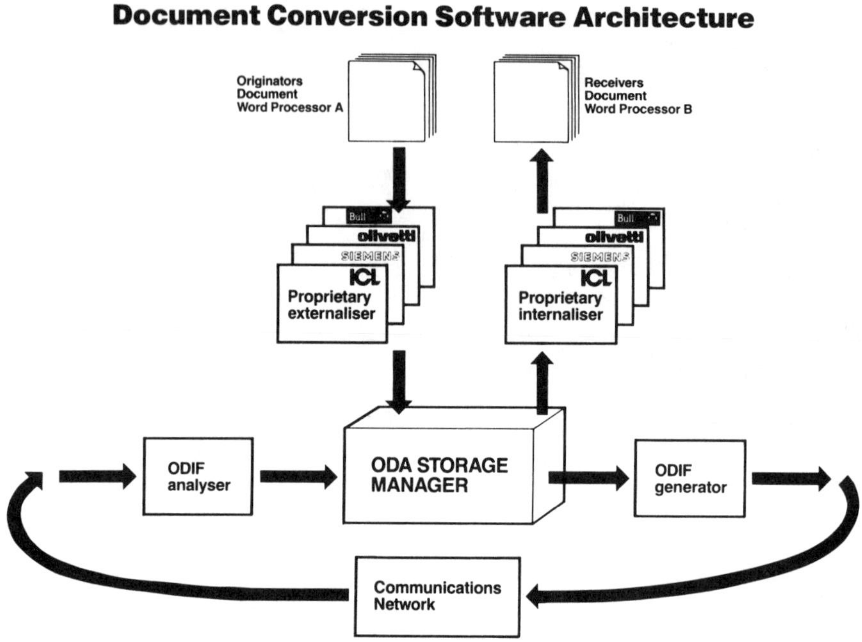

Figure 1. Overall System Diagram

The components of the software architecture are:

- Proprietary Format Externaliser;
- ODA Storage Manager;
- ODIF Generator;
- ODIF Analyser;
- Proprietary Format Internaliser;

Of these software components the ODA Storage Manager, the ODIF Generator and the ODIF Analyser were all written in the 'C' programming language and were ported to some of the partners' machines and operating systems. The ODA Storage Manager, ODIF Analyser, ODIF Generator and ODA diagnostic utility programs are available under licence from ICL.

Proprietary Format Externaliser and a Proprietary Format Internaliser were developed by each of the four PODA partners, one for each of the company word processor formats used in the Hanover demonstration. In addition to these major software components other components, such as utilities to print the stored ODA document in human readable form were developed to aid in testing the system. In addition an ODA Layout Process or Formatter was developed (not shown in figure 1). This was used to convert the processable form ODA documents interchanged between the word processors into the ODA formatted form, suitable for output to a printing system.

8.6.1 The Proprietary Format Externalisers

The Externaliser software is responsible for examining the word processor document, to determine which user-perceived features it uses as defined by the DAP it is working to. The externaliser then proceeds to represent these features in the appropriate ODA constructs, again as defined by the DAP. Each of the system conversion components represents the required ODA constructs in an in store, random access form of ODA. This random access form of ODA has been termed "SODA" by the project, as the acronym for "Stored ODA". The externaliser software component was made by all of the project partners, one for each of their chosen word processors used in the Hanover demonstration.

8.6.2 SODA and the ODA Storage Manager

The SODA form is created and accessed through the ODA Storage Manager, ODASM. The ODA Storage Manager [9] is a set of library functions for performing and managing access to ODA constituents in their stored form and simplifies certain of the operations required on the more complex types.

The document interchange format defined by the ODA standard is termed "ODIF", as the acronym for "ODA Interchange Format". ODIF has been specifically designed for the interchange of documents over communications networks. ODIF is a serial stream format and as such is unsuitable for the processing required for conversion to and from existing document formats. SODA has been specifically designed for such processes as document format conversion where random access to ODA constituents is of prime importance.

SODA is a data interface which defines 'C' programming language structures representing ODA constituents. These include structure members used by the interface access mechanism and structure members corresponding to, or related to all valid attributes in the DAP for each type of ODA constituent. The ODA Storage Manager was designed by ICL and was ported to both Unix and MS-DOS systems and used by the other project partners in their components of the system. The ODA storage format, SODA, was also designed by ICL.

8.6.3 The ODIF Generator

The ODIF generator reads the document in its stored SODA format and converts it to ODIF. This conversion process is facilitated by the design of SODA which closely matches the ODA architecture.

8.6.4 The ODIF Analyser

This component performs the inverse operation to that of the ODIF Generator: it reads a file of ODIF and converts it to the SODA form making use of the Storage Manager functions. The analyser also performs the essential check that the data stream is syntactically correct ODIF, a feature of great assistance during the development process.

The full details of the ODIF Generator and Analyser are described in [10]. Since the Hanover demonstration, improved ODIF Generator and Analyser components have been developed based on the ISO Development Environment software, (see [11]).

8.6.5 The Proprietary Format Internaliser

This component processes the SODA form of a document and converts it to the format required for the appropriate word processor. This component was constructed by each of the project partners, one for each of their particular word processors.

8.7 Conclusion

This paper has presented a brief overview of ODA and in particular the graphics aspects of this new standard for the interchange of compound documents.

The paper then described an important aspect of ODA, Document Application Profiles, now in the final stages of standardisation. The paper presented an overview of Document Application Profiles and gave details of the four profiles being defined, identifying Q112 and Q113 as those which include graphics.

Finally the paper gave details of the two ESPRIT PODA projects that have undertaken research into evaluation and advancement of the ODA standard. The paper gave details of the public demonstrations undertaken by these project and presented an overview of the software that has been developed.

ODA is an important step in office systems enabling compound documents to be interchanged between systems developed by different manufacturers. ODA, together with the development of OSI communications, will enable businesses to achieve some of the long promised cost benefits of office automation.

8.8 Acknowledgements

I would like to thank the assistance given to me in preparing this paper by my colleagues in ICL and other members of the PODA projects. Without their assistance and criticism, preparing this paper would not have been possible.

8.9 References

[1] Standard ECMA-101, Office Document Architecture, September 1985.

[2] ISO 8613 : Office Document Architecture (ODA) and Interchange Format.

[3] CCITT T.410 Series of Recommendations, Open Systems Architecture and Interchange Format.

[4] ISO 8824 : 1987 Information Processing - Open Systems Interconnection, Specification of Abstract Syntax Notation One (ASN.1).

[5] ISO 8825 : 1987 Information Processing - Open Systems Interconnection, Specification of basic encoding rules for Abstract Syntax Notation One (ASN.1).

[6] CCITT Recommendation X.400: 1988, Message Handling. (Seven parts).

[7] CCITT Recommendation T.4: 1988, Standardisation of Group 3 Facsimile apparatus for document transmission.
CCITT Recommendation T.6: 1988, Facsimile coding schemes and coding control functions for Group 4 facsimile apparatus.

[8] ISO 8632-1: 1987, Information processing systems - Computergraphics - Metafile for the storage and transfer of picture description information - Part 1: Functional specification.
ISO 8632-3: 1987, Information processing systems - Computergraphics - Metafile for the storage and transfer of picture description information - Part 3: Binary encoding.

[9] Pennell, R.F, Stored ODA Interface (SODA), ESPRIT project 1024 deliverable, December 1986.

[10] D'Amato, T and Guerra L, ODIFSM: Internalisation and Externalisation of an ODIF stream, ESPRIT project 1024 deliverable, June1987.

[11] ISO Development Environment. The Wollongong Group, 1129 San Antonio Road, Palo Alto, CA 94303, USA.

Chapter 9

Multipoint Protocol Aspects of Audiovisual Teleconferencing via one or two 64 Kbit/s Channels

David E. Lewis

1 INTRODUCTION

This paper is for contribution to the ESPRIT ARGOSI workshop, Breuberg Germany 15-17 October 1990. The ESPRIT project 2684 MIAS (Multipoint Interactive Audiovisual System) and its relationship to the International audiovisual standards is presented.

The ESPRIT MIAS project (Multipoint Interactive Audiovisual System) is developing the system protocols for a multipoint conference system with high quality audio, real time video and a range of meeting aids such as Facsimile, File Transfer and Editing. To verify the protocols, a practical demonstration will be based on the use of PC based hardware forming a personal multimedia workstation.

The earlier successful MIAC (Multipoint Interactive AudioConference) project demonstrated how a number of audioconference studios may be interconnected by 64 kbit/s links via a centrally located 4 port Multipoint Control Unit (MCU), to provide high quality audio (6 microphones per studio) with enhancements, for one 64 kbit/s channel. The work of the MIAC project is represented in a Draft ETSI Recommendation for Digital Audiographic Conference TN31-2.

Operating via two 64 kbit/s links, and targeted on the emerging ISDN network, project MIAS enhances the facilities and protocols demonstrated in the MIAC project.

The project has contributed to CCITT and ETSI in the area of multimedia systems infrastructure.

2 CONFERENCE FACILITIES

MIAS screen based facilities are provided on a desktop personal computer, in a windowed environment. A high quality audio multipoint environment is provided by a central audio bridge, and a range of multipoint conference enhancements are available. The system is intended for operation via two 64 kbit/s channels but a basic service is possible using a single channel.

Facilities available via one 64 kbit/s channel (MIAC):-

High quality audio (56 or 48 kbit/s) G722
Gp3 Facsimile transfer (8 kbit/s)
Still Picture TV (8 kbit/s)
Telewriter/pointer (800 bit/s)
Chairman control of audio (optional)
Text messages and conference status indications

Additional facilities with a second 64 kbit/s channels (MIAS):-

Real time video
Fast transfer of bulk data for:
- Gp4 Facsimile transfer
- File transfer
- Photovideotex
- Document Editing

3 APPLICATION OF INTERNATIONAL AUDIOVISUAL STANDARDS

The facilities described above are made possible by the services of a number of CCITT recommendations recently ratified or even still in the process of ratification.
The H series of recommendations covers the infrastructure for audiovisual services.

H221 defines the frame structure in a 64kbit/s digital link for audiovisual teleservices. Frame synchronous signalling allows numbers of 64 kbit/s links to be synchronised to form a larger single aggregate bandwidth, and the dynamic subdividision of that bandwidth to provide for multiplexed multimedia data.

H242 defines the procedures for establishing communication between terminals using one or more 64 kbit/s digital channels, up to 2 Mbit/s. These procedures define sequences of the BAS codes defined in H221, for communication establishment and mode changing during a conference.

H261 defines a video codec for real-time audiovisual services at px64 kbit/s. MIAS operates H261 in p=1 mode, thus providing moving video at 64 kbit/s in the B2 channel of the ISDN.

F711 from CCITT SG1 covers the service aspects of audiographic teleconferencing. MIAS complies with this recommendation.

G722 defines the coding technique for high quality audio in 56 or 48 kbit/s bandwidth. In addition to the essential aspect of high quality speech for teleconferencing services, the flexible bandwidth requirements of G722 allows the dynamic reassignment of bandwidth to multimedia conference enhancements.

4 LINK ASPECTS

The MIAS facilities defined in section 2 are multiplexed according to recommendation H221 from CCITT SGXV.

Pioneered in CEPT/NA3/HP6 and the earlier ESPRIT MIAC project, CCITT H221 provides for multiplexed multimedia data by dynamically subdividing a single 64kbit/s channel, or a number of such channels synchronised to form a single channel of larger aggregate bandwidth.

A single 64kbit/s channel is structured into octets at 8kHz. Each bit position of the octets may be regarded as a sub-channel of 8 kbit/s, the eighth sub-channel being called the Service Channel (SC). The service channel contains two repetitive, frame synchronous, signals FAS and BAS which occupy 800 bit/s each.

FAS (Frame Alignment Signal) provides the means for synchronising each 64 kbit/s frame, and also provides for control and alarm information, and end-to-end error performance monitoring.

BAS (Bitrate Allocation Signal) provides the means for dynamically allocating the sub-channels of each 64 kbit/s frame according to the immediate needs of the multimedia facilities. BAS may also be used to signal terminal capability, for instance during the initialisation phase, and for simple conference control signals. However in MIAS a more comprehensive messaging facility is employed, via the H221 MLP (MultiLayer Protocol) channel. MLP is currently under discussion in CCITT SGVIII.

The remaining capacity of the channel (including the remainder of the Service Channel) may convey a variety of signals within the framework of a multimedia service under the control of BAS. Some MIAS scenarios are as follows:-

Option 1: Basic conducted or non-conducted conference mode.
B1 channel - Audio at 56 kbit/s, MLP at 6.4 kbit/s
B2 channel - Moving video at 62.4 kbit/s

Option 2: Slow data transfer with moving video.
B1 channel - Audio at 48 kbit/s, MLP at 14.4 kbit/s
B2 channel - Moving video at 62.4 kbit/s

Option 3: Fast data transfer without moving video.
B1 channel - Audio at 56 kbit/s, MLP at 68.8 kbit/s (residue of B1 plus all of B2).
Moving video temporarily disabled.

5 NETWORK ASPECTS

The MIAS terminals may be operated in a two way terminal to terminal mode via an ISDN 2B connection or via 64 kbit/s leased lines. Conferences of more than two terminals may be created by the use of a central Multipoint Control Unit (MCU), to which each terminal in the conference is connected again via the ISDN or leased lines.

The central MCU, or 'star' configuration as defined in CCITT recommendation F711, is generally adopted as the most efficient method of providing multipoint services in a wide area network. The MCU would typically be a PTT network resource, or may be part of a large company private network.

A number of MIAS MCUs maybe interconnected to increase the size of a conference, the interconnected MCUs behaving effectively as a single larger MCU. A typical reason for using two or more MCUs would be the linking of geographically separated clusters of terminals, thus saving on the expense of long distance links, for instance an international conference between two or more countries.

6 THE MULTIPOINT CONTROL UNIT (MCU)

The MIAS multipoint control unit performs three basic functions:-
i) Audio bridge
ii) Video switch
iii) Control message and bulk data switch

The control protocol aspects of the MCU depend on the services of the message switch, function iii. above. Packetised control information and data is transferred on a link basis between terminals and the MCU in the Multilayer Protocol (MLP) channel of the H221 frame structure as explained in section 4. The MCU distributes messages and data between the connected terminals according to a multipoint addressing facility which creates a true multipoint environment in which all routings are possible including terminal to terminal, broadcast one to all and selective routing to a sub group of terminals.

7 MULTIPOINT PROTOCOLS

Protocols are required for two basic tasks:-
i) Multipoint conference control
ii) Multipoint control/data transport

7.1 MULTIPOINT CONFERENCE CONTROL

MIAS has adopted a distributed approach to the control of the multipoint conference. Tokens for the use of any conference facility are negotiated by the terminals themselves with the MCU acting as a message distributor, but taking no part in the negotiation procedure. Thus the conference control protocols reside in the terminals, and operate identically in the terminal to terminal direct connection, or the multipoint environment via a central MCU. A distributed multipoint environment has been created resulting in an application independent central multipoint control unit.

The distributed conference control protocol relies upon message flows between all points in a multipoint conference, and to achieve this a multipoint data transfer protocol has been developed.

7.2 MULTIPOINT DATA TRANSFER

The control messages, and bulk data between the MIAS facilities, are transferred in dedicated 'multipoint pipes' transparent to the multipoint system, and only the end terminal processes need to understand the message content. Since bulk data between conference facilities such as facsimile or file transfer may coexist in the MLP channel with information of an interactive real-time nature, the latter must be given priority during periods of contention for transmission.

The layered architecture relies upon LapB to provide a secure data transfer on a link by link basis. The higher layers, while bearing superficial similarity with the OSI Reference Model functionality, are customised for the specific task of audiovisual conference control, via a dedicated framed channel as defined in CCITT H221.

The multipoint routing of messages is achieved by a layer 3 addressing field consisting of MCU and Terminal addresses. The priority of the information is also signalled in the layer 3 field. The Session field effectively identifies a transparent 'pipe' as described above. Some messages having a complex data structure are encoded according to ASN1/X208, however the bulk data packets bypass this encoding process for reasons of efficiency.

The MIAS Protocol Architecture

```
---------------------------------
| N | 6 | 5 | 4 | 3 | 2 | 1 | 0 |      APPLICATION
|   |   |   |   |   |---|---|---|
|   |   |   |   |   |   |   |   |      PRESENTATION (ASN1)
|---|---|---|---|---|---|---|---|
|   |   |   |   |   |   |   |   |      SESSION (Multipoint)
|-------------------------------|
|   non-priority    | priority  |      ROUTING (Multipoint)
|-------------------------------|
|            LapB               |      LINK
|-------------------------------|
|   H221 (4.0 - 66.8 kbit/s)    |      PHYSICAL
---------------------------------
```

Control/Interactive sessions:-
0=Control 1=Editing 2=Pointing

Bulk data sessions:-
3=FAX Gp4 4=File Transfer

8 THE MULTIPOINT OPERATION OF MEETING AIDS

Meeting aids are generally designed for operation on a point to point basis and a fundamental task of a multipoint conference system is to provide real-time interactive multipoint environment for facilities such as group editing and pointing, and multipoint operation of standard equipment such as Gp4 facsimile. The concept of the Interface and Protocol Adaptor (IPA) was adopted to map terminal applications onto the MIAS multipoint environment. In this way both integrated screen based facilities and proprietary equipment may be operated in a multipoint environment provided by an application independent MCU.

The Interface and Protocol Adaptor (IPA)

```
            terminal 1                                  terminals
                                                    (as terminal 1)
              IPA          -------------
            -------        |           |-----------| 2
------      |  :  |        |           |
|FAX4|------|  :  |--------|    MCU    |-----------| 3
------      |  :  |        |           |
            -------        |           |-----------| 4
            terminal       -------------

<-- pt-pt --> <----------- multipoint ----------->
                           environment
```

9 STANDARDISATION OF AUDIOGRAPHIC PROTOCOLS IN CCITT

The MIAS approach as described above has been the basis of an input to CCITT SGVIII rapporteurs group for question 23, where the subject for discussion covers protocols for AudioGraphic Conferencing (AGC). Naturarally, there are other approaches and the current input to discussion on AGC protocols will be briefly reviewed. The discussions cover two main areas, i) conference control protocols and ii) multipoint data transfer.

9.1 CONFERENCE CONTROL PROTOCOL

In SGVIII the term Conference Control Service (CCS) has been adopted.

The MIAS approach to CCS as described above is one of DISTRIBUTED control, with the advantage of an application independent MCU. Other approaches range from the totally CENTRAL control where the central MCU is the master with total control over the issue of tokens for conference services, to a hybrid proposal with a mixture of Central and Distributed controls.

9.2 MULTIPOINT DATA TRANSFER PROTOCOL

In SGVIII the term Multipoint Communication Service (MCS) has been adopted.

The MIAS approach to MCS as described above is totally customised to the specific requirements of Audiovisual conferencing in an 'in band' environment provided by the MLP channel of the H221 frame structure.

Other approaches adopt some or all of the protocols from the OSI 7-layer reference model, in a minimal functionality. The full OSI stack approach implies that the 7 layer stack must be terminated on a point to point basis in the MCU ie per MCU port. It is not clear if an application independent transfer of data is possible on a multipoint basis, and it is probable that this approach requires the termination of each terminal application in the MCU. The hybrid approach adopts OSI layers up to session, with a customised MCS above.

9.3 REVIEW OF APPROACHES

It is seen that there are two major areas of contention in the discussions of the AGC protocols CCS and MCS :-

i) CCS - Distributed control versus Centralised control.
ii) MCS - Customised protocols versus protocols from the existing OSI repertoire.

Currently it is difficult to see how a common appoach to a specification for AGC protocols can be achieved from these widely differing viewpoints, without some major compromise on the part of one or all the proponents. All approaches can be claimed to work, although the various implementations are not directly comparable in the services offered.

10 CONCLUSION

The customised multipoint conference control protocols described have been successfully demonstrated for basic conference control purposes with an in-band control channel. The protocols have been further enhanced as described to cater for more sophisticated audiovisual conference facilities.

The relationship of the MIAS protocols to the current AGC protocol discussions in CCITT SGVIII has been reviewed. It is seen that some major differences in approach must be overcome before significant progress can be made towards the drafting of a recommendation for AGC protocols.

ACKNOWLEDGEMENT

The above article is based on the work of the following ESPRIT MIAS partners:

Alcatel (France)
Amper (Spain)
BTRL (UK)
CNET (France)
CSELT (Italy)
RNL (Netherlands)
Telefonica (Spain)

Thanks are also due to the General Manager Network Systems at BTRL for permission to publish this paper.

Chapter 10

The ARGOSI Classification Scheme for Graphics and Networking Applications

Julian R. Gallop

1 The Place of Classification in the ARGOSI Project

Transferring graphics networks in a heterogenous environment introduces its own set of considerations, that are not present when graphics and networking are treated in isolation. The project aims to advance the state of the art of graphics over networks by study and by a prototype, the results of this work being directed to the responsible standards bodies. It is important to relate the work of the project to real applications and to identify aspects of the graphics and networking requirements which applications have in common; this is the task of the classification workpackage in the project.

2 Investigations

Information needs to be obtained about the requirements of applications. This was done by going to the organisations responsible for the applications, either the user organisations themselves or implementors. Two major methods were chosen - interviews and postal questionnaire.

Visits were made by ARGOSI partners to organisations developing applications which use graphics and networking, either now or in the future. Experienced and knowledgeable people in these organizations were approached and a questionnaire was used to guide the interviews.

To gather information more widely, a postal questionnaire was constructed and sent to a wide range of organizations.

2.1 Questions

Although it was not possible to develop the classification scheme before obtaining the information, it was possible to identify the important questions. It is worth mentioning some examples here.

The level of picture elaboration is important. The data could be image data, multi-media data, device-dependent or device-independent graphics data, spatial data, product data, application data etc. The choice here is often governed by the manipulations that the receiver of the data is expected to perform.

Structure in the graphics data is important as this determines whether instancing and subsets can be used.

Data volumes are significant not only for determining communication speeds, but it is also important to know if large primitives are used by the application. In general, graphics standards do not place such requirements on implementations.

Information about the user interaction - occasional or frequent, response time, its purpose - determines the round trip requirements.

Questions were also asked about specific graphics and networking standards and technologies used.

2.2 Interviews

About 50 interviews have been conducted by various ARGOSI partners. Particularly when conducted by a personal visit, this method allows a good understanding of the expert's or user's work. It is possible to understand the reasons for their decisions and to gain an appraisal of the architecture of the application.

In the ARGOSI project, the application demonstrator needed to be selected early to allow time for the demonstrator to be built, but also needed to be guided as much as possible by the classification. A number of factors emerged from the interviews that were conducted early on.

Some applications are inherently spatial and distributed. In these applications which are drawn from application areas such as transport planning and meteorology, there is a useful distinction between high volume but slowly changing data (for example the map) and the data that changes. In some situations this changing data is low volume and useful savings can be made by only transmitting this data.

In other situations also in spatially oriented application areas, the volume of data that needs to be transmitted can be very large - not only the total data, but the amount of data per output primitive. In meteorology, satellite images and complex contours are examples of this. Since graphics standards do not in general make statements about the data volumes, many implementations are not able to handle the large output primitives involved.

In several applications areas, it was commonly found that a user was consulting a portion of existing graphical data.

The features that were emerging from the interviews led the project to consider a prototype application based on consultation of graphical data in a geographical application area. Other factors were taken into account including the decision to use Public Data Networks across Europe and the desire to be able to scale up and use faster networks if they were available. The project decided that a prototype for a freight transport information system would be a suitable demonstration of the relevant graphics and networking standards, which for this purpose was CGM and FTAM.

2.3 Postal Questionnaire

The postal questionnaire was sent to some 2500 people on relevant mailing lists. Mailing lists that spanned Europe were preferred, but lists available to particular partners were also used.

Because the method is entirely non-interactive, the questions were simplified, but with background information about the project. About 140 replies were received and some simple analysis tools were used.

Further information on the postal questionnaire is provided in the workshop paper that describes the project as a whole.

3 Taxonomy

Using the experience and information gained from the surveys, a taxonomy has been derived.

The taxonomy for graphics and networking is based on a set of metrics which characterise applications. For each application, each metric takes a particular value. All the metrics can be thought of as forming an n-dimensional array of n-dimensional boxes. Classifying the application identifies the box in which the application belongs.

Graphical information can exist at a variety of semantic levels within the application and its supporting subsystems. Potentially classifying an application is complex if the problem is not reduced. It was decided that to characterise an application, the place at which data flows across a network is identified. This is the place where the integration of graphics with networking OSI services has significance. When this is done, it is normally possible to identify the values of each metric. This led to the decision that the graphics API used in the user's local workstation had less significance in constructing the present taxonomy than was at first envisaged.

Some applications are more complex in that data may cross a network at more than place in the application. For such an application, each link is studied and the application may be represented in more than one box in the classification.

On occasion, it may be difficult to determine which box an application falls into. This could point to a fault in the taxonomy in which case the taxonomy would need further refinement. Alternatively this difficulty could represent a genuine design decision that needs to be made in the application.

The metrics will now be described.

3.1 Semantic Content

This is the semantic content of graphics data transferred across a network link. The characterisation used is an extended version of a recent draft of the ISO/IEC Reference Model for Computer Graphics.

APPLICATION-DATA refers to all kinds of data other than that identified by the remaining categories. It is noted here for completeness, but does not play a further part in the taxonomy. GRAPHICS-RELATED refers to data that is in some way graphics related, but does not contain graphical information that could be directly executed to produce an image. For example, geographical data, product data (e.g. STEP) or business presentation graphics could be considered in this category.

At all subsequent levels, the concept of graphical input exists but is not explicitly described here.

Data at the CONSTRUCTION level represents a model from which specific graphical scenes can be produced. At the VIRTUAL level, the scene is constructed. The VIEWING level takes a specific view of the scene. Output primitives at this level may have a lower dimensionality than in the virtual environment. The LOGICAL level renders the picture as an image ready for presentation. The image may still be considered to consist of a set of logical output primitives, but attributes which determine the visual appearance have been bound at this level. The PHYSICAL level presents the image for display to a specific device. The data representing the picture at this level is device dependent, for example device opcodes or pixels and colours.

The semantic level determines the processing that needs to take place in the receiving end of the graphical data. It also determines what manipulations are possible in the receiving end, without requiring additional data to be received. To take a simple case, if data at the virtual level is transmitted, the view can be changed in the receiver. If data is transmitted at the logical level, the receiver in general cannot display a new view without receiving more data.

This metric is not necessarily single valued. For example, a cartographic application may display a satellite image overlaid with a map, overlaid with contours. As a result, several kinds of graphics data may need to be accessed and potentially transferred across a network.

3.2 Dimensionality

This metric refers to the dimensionality of graphics data transferred across the network. Dimensionality can refer to the Euclidean or non-Euclidean geometry (for example data expressed in homogeneous coordinates); time; and data associated with the geometry. In this version of the taxonomy, a limited range of values is considered: 2D, 3D, 4D (includes time) and HIGHER.

3.3 Data Source

This metric indicates whether the data to be accessed is a complete known body of structured information (such as a picture or part of a picture) or whether the body of information is being generated to interact with or construct a picture. The values of the metric are COMPLETE and PARTIAL.

3.4 Session Control

This metric characterises a session, rather than individual transactions within a session. The metric indicates which component of the distributed system has control over the selection of data and initiates the transfer. The values of the metric are GIVE-ME, TAKE-THIS and TWO-WAY. For the GIVE-ME and TAKE-THIS styles of session control, the initiator of each transaction is the same throughout the session. For the TWO-WAY style of session control, the initiative for each transaction may pass freely between the parties involved.

3.5 Selection Criteria

The selection of graphical information is another important metric in the classification. The metric is subdivided into three principal categories. A value of WHOLE means that the whole data structure is selected. A value of STATIC-SUBSET refers to a method of selection that is based on the predetermined structure of the data. Within a file of pictures, this could mean selecting a picture. Within a picture, this could refer to a specific grid square if the data were organised in that manner. A value of DYNAMIC-SUBSET refers to a method of selection that need not bear a direct relationship to the predetermined structure or organisation of the stored information.

The dynamic method may be further subdivided. GEOMETRIC selection would take place by satisfying some geometric relationship: examples could be, select all graphical information contained within a given window or select front faces. Selection by ATTRIBUTE involves using non-geometric attributes: select all green primitives.

3.6 Quality of Service

The metrics defined so far distinguish applications in fundamental ways. It is likely that the applications falling within different boxes would be satisfied by different standards. There is a further set of parameters which are not fundamental, but instead refer to how the graphics over networking service scales up or down.

DATA VOLUME refers to the amount of graphics data transferred in a single transaction. It is measured in terms of target data. For this version of the classification, the simple approach of using a pair of numbers has been taken: total number of coordinates plus total number of cells; and number of primitives. There is not a precise identity between a coordinate and a cell but since each number is expressed as an order of magnitude this lack of equivalence is not serious.

The TRANSACTION TIME is the minimum time for a single user interaction, measured from the user request leaving the user's local system to the completion of the response to the user. Units are (FRAME RATE, SECONDS, MINUTES, HOURS, DAY, LONGER).

The TRANSACTION INTERVAL is concerned with the frequency of transactions. The units are the same as for TRANSACTION TIME.

The ACCEPTABLE ERROR COUNT refers to error rate at lower layers in the network system where an error rate is measurable. It indicates the error count that is acceptable to the application. If this metric takes the value NO-ERRORS, the acceptable count is 0. SPECIFIED ACCEPTABLE indicates a particular acceptable count. DON'T-BOTHER means that error detection is of less importance to the application: some data could be lost, as (for example) replacement data follows.

4 Examples of Cells in the Taxonomy

To show how the taxonomy works we show examples of some boxes in the taxonomy.

semantic level	VIRTUAL
dimension	2D
data source	COMPLETE
session control	GIVE-ME
selection criteria	STATIC-SUBSET

The user requests that a subset of a file of 2D virtual graphics data is delivered to the local node. The subset is selected by a mechanism that reflects the structure of the file. Being at the virtual semantic level, the local node has control over viewing and the binding of attributes which determine the visual appearance of the graphics data. For example, a user at a workstation may request a selected picture from a large number of pre-stored pictures.

To achieve this kind of application, the CGM and FTAM standards are relevant. In particular FTAM needs to be able to access part of the remote file, as determined by the graphical structure.

An application of this is a meteorologist wishing to examine a selection of centrally stored weather maps. Transmitting application data is a possible alternative, but if the local workstation is not manipulating the data in any way, the additional semantic content is of no importance. If data closer to the physical layer in the reference model is transmitted, the ability to deal with variation in the local display equipment is lost.

Another application is access to a remote picture library, which could be used for slide production. The user may wish to obtain a selection of pictures on their local workstation display and request some to be printed. An interesting design issue is, how does the user find out what is in the library? It may seem that the user's workstation needs to be sent all the pictures, which could involve high network usage. Depending on the numbers, it may be preferable to transmit images, each containing many of the pictures in the library, to enable the user to browse without consuming considerable network resources. In this phase of the application, the semantic level is likely to be physical. This example illustrates that it is possible for an application to have operations that fall into different boxes in the taxonomy.

The ARGOSI prototype application is of this type. The user consults predetermined regions of a total area in order to obtain information relevant to the management of a road freight service.

Another example of a box in the taxonomy has just one metric altered, compared with the one just elaborated.

semantic level	VIRTUAL
dimension	2D
data source	COMPLETE
session control	GIVE-ME
selection criteria	DYNAMIC-SUBSET

The meteorological application would fall into this box in the taxonomy if the user needed to obtain over the network the data for a particular region, whose limits are under the user's control. The assumption is that the picture is sufficiently large that transmitting the whole picture is onerous and that storing predetermined regions is inappropriate.

Inspecting a portion of a remotely stored engineering drawing is another example of this.

5 The Role of the Taxonomy

Classifying an application is the beginning of the procedure to determine the strategy for future standards and the use of existing ones. Once applications that have similar characteristics in the taxonomy are identified, they can be studied in further detail. For example, a major distinction between the CGM (1987) and CGM with Amendment 1 is the segment facilities. The classification would show whether STATIC-SUBSET is required, but further study of the applications would be needed to determine how the subset would be formed, which could be achieved by extracting a picture from a metafile or a picture part from a picture.

6 Summary

A taxonomy for applications of graphics over networks has been produced based on the experience and information gained in the user surveys carried out to date. Classifying applications according to the metrics defined in the taxonomy provides a basis for the required networked graphics services to be examined in the Study of Services workpackage in the Project.

Chapter 11

Meteorological Communications and Graphics

Christopher T. Little

1 Introduction

Meteorologists first started producing weather maps regularly in the mid- 1800s. The Palatinate states were the first to issue them on a daily basis and the UK meteorological service first issued them on 11th March 1872. See Figure 1. Prior to this, weather information had been regularly transmitted by telegraph and published. Admiral Beaufort, who invented the standard classification of wind speeds, spent part of his career constructing a telegraph across Ireland. He also evolved a notation for concisely recording weather [1]. This notation, based on the letters of the Latin alphabet, was convenient for typesetters and telegraphic transmission, but did not give a readily assimilable representation on maps, and more graphical representations evolved rapidly after the invention of chromolithography in the 1830s and its widespread adoption in the 1860s. A series of international meteorological congresses met to agree on standard procedures and codes for the telegraphic communication of data and its representation on maps. By the 1920s maps were very close to modern international standards agreed by the World Meteorological Organisation.

2 The Global Telecommunications System

Current procedures are to transmit observed data in language-independent, all-figure codes [2], (and see Figure 2), over character based communications and to plot a graphical map from the collated data at central sites, and typically re-transmit the plotted map (see Figure 3) over analogue facsimile circuits to forecasters. This observed data is transmitted using message orientated protocols. Typically, at the terminal nodes of the network, data quantities are less than 1000 bytes per hour, transmitted over 50 baud lines. However, at the central national and international collecting nodes, quantities rise to one million characters per hour, excluding satellite data and imagery. The 2400 baud lines circling the globe are slowly being upgraded to faster speeds. Progress is also being made in establishing binary protocols and digital networks. Figure 4 indicates the more important nodes of the global communications network.

The plotted charts are usually converted to contour charts (see Figure 5), as are the outputs of numerical models run from the observations. The charts are often combined with satellite and radar imagery. The charts may also be modified by human intervention to show atmospheric discontinuities (fronts) or areas of interest that objective systems cannot easily handle. See Figure 6 taken from [4]. The interpolated data underlying the charts, represented as 2D arrays of values, are often transmitted using file-transfer orientated protocols. The graphical representations of the charts are widely disseminated also, using bit-map orientated protocols, such as CCITT T.4.

The WMO has recognised the importance of the Computer Graphics Metafile, CGM, and recommended its adoption where recipients do not have significant data processing capabilities, though CGM is not yet used operationally [3]. A typical CGM, such as surface pressure isobars combined with isotherms over the North Atlantic area may be 100 Kilobytes in size, in the most compact, binary, encoding.

Currently imagery is transmitted directly, in either analogue or digital form, from the satellite direct to ground stations. Transmissions over landlines is expensive and hence restricted. Typically, images are one to five Megabytes in size and are available every two hours in both visible and infrared wavelengths.

The higher resolution model arrays are starting to be comparable in size to satellite images. Model arrays typically contain 20,000 values, usually 4 or 8 byte numbers, but can be compressed into 16 bits. A model would contain five such arrays of different variables (pressure, temperature, humidity, wind velocity) for each of twenty levels, though a meteorologist in general would only inspect up to a dozen such single fields for each forecast. A forecaster making 5 day forecasts would inspect charts at 12 hourly intervals, whereas for a one day forecast, charts at 3 hourly or even hourly intervals, would be used.

The transmission of original data has been preferred to data in pictorial format. This is to save bandwidth, and applies for arrays of global data with resolutions of the order of 5 degrees of latitude and longitude. However, current numerical models are achieving resolutions of the order of one degree on the global scale, and at this resolution, it is more efficient to transmit metafiles, or heavily filtered data, for human interpretation. (The higher resolution models are used, even if the observed data does not seem to warrant it because of the more accurate simulations of phase speeds and energy transfers to different scales that can be obtained.)

As calculated from above, a forecaster could easily inspect ten to fifteen Megabytes of data (stored in compact, efficient formats) in making a forecast. The forecaster may be very near the computer storing this data, or may be literally thousands of kilometres away.

3 Graphical Interaction

The above scheme is a network to collect and centralise global data very rapidly and also a dissemination network, often overlapping the observing network, for analyses, imagery and forecasts. Even at highly developed meteorological centres, the level of interactivity in graphics is relatively low compared to a CAD system, for example. When a full range of products is available on workstations as opposed to hardcopy, most interaction is to choose the next product to be viewed (e.g. a picture within a metafile), or to decide which products should be viewed together and overlaid (e.g. choosing global segments within a CGM). For example, an eight bit pseudo- colour or monochrome satellite image may be overlaid with three contour charts (pressure, temperature and wind velocity) plus a selection of the original plotted data and the visibility of the overlays selected via the colour look-up table of the display. The preferred solution is to interact with local data. This gives improved response for a time critical application, and gives increased resilience if the network fails. The forecaster can work independently with the local data until the network is restored. Networks usually fail in bad weather- exactly when the forecaster has crucial work! This approach is a straightforward computerisation of previous and existing practices based on paper.

The second major requirement for interactivity is to augment machinable products according to the forecaster's professional judgement. See Figure 6. Direct intervention in numerical models is not done. Again this interaction can be done locally, using local segment manipulations. When the forecaster is satisfied with the modifications, then the finished product can be transmitted to the recipients. Such products will not be used as input to a numerical model, as the model's mathematical-dynamical balance will be ruined. Systems to meet this requirement are being developed only now on graphical displays, and even in the most developed centres these tasks are done mainly on paper.

There is a research requirement to interact fully with analysis systems to produce a blend of diverse and sometimes subjective data types, on a relatively small scale, typically a model covering a small country, or even a single thunderstorm, where the meteorological parameters are not observed well by the global observing system. Such mesoscale meteorological systems are typically much more three dimensional, rather than two dimensional as assumed previously. Such systems are likely to be very closely coupled with large powerful computers to bring the correct dynamical balance to the interactive data generation, and are unlikely to have a major impact except at a very few advanced centres. If these systems are introduced operationally, the results of such models will be disseminated as described previously.

4 Summary

File transfer and message handling protocols over character and binary global networks are required in a wide variety of speeds to meet economic constraints. All systems must be robust and resilient. Application data transmission occurs at present, but metafile and bit-map transfers will increase in the future.

5 References

1. Napier Shaw, Manual on Meteorology, Vol 1, Cambridge University Press, Cambridge, 1926
2. WMO Manual on Codes, Vol 1 - International codes, WMO No. 306, WMO, Geneva, 1988
3. Final Report of First Session, Working Group on Data Management, Sub-group on Data Representation, WMO, Geneva, 15-19 May 1989
4. Interactive Support System for Drawing Weather Chart, pp181-191, Weather Service Bulletin, Vol 55 No. 4, Japan Met. Agency, Tokyo, 1988

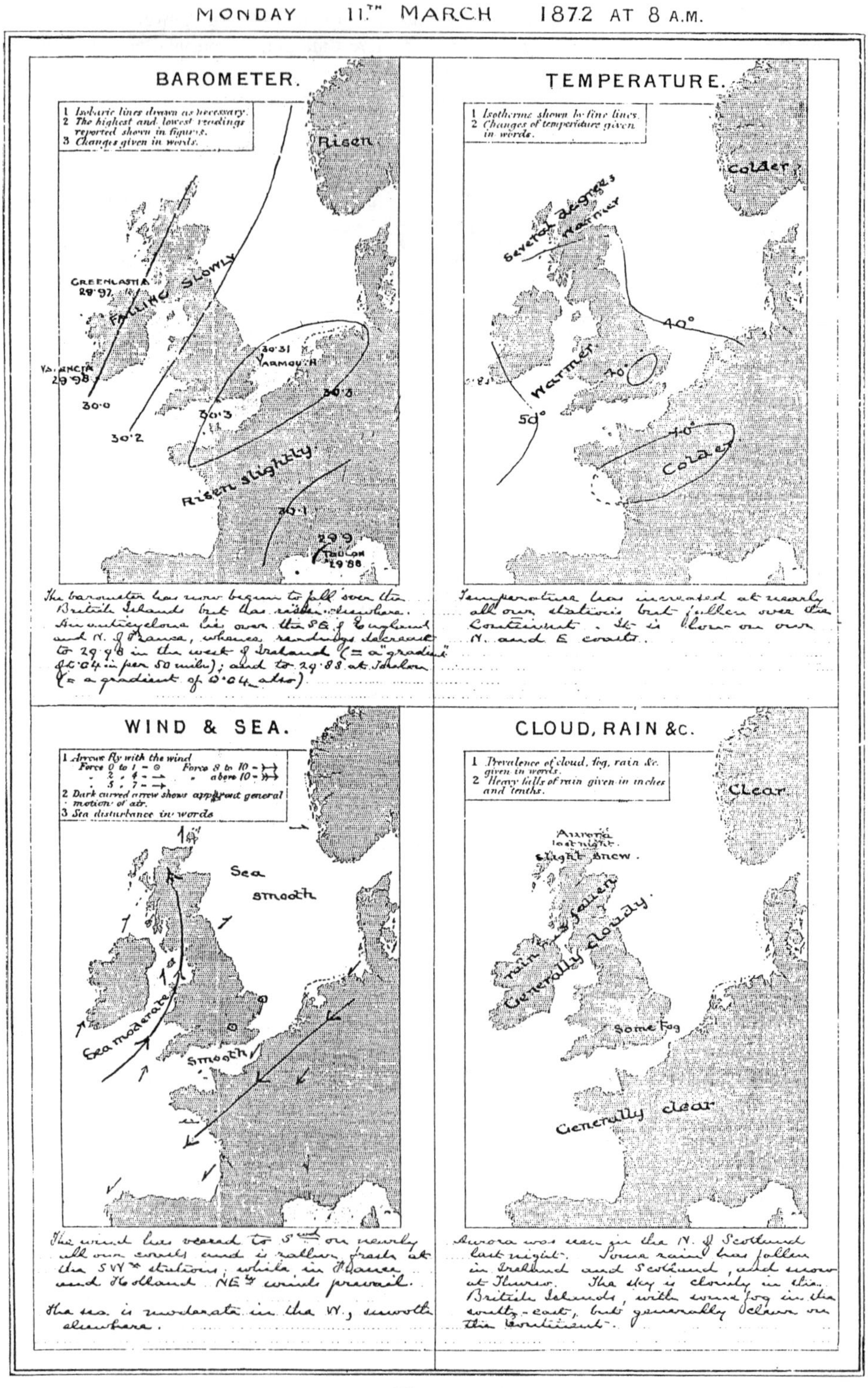
MONDAY 11TH MARCH 1872 AT 8 A.M.
BAROMETER.
1 Isobaric lines drawn as necessary.
2 The highest and lowest readings reported shown in figures.
3 Changes given in words.
Risen
Falling slowly
Greencastle 29·97
Valencia 29·98
30·0
30·2
30·31
Yarmouth
30·3
Risen slightly
30·1
29·9
Toulon 29·88
The barometer has now begun to fall over the British Islands but has risen elsewhere. An anticyclone lies over the S.E. of England and N. of France, whence readings decrease to 29·98 in the west of Ireland (= a gradient of ·04 in per 50 miles); and to 29·88 at Toulon (= a gradient of 0·04 also).
TEMPERATURE.
1 Isotherms shown by fine lines.
2 Changes of temperature given in words.
Colder
Several degrees warmer
40°
Warmer
50°
Colder
Temperature has increased at nearly all our stations but fallen over the Continent. It is low on our N. and E coasts.
WIND & SEA.
1 Arrows fly with the wind
2 Dark curved arrow shows apparent general motion of air.
3 Sea disturbance in words
Sea smooth
Sea moderate
Smooth
The wind has veered to Sward on nearly all our coasts and is rather fresh at the SWrn stations; while in France and Holland NEly winds prevail.
The sea is moderate in the W., smooth elsewhere.
CLOUD, RAIN &c.
1 Prevalence of cloud, fog, rain &c. given in words.
2 Heavy falls of rain given in inches and tenths.
Clear
Aurora last night.
Slight snow.
Rain has fallen
Generally cloudy.
Some Fog
Generally clear
Aurora was seen in the N. of Scotland last night. Some rain has fallen in Ireland and Scotland, and snow at Thurso. The sky is cloudy in the British Islands, with some fog in the south-east, but generally clear on the Continent.

Figure 1

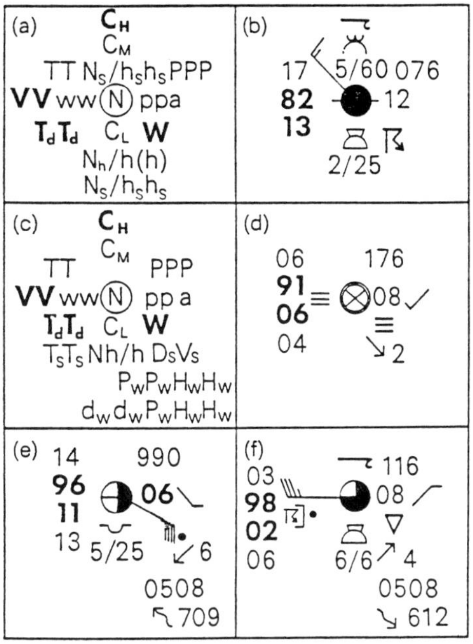

Figure 2 **Station model with typical examples**
(**bold** type represents red ink)

(*a*) Model for land station report.
(*b*) Land station report—83314 82029 07617 29563 13212 82925 85460.
(*c*) Model for ship report.

Ship reports:

(*d*) — — — 90000 91454 17606 9//// 32308 00406.
(*e*) — — — 51140 96036 99014 55500 56606 85625 01311 30508 13709.
(*f*) — — — 62735 98918 11603 69603 14108 00602 30508 31612.

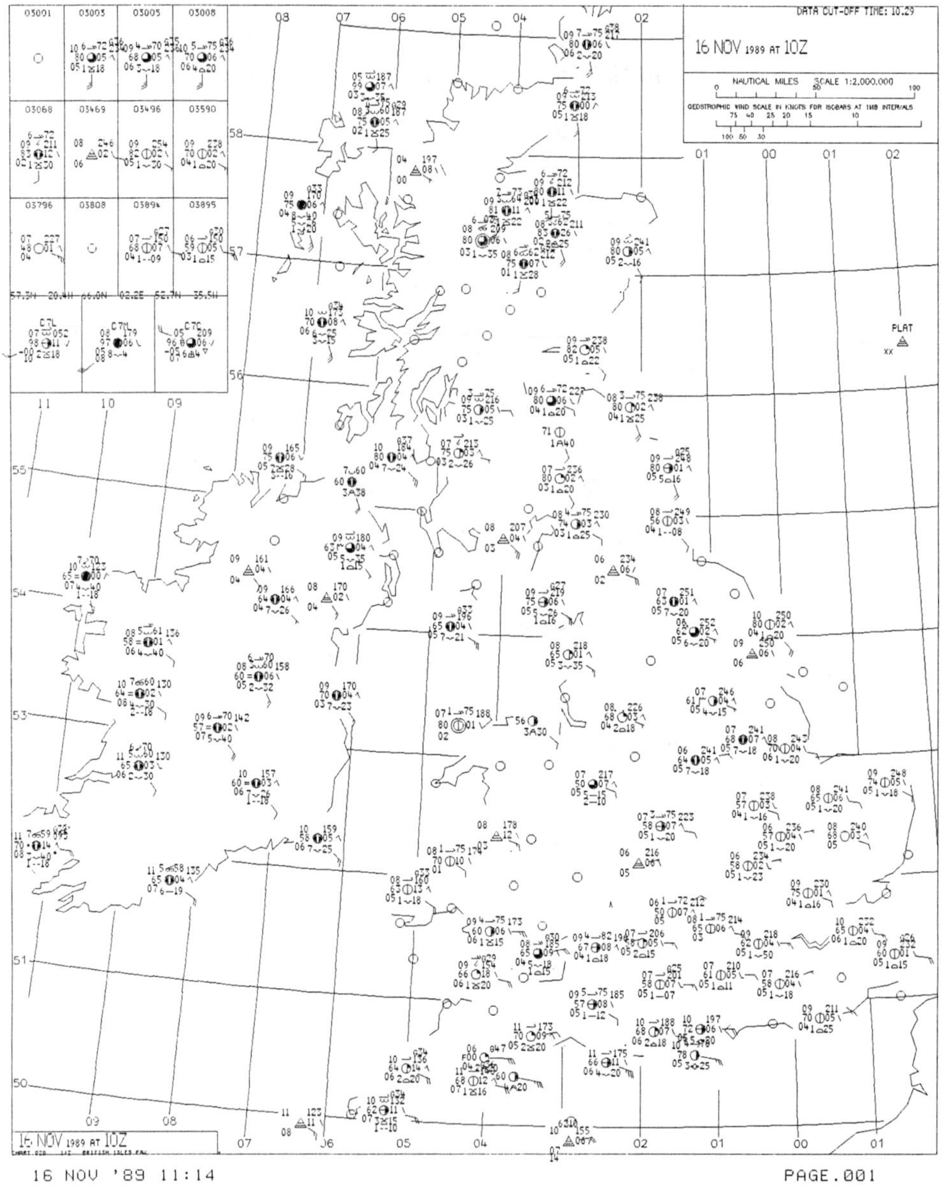
DATA CUT-OFF TIME: 10.29
16 NOV 1989 AT 10Z
NAUTICAL MILES SCALE 1:2,000,000
GEOSTROPHIC WIND SCALE IN KNOTS FOR ISOBARS AT 1MB INTERVALS
PLAT
16 NOV 1989 AT 10Z
16 NOV '89 11:14
PAGE.001

Figure 3

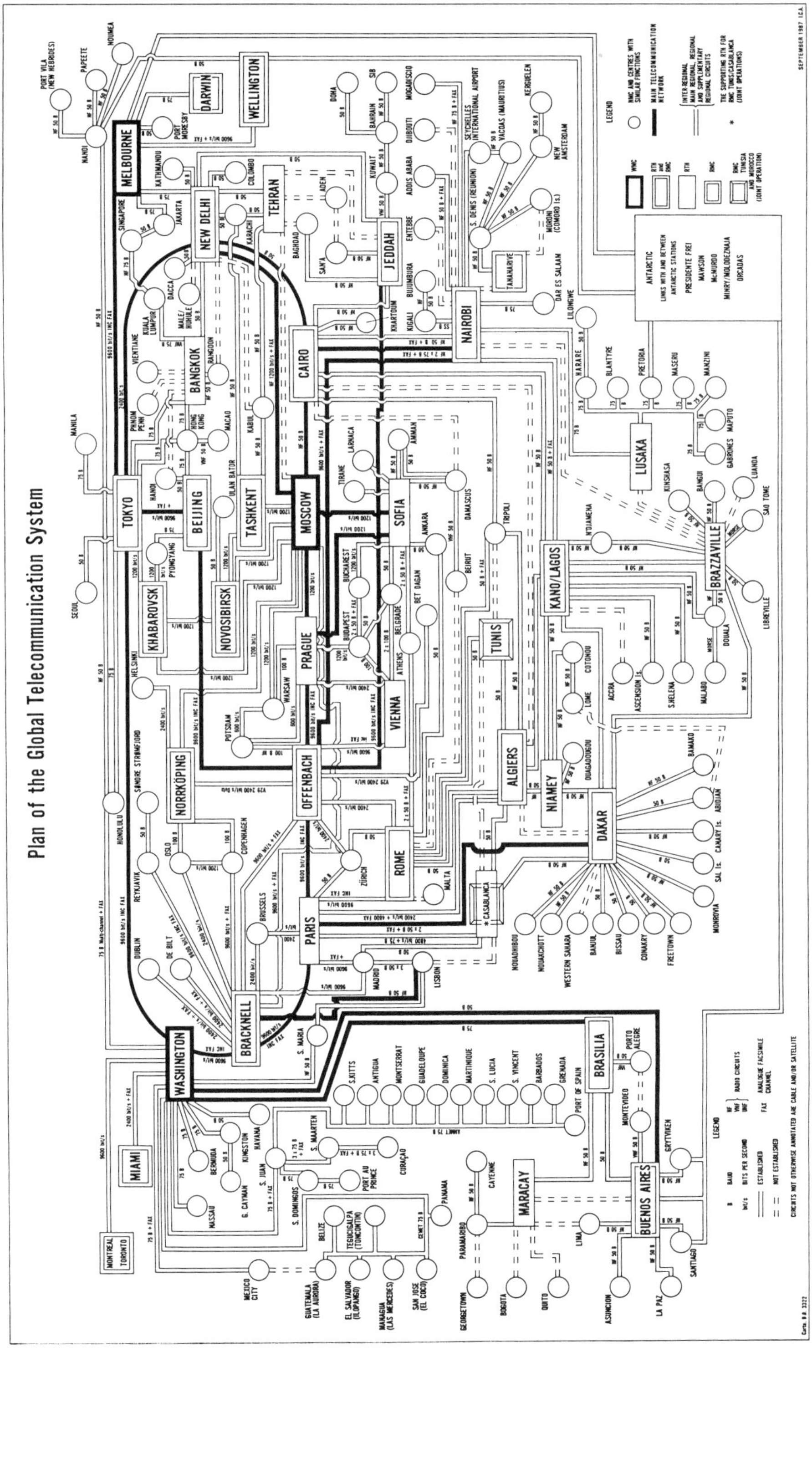

Plan of the Global Telecommunication System
ANNEX IC
WASHINGTON
BRACKNELL
OFFENBACH
PARIS
PRAGUE
MOSCOW
SOFIA
VIENNA
ROME
NORRKÖPING
NOVOSIBIRSK
KHABAROVSK
TASHKENT
BEIJING
TOKYO
BANGKOK
NEW DELHI
MELBOURNE
DARWIN
WELLINGTON
TEHRAN
JEDDAH
CAIRO
NAIROBI
LUSAKA
BRAZZAVILLE
KANO/LAGOS
TUNIS
ALGIERS
NIAMEY
DAKAR
CASABLANCA
BRASILIA
BUENOS AIRES
MARACAY
MIAMI
MONTREAL
TORONTO
LEGEND
ANTARCTIC

Figure 4

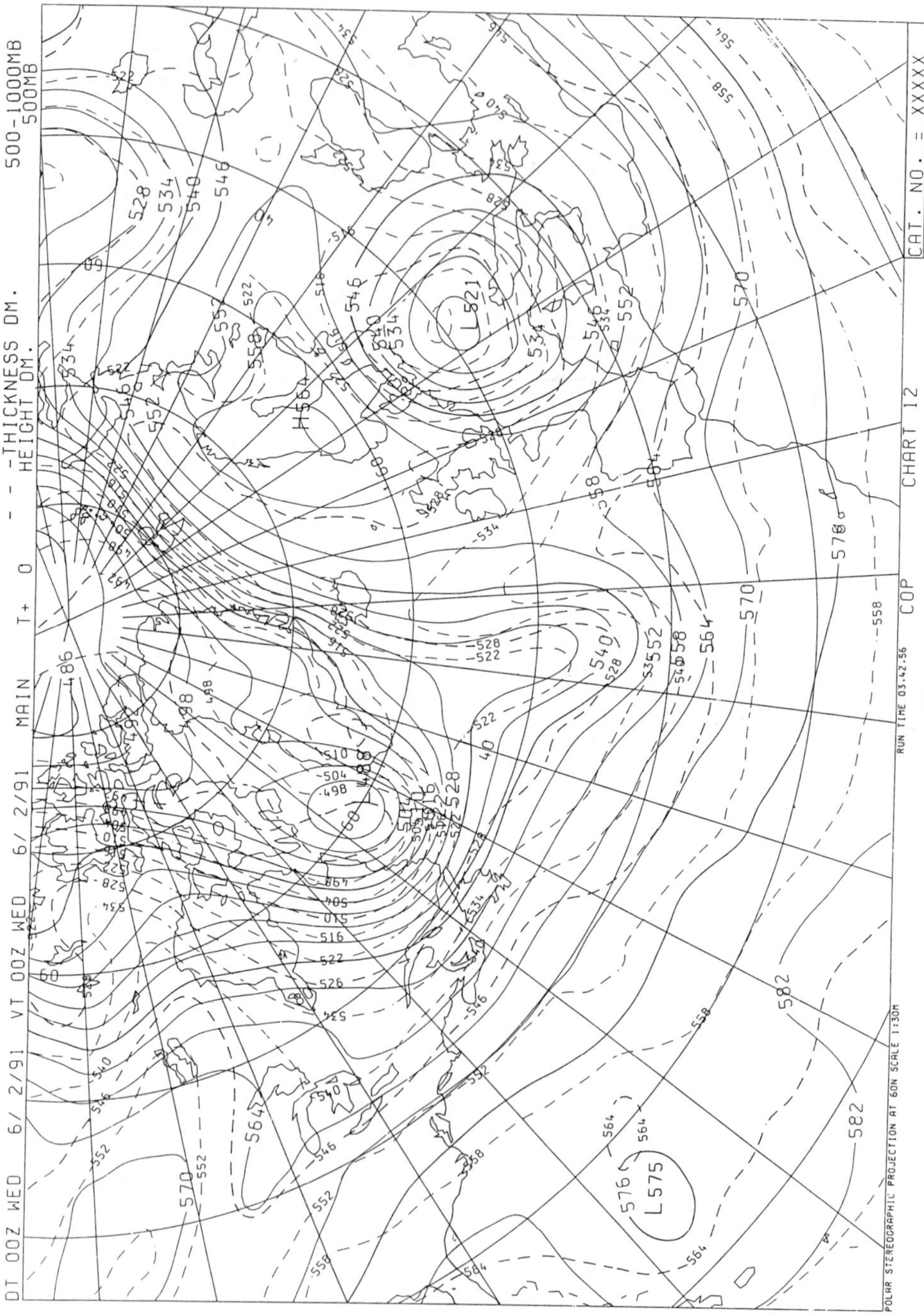
DT 00Z WED 6/ 2/91 VT 00Z WED 6/ 2/91 MAIN T+ 0
- - -THICKNESS DM. 500-1000MB
HEIGHT DM. 500MB
POLAR STEREOGRAPHIC PROJECTION AT 60N SCALE 1:30M
RUN TIME 03.42.56
COP
CHART 12
CAT. NO. = XXXXX

Figure 5

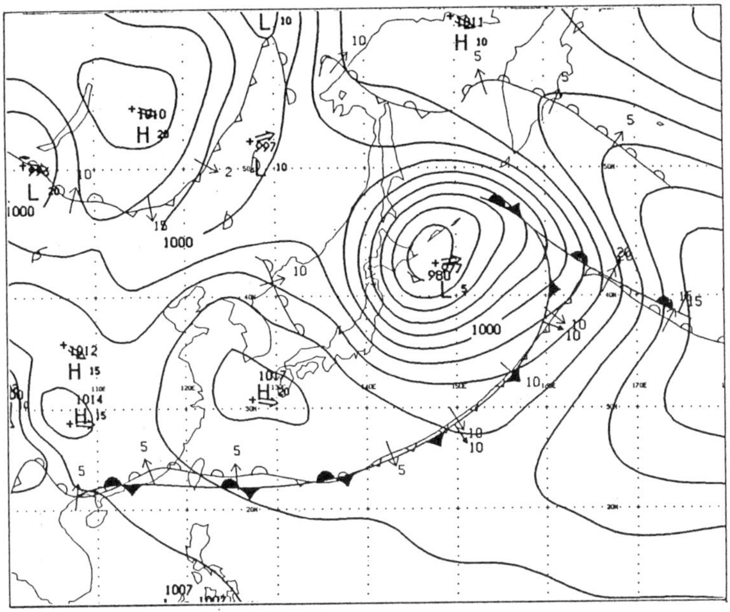

第 7. c 図　作業画面の例 3
作成された前線（移動速度記号も含む）.

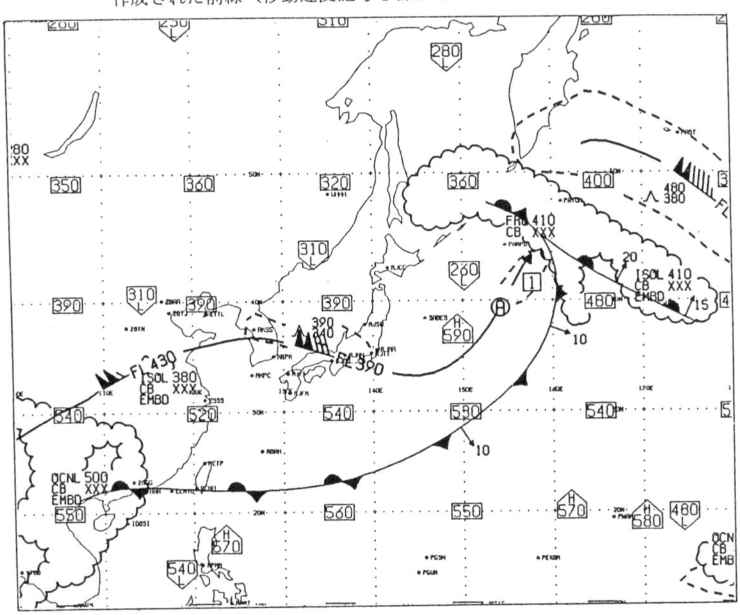

第 7. d 図　製品図の一部分
（表示されている記号については,「国際航空用悪天予想図について」（予報部数値予報課，1988）を参照）

Figure 6

Chapter 12

Multimedia Applications in a Broadband Environment. Framework for Integrated Services

Peter Egloff

1 Introduction

The following paper reflects a subset of the work done within the BERKOM project (BERliner KOMmunikationssystem) since the beginning of 1988. The purpose of this activity is to describe a framework which can be used as a tool for the design of future-oriented integrated telecommunication services. Based on the fundamental ideas of the Reference Model for Open Systems Interconnection (OSI Model), and keeping in mind its functional limits, this framework - called **BERKOM Reference Model** - will help to identify the needs of future applications and the necessary structure of protocol stacks based on existing standards and/or recommendations. Additionally this framework permits the identification of areas in which functional standards are not available and therefore future standardization activities are necessary. One of the basic ideas of this work is to provide for future integrated telecommunication services supporting multimedia applications. It should be possible to construct these telecommunication services dynamically using building blocks for communication services as well as for data structures.

This work has been performed and the following paper was prepared under the oversight of the team at the *Forschungszentrum für Offene Kommunikationssysteme (FOKUS)* of the *Gesellschaft für Mathematik und Datenverarbeitung (GMD), Berlin - Germany* (G. Schuermann, A. Scheller, M. Tschichholz, A. Dittrich, C. Egelhaaf, K.-D. Engel, J. Hall, U. Holzmann-Kaiser, E. Moeller, K.-H. Weiss). In addition this work was assisted by people at FhG/AGD in Darmstadt (D. Kroemker, C. Blum, G.R. Hofmann) and by people at TU Berlin / ISM (H. Nowacki, D. Bauch). This work was granted by the BERKOM project, a broadband communication pilot project of the German PTT (Deutsche Bundespost - Telekom).

2 Scope and Goals

The BERKOM project (BERliner KOMmunikationssystem) has been launched to promote the development of future services and end systems for broadband ISDN, so that various kinds of applications may profit from this new technology. Several examples of future application areas include the office environment, computer aided design, image communication and digital image interchange, printing and publishing, medicine, information systems and the distribution of high definition television (HDTV).

In order to provide services, which allow communication between arbitrary communication partners in an open systems environment, future developments have to be based on international standards. An analysis of relevant standards in the fields of communication, application environment, and information and data structures and interchange formats has shown that these developments have not been adequately coordinated. In several areas, an overlapping of functionality exists, while other areas are not even considered within the standards. Going beyond the definition of base standards, a number of application profiles have been developed within CCITT and numerous regional workshops, which further restrict the range of functionality of the base standards within certain fields of application. For this reason, future products which are based upon the same standard may not even have the same functionality. This will greatly disturb the capability for open communication.

As integrated services, which are provided by distributed applications, have a lot of common functionality the application developer should be supported in respect to the selection of suitable combinations of standards and application profiles. Additionally similar services should use the same profiles to provide interoperability. Using the framework for integrated services, many distributed applications which have common functionality can use products based on the appropriate standards - if available at all.

An objective of the framework is to give a comprehensive description for the structuring of the integrated services provided by distributed applications. It is a framework for existing standards which also supports the identification of functional areas where no standards are available ("white spots").

In recent years, many application oriented standards have been developed in the area of communication and information and data structures. Additionally, many application standards, such as for storage and retrieval, have been published or are under development in the context of integrated services, which cover aspects that go beyond communication. These standards are categorized as the application environment.

The framework categorizes the standards and specific profiles into

- information and data structure profiles,
- communication profiles for upper layers
- profiles for the application environment.

Distributed applications require identification, localization and management support. These related functions, information and data structures and communication protocols are grouped in this document under the overall term *administration*. A globally available information system is needed to fulfill identification and localization requirements.

This paper introduces functions and data structures required for such administrative support. Because administration aspects are integrated in most applications and related to all the categories listed above, they are referred to throughout this paper, and are not described separately.

The presently available framework contains short-term and medium-term profile recommendations, which should serve as a basis for the development of applications within this framework. The profile recommendations are based on the OSI Basic Reference Model, existing CCITT telematic services, distributed applications already standardized within OSI, and other international standards and profiles in the areas of communication and data structures for information interchange. Hereby, existing telematic services are taken into consideration. The telematic services cover complete service descriptions including communication protocols, interchange formats, and terminal characteristics. The present version of the framework concentrates, however, upon communication and management aspects and data structures and interchange formats. In addition to these profile recommendations, areas are identified for which the available standards do not yet offer any solutions.

The disadvantage of standards which do not complement each other in most cases, but which are of overlapping functionality, is not solved by the current approach which can be regarded as a first step to an architecture providing generic or common functions which can be combined according to general rules. In order to eliminate, in the long term, the inadequacies of the presently available standards, an architecture for distributed processing (including homogeneous concepts, generic functions and common data and information facilities) has to be developed in addition to the current approach.

The architecture should permit the modelling of distributed applications and the integration of services independent of available technological constraints and transmission mechanisms. The approach to such general concepts is not, however, part of this paper.

3 Description of the Model

Integrated services are provided by distributed applications, which can be based on the information and data structure standards and profiles together with the communication and application environment standards and profiles.

Presented in Figure 1 are the three categories of profiles upon which distributed applications and integrated services are based. Suitable profiles selected from each category can be used to develop specific distributed applications. One main reason for the distinction of communication on the one hand and information and data structure on the other hand is motivated by the historically separate development of standards in these areas. Additionally many standards have been developed which have non-communication specific aspects, and some communication-specific standards have been developed, which also possess aspects going beyond communication. These are categorized as an application environment.

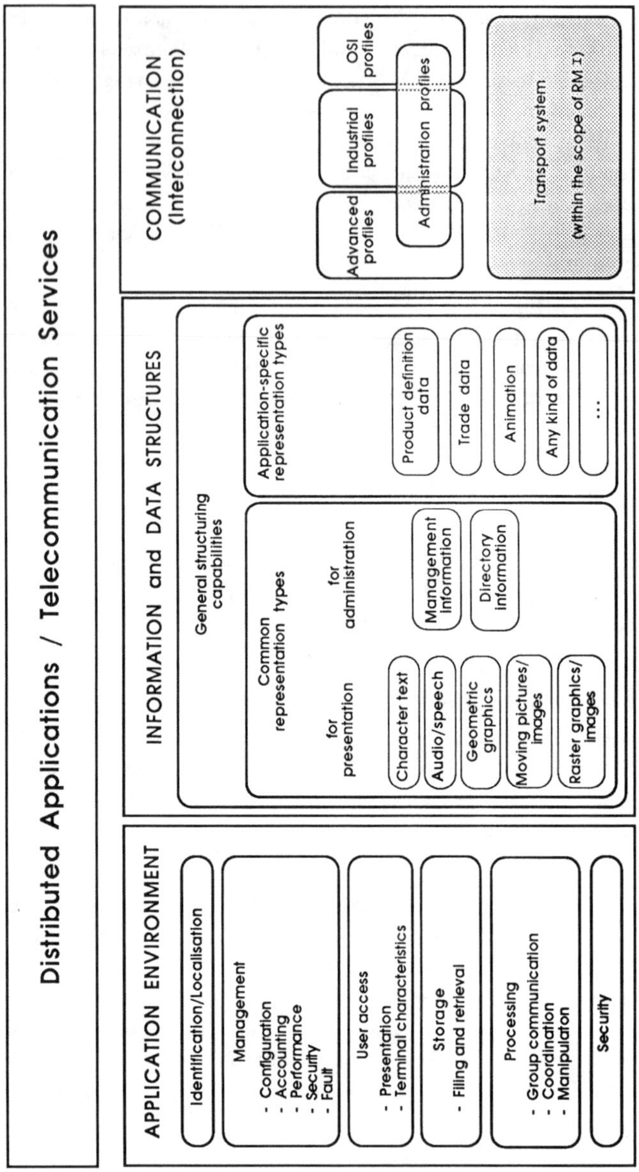

Figure 1 : Scheme of the Framework for Integrated Services

The three parts of the framework, which are described in more detail in the sections below, are:

- Information and data structures,

  The information and data structures comprise *general structuring capabilities*, *common* information representation types and *application-specific* information representation types. The representation types character text, audio/speech, geometric graphics, moving pictures and raster graphics are classified as representation types for presentation. The representation types for presentation, which are used to present information in many different application areas and representation types for administration, such as management and directory are classified as common representation types.

  In addition to these common representation types, many applications require the interchange of specific information. Some of this *application-specific* information is not intended to be humanly perceptible, and therefore must undergo further processing before presentation as a common representation type (e.g. product definition data).

- Communication (interconnection)

  The communication aspect can be classified in

  - OSI application profiles,
  - Advanced application profiles encompassing
    - light weight protocols for isochronous communication
    - and multipoint communication, such as multicasting and
  - Industrial profiles such as FTP and Telnet
  - Administration profiles
    - directory
    - management

- Application Environment

  The functionality needed for the development of distributed applications in different application areas in addition to communication aspects and information and data structures is classified according to aspects.

  - processing
  - storage
  - user access
  - identification and localization
  - management
  - security

Standards and profiles from each of those parts can be combined to fulfill specific application requirements. Some application profiles are data structure independent. They are transparent in relation to data structures. Some application profiles need only profiles from the communication part.

Attention must be paid to the fact that the developer finds no support for the concept of *how* (in the sense of design guidelines or architectural concepts) to build an integrated service as a distributed application. The realization of integrated services by developers using these standards requires additional work. This will be reserved for a future architecture within Open Distributed Processing (ODP) and distributed applications. But, as already mentioned, this report does provide recommendations for some of the identified "white spots", where no solutions are given by standards today.

3.1 Information and Data Structures

The analysis of standards has shown that the different standards contain many data and information models which are partially incompatible. What is needed is a consistent approach in the modelling of information and data structures. The approach discussed below can be considered as a first step in this direction.

An important characteristic of information interchange is the kind of information representations supported by the underlying information model and data structures. Different kinds of information representation are often referred to as **representation types.** There are a number of representation types which are used in many different fields of application, while others are specific to a certain class of applications. Accordingly, the notions of **common representation types** and **application-specific representation types** have been introduced.

Typically, **character text, geometric graphics and raster graphics (images)** in various degrees of complexity are mandated by today's document processing systems. Developments in recent years in the area of workstation and network technology have made it possible to include time-variant information such as **moving pictures and audio.** As these representation types are used to present information in many different application areas, they are classified as common representation types.

Representation types for the administration of distributed applications, such as management and directory information representation types, are also regarded as common representation types because they may be used by many different applications. Directory information is represented as *attributes* which specify the semantics (*attribute type)*, the syntax (*attribute syntax*) and the information itself by means of the *attribute value(s)*. Globally relevant information such as names and addresses will be stored using the standardized *Directory System* ,e.g. identification and localization.

Management Information is also represented as attributes which form logical units called *Managed Objects*. A *Management Information Base* conceptually contains all the Managed Objects of one OSI end system.

The concept of attributes, identified by globally known object identifiers, makes a common understanding of heterogeneous components possible. This is a fundamental concept for really *open communication*. For both types of administration information, specific information models have been standardized.

In addition to these common representation types, many applications require the interchange of specific information. Some of this application-specific information is not intended to be human perceptible at all (e.g. robot control), others must undergo further processing before being representable in a common representation type (e.g. product definition data). For clarity a few additional remarks concerning the difference between application-specific representation types, such as product definition data, and common representation types are necessary. As it has been mentioned above, an application-specific representation type has to be transformed into a common representation type before it becomes humanly perceptible. This is because the intension product information in the first place is to describe the technical product for special purposes such as manufacturing, simulation etc., and not to derive a representation suitable for human perception. If the latter case is required, it can be done by preprocessing, but in general a certain amount of product information is lost. If a technical product consisting of different assemblies and parts is, for example, described using the representation type product definition data, all the structural information is included. In an image representation, however, this information may be lost, since there may be no direct correspondence between product structure and image structure.

Even for the exchange of technical drawings it is not the same when the product definition data type or the common representation type geometric graphics is used. In the first case all the annotations such as dimension and tolerance are given explicitly, while in the second case the symbols representing such information are aggregations of graphical elements, which can only be understood by an engineer who knows the semantics of the symbols.

For applications it is therefore important to decide if the complete model description is needed or if a reduced informational content as represented by the common representation types is sufficient.

For some reasons, such as further developments in the technology and standardization area, representation types classified as being application-specific today might become common in the future.

The term "multimedia" is generally associated with information in a form receptible to humans, i.e. representable through common representation types. However, as many applications require the integrated processing of common and application-specific representation types, multimedia information in the framework is understood in a more general sense to include the application-specific representation types.

> **Multimedia information comprises common and application--specific representation types, i.e. it is intended for visual and auditory perception as well as for automated processing. The information is not restricted to local existence, but may be distributed. The information may, but does not have to be, presented on different presentation media.**

Today, no precise terminology in the area of multi/hypermedia is being provided uniquely within standardization bodies. Such a precise terminology is currently under development, e.g. in ISO/IEC JTC1/SC2/WG8 – Coded Representation of Picture and Audio Information. For example, basic representation type is denoted there as "representation medium" and raster graphics as "still pictures". In cases where there is common agreement concerning terminology, it might be adopted in future versions of the framework document.

The following list contains a brief description of the common representation types identified so far, and some examples for application-specific representation types:

- **Common representation types**
  - Representation types for presentation
    - character text
      describes character set selection, character positioning, character imaging (emphasis, font selection);
    - geometric graphics
      describe graphical objects of 2- and 3-dimensional geometry of diverse appearance, such as line, marker, and filled-area elements, and their spatial transformations;
    - images (raster graphics)
      describe discrete structures for visual presentations; images are discrete in geometry (rasters, lines, columns, pixels), amplitude, colour channels (either spectral bands, colour separations or key masks), and time (see: moving pictures);
    - images (moving pictures)
      describe sequences of elementary images, requiring a minimum temporal frequency for human perception in order to simulate a continuous motion;
    - audio
      describe digital audio in form of sequences of samples, type of coding, such as PCM and ADPCM, and coding attributes, such as sample resolution and companding laws;
  - Representation types for administration
    - directory information
      describes standardized and registered (application-specific) *attributes* which can be published globally by the Directory System;
    - management information
      describes standardized and registered (application-specific) *attributes* which are required for the management of objects in an open distributed environment.

  both representation types are based on standards. Application-specific or private (local scope) extensions are possible.

- **Application-specific representation types**
  - product definition data
    describes geometrical, topological, presentation, and non-geometric aspects of product data;

- data for animation and simulation applications

  serves the manipulation of motion sequences and generation of moving pictures including the synchronization with audio; supports the interchange of scene description (geometry, light sources, camera model), surface characteristics and optical properties, wire frames, scripts, moving pictures and audio;
- trade data

  provides common structures for the interchange of trade data, such as invoices and order forms;
- ...

In addition to specific representation types, **general information structuring capabilities** are of importance. The definition of the general structuring capabilities is for further study. The Office Document Architecture and the Standard Generalized Markup Language , emerging from the office and publishing environment, play a major role. Both standards are considered as relevant document interchange formats, although with its layout description and the Document Application Profiles (DAPs) under development, ODA has at present the advantage of allowing document interchange without prior agreement between the communicating parties. However, with the development of the Document Style Semantics and Specification Language (DSSSL) and EWOS planning profiles for SGML, the use of this standard will be less restricted to closed user groups, as is currently the case.

Two descriptions of *general structuring capabilities* which have already been standardized can be found in the Directory Standard. Terms such as *Directory Information Tree (DIT), entry, attribute, managed object, containment tree, etc.* are introduced and defined in these standards. These concepts should be considered when an information model is being defined.

3.2 Communication

In a distributed environment, applications composed of a number of components are split among the different nodes of systems. These components, called *application-processes* (in the sense of the OSI Reference Model) interwork to carry out a distributed information processing task, e.g. providing a telecommunication service. To interact, distributed application-processes require well defined sets of procedures along with the information types required to carry out a specific type of application. *Application-entities* model the aspects of an application-process relevant to open system interconnection - called communication aspects. A part (grouping of functions) of an application-entity, which provides an OSI capability, using underlying services provided by layers below the application layer, is called *application-service-element.*

The application layer provides means for the application-processes to access OSI capabilities. Hence the application layer does not interface with a higher layer, the application layer serves as a window between correspondent application-processes which use OSI for information interchange.

The communication specific profiles can be classified in

- OSI application profiles,
- advanced application profiles encompassing
  - light weight protocols for isochronous communication
  - and multipoint communication, such as multicasting.
- administration profiles

The functionality common to many applications either defined in standards and profiles or still not defined must be identified. They describe those communication functions, which can be used by many applications.

3.2.1 OSI Application Profiles

The *OSI application profiles* can be derived from combinations of the communication standards and profiles.The communication protocols are defined without extension of the capabilities and definitions of the OSI Basic Reference Model.

3.2.2 Advanced Application Profiles

Advanced application profiles encompass

- real-time communication support
- multi-point communication support, such as multicasting.

Real-time communication profiles can be used for example for real-time audio and real-time moving picture communication. From the service point of view this is an OSI extension, and from the protocol point of view, the protocols are reduced in their complexity (light-weight protocols).

For real-time communication, the following advanced application profiles, which may be supplemented if required, are proposed:

- Audio communication
- Moving pictures communication

3.2.3 Industrial Profiles

Application oriented industrial profiles are based on 'industrial standards' such as the suite of protocols developed by the ARPAnet community, which have raised to the level of a standard by the US Department of Defense (DoD). The later are known as TCP/IP (Transport Control Protocol / Internet Protocol). IP is the equivalent of the (upper sub-layer of the) Network Layer in the OSI Reference Model and TCP is roughly the equivalent of the Transport layer (Class 4) in the OSI Model. But TCP/IP also stands for a full stack of protocols which have been defined for the use on top of TCP/IP:

- TELENET for remote login (ie. access from a terminal to a remote computer), the equivalent of the OSI Virtual Terminal Protocol,
- FTP for file transfer,
- SMPT (Simple Mail Transfer Protocol) for electronic mail between users of the internet service,
- X Windows for advanced workstation functions.

Another popular protocol developed on top of IP is the Network File System (NFS) developed by SUN (comparable to OSI FTAM). There is no major focus on those profiles in the scope of this framework.

3.2.4 Administration Profiles

OSI-Profiles

- Directory Profiles
  - The X.500/ISO-9594 standard is described in a series of eight documents which define the information model and the protocols to be used when developing a standardized directory service.
  - The EWOS Profiles are being produced to provide guidelines for consistent interworking between different implementations of X.500. The documents *Access to the Directory*, and *Common Directory Use* are being voted on. The other functional standards exist in draft form at present (EWOSA-712), (EWOSA-713), (EWOS-A714), (EWOSQ-512), (EWOSQ-513).
  - The BERKOM extensions (B/1) to the initial schema defined in the X.500 standard provide additional object classes, attribute types and attribute syntaxes that can be used by applications. The extensions are defined in and will be published separately as a revised document by the end of 1990.
- Management Profiles
  - The OSI Management standards are concerned with the monitoring and controlling of resources involved in an OSI communication activity. The concepts, terminology and management model are described in, which provides the framework for further OSI management standardization.

  - The Systems Management Functions specify standard mechanisms for a broad range of management activities.
  - The CMIS / CMIP standards are concerned with the set of common services and protocols for transmitting and manipulating management information.
  - The BERKOM extensions (B/2)will provide generic OSI-conforming management tools to support the management functions required by distributed applications in the BERKOM environment. The extensions are in the process of being defined and will be published at a later date.

Non-OSI-Profiles

- Management Profiles
  - The Simple Network Management Protocol (SNMP) has been developed for TCP/IP-based internets. It comprises both the architecture and the information model used for describing managed objects. Although designed for use over TCP/IP it is currently being implemented experimentally over the OSI Transport Service.
  - The Telecommunications Management Network (TMN) is being defined by CCITT. It covers a range of functions needed to manage a telecommunications network.
  - In the ISDN Protocol Reference Model it is stated that ISDN Management is for further study.

3.3 Application Environment

In addition to communication-specific aspects, as described above, and data structure aspects, telecommunication specific characteristics, such as terminal characteristics of telematic services, which are beyond the scope of OSI, are within the scope of this framework.

The functionality needed for the development of distributed applications in different application areas is classified according to ODP aspects , although there is some overlapping functionality between the different classes. The classification depends on its main characteristics.

Application environment profiles encompass non-communication specific aspects such as filing and retrieval, security, presentation of multimedia information and terminal characteristics. The following aspects structure the functionality. The aspects which are supported within the scope of this framework are listed below. The functions listed under each aspect are part of the conceptional work within the scope of the framework.

- Processing
  - generation or manipulation

    supports the distributed creation, manipulation, processing and deletion of the contents and structures of multimedia information.

  - coordination of group communication

    is necessary for the synchronous, asynchronous, simultaneous editing and processing of information by user groups; mechanisms must be provided for multimedia information and user groups working in a group communication environment.

- Storage

  - filing and retrieval of multimedia information

    deals with different storage aspects such as private, common, local, remote and search strategies for multimedia information.

- User Access

  - presentation of multimedia information

    has to cover the simultaneous presentation of several basic information types at the same or at different locations.

- Identification and localization

  - Identification: global or context-specific unique object name
  - Localization: name / address mapping the name resolution process must be supported, such as name address resolution (directory).

- Management

  - OSI-Management
  - management of distributed applications

    provides facilities to support distributed applications with respect to their administration and covers more than OSI communication management (e.g. managing the coordination between various components of a distributed application).

  - time coordination (time management)

    involves synchronization of clocks across two or more distributed open systems.

- Security

  covers the areas of authentication, authorization, audit and cryptographic support facilities etc. Security is not supported by the framework at the moment.

Application program interfaces (APIs) are either part of the application environment or communication, if access to communication functions is defined.

3.4 Relationship between Information and Data Structures, Communication and Application Environment

Three parts of the framework have been described in the previous sections. These parts are not independent: Firstly the relationship between information and data structures and communication, secondly the relationship between communication and application environment and last but not least the relationship between information/data structures and application environment are described.

The relationship between information/data structures and communication can be described by means of some basic principles of the OSI Reference Model. As already mentioned information processing for a particular application is performed by application-processes. The application-entities (AEs) model the aspects pertinent to interconnection. Application-processes exchange information by means of application-entities, application-protocols and presentation-service. The presentation layer provides for the representation of information that either AEs communicate or refer to in their communication. Two complementary aspects of this representation of information are covered:

- the representation of data to be transferred between AEs;
- the representation of the data structure which AEs refer to in their communication, along with the representation of the set of actions which may be performed on this data structure.

Thus the presentation layer is concerned only with the syntax and not with its semantics, which is known only by the AEs of the application layer. The presentation layer provides for a common representation to be used between AEs. So the AEs are provided with syntax independence, which is described in the OSI Reference Model in two ways:

- the presentation layer provides common syntactical elements which are used by AEs;
- the AEs can use any syntax and the presentation layer provides the transformation between these syntaxes and the common syntax needed for communication between AEs. This transformation is performed inside the open system and therefore has no impact on the standardization of the presentation protocol.

The presentation-service provides to the application layer the session-service in form of presentation facilities and transformation and selection of syntax. Transformation is concerned with code and character set conversions, with the modification of the layout of the data and the adaption of actions on the data structures. Selection of syntax provides the means of initially selecting a syntax and subsequently modifying the selection, e.g. choosing a different agreed syntax.

There are three different set of syntaxes, the syntax used by the originating AE, the syntax used by the receiving AE – the abstract syntaxes – and the syntax used between presentation entities – the transfer syntax. Any of these syntaxes may be identical. The presentation layer is capable of the transformation between the transfer syntax and each of the other syntaxes if required. So a presentation-entity must know the syntax of its AE and the agreed transfer syntax. Syntax transformation (e.g. special transformations for compressing) may be performed either as a specific syntax-matching service provided to the application entities, or as a function internal to the presentation layer.

From the excursion to the OSI Reference Model above (some parts are quoted literally), we conclude that information/data structures are related to the application layer in respect to semantics and to the presentation layer in respect to the transfer syntax (representation of data). If an application is modelled adequately, from communication point of view AEs or ASEs must be selected or developed. The definition of AEs and transfer syntaxes are influenced by the information/data structures of the framework.

Consider, for example, the exchange of geometric graphics information as defined in the Computer Graphics Metafile (CGM) using the File Transfer, Access and Management (FTAM) service. Existing document type definitions within FTAM are sufficient for the exchange of a CGM in one of its three encodings:

CGM encoding	Constraint set	FTAM document type
character encoding	unstructured	FTAM-3: unstructured binary file
binary encoding	unstructured	FTAM-3: unstructured binary file
clear text encoding	unstructured	FTAM-1: unstructured text file

The abstract and transfer syntaxes for these document types are the following.

FTAM-1: *abstract syntax:* An indefinite series of instances of the ASN.1 data type GraphicString.

transfer syntax: application of the ASN.1 Basic Encoding Rules to each data type in the data value and concatenating the resulting octets (an implementation may optionally support other transfer syntaxes for this abstract syntax).

FTAM-3: *abstract syntax:* An indefinite series of instances of the ASN.1 data type OctetString.

transfer syntax: application of the ASN.1 Basic Encoding Rules to each data type in the data value and concatenating the resulting octets (an implementation may optionally support other transfer syntaxes for this abstract syntax).

In this case, FTAM need not to have any knowledge of the CGM; the application decides which FTAM document type to use for the exchange of a CGM in a given encoding (via the FTAM service element F-open). The receiver of a file would not know that it contains a CGM, unless this information is exchanged additionally by other means.

However, registration of a CGM-related FTAM document type could provide FTAM with relevant information regarding CGM. The extent as to which FTAM service elements and the presentation layer have to know the CGM syntax depends on the intended access to CGM. If no access is required to individual metafiles within a CGM file, the unstructured constraint set would be sufficient. In comparison to the document types FTAM-1 and FTAM-3, however, the receiver could identify the file contents as being CGMs. On the other hand, if access to individual pictures of a CGM is required, a 'two levels depth hierarchical' constraint set has to be used Thus, FTAM has knowledge of almost all structural information within the CGM (except for the CGM Picture Descriptor). This has to be reflected in the abstract and transfer syntaxes.

The relationship between communication and application environment can be described by means of the ODP aspects, which are high-level categories of useful groupings of functionality in respect to open distributed processing. The aspects are interrelated and offer no definite boundaries for classifying functionality. The OSI Reference Model has been defined for one aspect - the communication aspect - which enables the distribution of objects in open distributed processing. Because of the importance of the communication aspect and the given OSI Reference Model the communication part is regarded separately in this document. All non-communication specific aspects, which are by definition not part of the OSI Reference Model are called application environment.

The relationship between information/data structures and application environment can be described by means of the functionality of the different aspects. As already mentioned the processing aspect encompasses, for example, the generation and manipulation of multimedia structures, and the storage aspect the filing and retrieval of multimedia structures. The functionality classified by the different aspects and the data structures are very strongly related to each other and it depends on the modelling approach for each aspect how the information/data structures are defined. In many cases the definition of functions within the various aspects are governed by the data structures they are intended to act upon.

3.5 Combinations of Profiles

The combination of profiles is necessary because some applications require the functionality of more than one application profile. The combination of profiles requires an adequate modelling approach. Solutions for the following working areas must be developed:

- Combinations of information and data structure profiles
- Combination of communication profiles

  One main task from the communication point of view is the development of solutions for the coordination of isochronous and anisochronous communication including the synchronization of isochronous communications, such as audio together with moving pictures, if no integrated coding is used. This combination of advanced and OSI communication profiles is outlined below but still for further study.

  From OSI application layer point of view two solution are obvious. The Application Layer Structure (ALS) standard supports the modelling of a combination of application entities and application service elements in the OSI application layer and the management of multiple associations. So isochronous and anisochronous communication can be modelled as two application service elements, based on two different associations and protocol stacks. The coordination of the associations is provided by a specific Multiple Association Control Function (MACF). An alternative approach is the use of two different application entities. In the later case the associations must be coordinated by the application itself.

- Combination of application environment profiles

  If profiles of the environment are required by applications and have to be combined with communication profiles, further modelling approaches are needed:

  - In some cases interworking between profiles must be defined.
  - The DOAM activities can be used in the office environment. It is based on a client-server model and allows the modelling of distributed applications based on non-interacting or interacting servers.
  - More general approaches will be developed in the approach based on Open Distributed Processing (ODP) and DAF. These are not at this time within the scope of this version, but relevant concepts will be integrated when available.

4 Necessary work beyond existing Standards

There are many enhanced requirements from expected application needs that cannot be fulfilled by existing standards and profiles. The requirements are listed below. After each list an enumeration of standards follows, covering parts or single items of the listed requirements, or identifies standards where solutions are currently under development. It is intended to develop concepts for several of these topics in the scope of the framework. Results of this work will be included in further versions of this document or in separate documents.

Data structure area

- adequate specification of the common representation type moving picture;
- integration of moving picture and/or audio with the other common representation types;
- integration of application-specific representation types;
- advanced functionality of the common representation types, such as character text along arbitrary paths;
- advanced document architecture regarding general structuring capabilities, such as network structures to support hypermedia applications, synchronization, alternative structures, etc.;
- external references to support distributed applications, such as joint editing;

- variants of a document with partially the same content and partially different content, such as an extensive Instruction Manual and a brief Pocket Guide;
- versions (revision history),
- tables,
- forms,
- colour reference model integration,

  incorporation of CIE colour reference models in information and data modelling,
- role support in group communication,
- specification of directory information required for integrated broadband services and distributed applications,
- specification of management information required for integrated broadband services and distributed applications,
- extensions to the directory and management information models.

Standards under development in this area are:

- Office Document Architecture (ODA) extensions,
- Document Architecture, Transfer, Access and Manipulation (DATAM),
- High Definition TeleVision (HDTV),
- Image Processing and Interchange Standard (IPI) ISO/IEC JTC1 SC24 WG1
  - Abstract Image Data Model
  - Application Programmers Interface (API)
  - Image Interchange Format (IIF),
- Digital Audio and Picture Architecture (DAPA) of ISO/IEC JTC1/SC2/WG8 and CCITT New Image Communication (NIC) Group working on Raster Image Communication Architecture (RICA),
- Computer Graphics Metafile (CGM) extensions,
- Directory Information Model extensions,
- Structure of Management (SMI) extensions.

Communication area

- development of advanced communication profiles for moving picture and audio real-time applications,

- synchronization mechanisms between isochronous communications (e.g. moving pictures and audio),
- synchronization mechanisms between isochronous and anisochronous communication,
- solutions for combinations of different communication profiles.

Existing standards or those under development in this area are:

- Distributed Applications Framework (DAF),
- ISDN Protocol Reference Model,
- Digital Audio and Picture Architecture (DAPA) of ISO/IEC JTC1/SC2/WG8 and CCITT New Image Communication (NIC) Group working on Raster Image Communication Architecture (RICA),
- Telecommunications Network Management (TMN).

Application environment area

- processing

  generation and processing of multimedia information, supporting distributed creation, manipulation, processing, and deletion of content and structures of multimedia information,

  coordination of group communication, allowing for asynchronous and synchronous processing of documents within a user group,

  concepts for distributed operations within the Directory System (Directory Operational Model),

  concepts for the relationship of managed objects and related resources,

  image processing

- storage

  storage and retrieval of multimedia information, allowing for private and group storage, different types of access privilege as well as information search based upon a variety of criteria,

- user access

  presentation of multimedia information,

- identification and localization,

  covering information retrieval as well as information about user groups,

  global identification and localization of managed objects,

  integration of Directory use in (existing) applications,

- security

- management

  of distributed applications,

  integration of management in (existing) applications,

  universal time coordination, involving synchronization of clocks across two or more distributed open systems.

Existing standards or those under development in this area are:

- Open Distributed Processing (ODP),
- Distributed Applications Framework (DAF),
- Document Transfer, Access and Manipulation (DTAM),
- Document Filing and Retrieval (DFR),
- Distributed Office Application Model (DOAM),
- Directory System (DS) extensions,
- OSI Management standards and extensions,
- Systems Management Functions.
- Image Processing and Interchange (IPI)

5 Conclusion

As mentioned in the introduction this paper is a subset of a document titled **BERKOM Reference Model - Application-Oriented Recommendations, Version 3.2, May 1991**. The full document including several annexes and a reference list can be obtained from DETECON - Deutsche Telepost Consulting GmbH - , Technisches Zentrum Berlin, Voltastrasse 5, W 1000 Berlin 65, Germany.

Chapter 13

Towards Standards for Combining Database, Knowledge Base and Communication Technologies in the Field of Road Transport Management

Jef F. Mortelmans

Abstract

Building up a Road Transport Management System needs the combinaton of:

- Database technologies
- Knowledge Base technologies
- Communication technologies

in a cost-effective and user-friendly way.

The combination of the technologies can be done in different management tasks with the Road Transport domain:

- Transport Operations
- Road Safety
- Road Maintenance
- Other road related activities (saving of Energy, fulfilling of Environmental Needs, etc.)

Management systems for different tasks have to work together within a global system or ''Road Transport Environment'' management system.

The development of particular systems - the same as the development system of a global system - is only possible through prototyping and field trials. In an early stage of the development we already have to think about standardization, especially about:

- the standardization concerning the practical transfer of data and knowledge.
- the standardization of information patterns (mostly in a graphical form) used by e.g. the road administrators (see among others information on road maps).

1 Background and Problems

For each management system, we need

DATA

At the same time we need also knowledge (natural and/or artificial knowledge) which is to be used for working with data.

Working with data means:

COLLECTION
STORAGE
RETRIEVAL

and

PROCESSING

For managerial activities on a large scale we need also

COMMUNICATION

of data in a network. Together with the communication of the data we can also transfer rule-based

KNOWLEDGE

This knowledge can be used not only for data handling but also for communication purposes.

For building up of an efficient management system different technologies have to be combined. This is to be done also for the technology concerning the transmission of

GRAPHICAL INFORMATION

It is felt that there would be a great need in the next years for the transfer of large amounts of data on maps.

The display of pictures is frequently used in road transport management and therefore an adequate mechanism for the transfer of pictures has to be provided.

For road transport management we need practical solutions for the transfer of graphics in a network.

2 Knowledge and Data for Road Transport Management

For prototyping a transport management system we can start with the information given in Figure 1. Two main applications play a role in the system:

- applications on the spot;
- applications on term.

The data and also the knowledge to handle these data in a way to perform the system, concern a number of elements with particular characteristics which can be bundled in groups. Each group of elements is more or less connected with the applications on the spot and the applications on term.

The groups we can mention are:

- mobility;
- accessibility;
- road maintenance;
- energy consumption;
- environmental needs;
- road safety.

Knowledge which can be used with Expert Systems for the transfer, the retrieval and the processing of data can also serve for solving problems with

PARTIAL DATA
NON-ERROR-FREE-DATA (see: maximum error rate).

3 Communication in the Road Transport Management Field

In the seventies and in the early eighties people in Road Transport research centres were primarily interested in gathering and processing data on a small scale (local situations e.g. a particular intersection). In the late eighties more and more researchers became aware of the possibilities for management tasks on a large scale. These possibilities result from combining

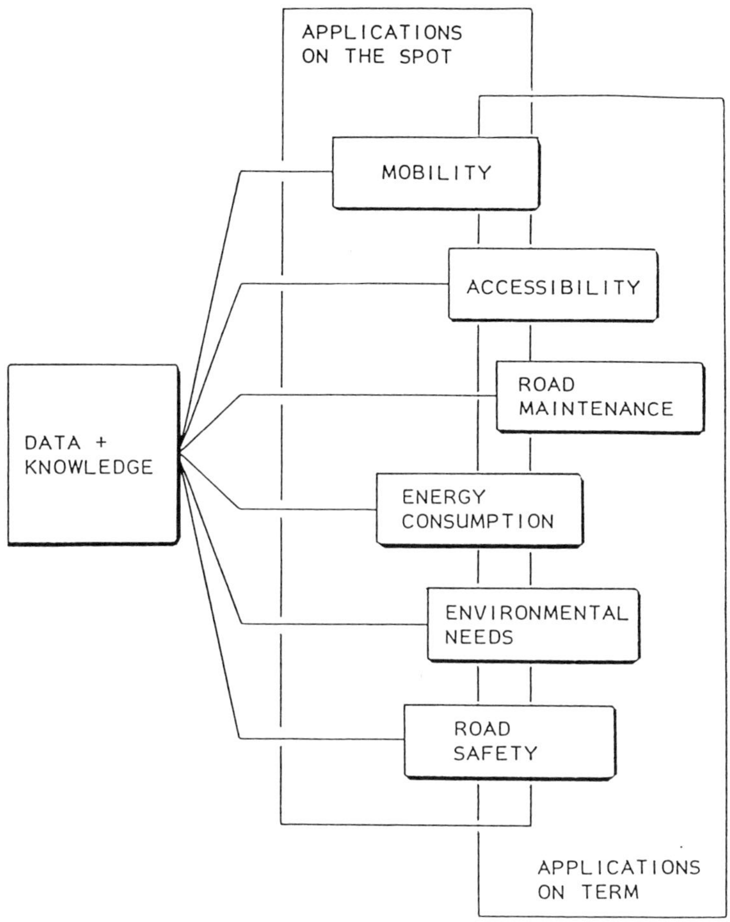

ELEMENTS OF A GLOBAL ROAD TRANSPORT ENVIRONMENT MANAGEMENT SYSTEM

FIG. 1

DATABASE TECHNOLOGIES
KNOWLEDGE BASE TECHNOLOGIES
COMMUNICATION TECHNOLOGIES

in a cost-effective and user-friendly way.

Some practical applications of the communication technology in combination with Database and Knowledge base technologies can be seen in Figure 2.

At the moment results of studies, say, about unsafe driving actions, set up in different countries, can now be transmitted in an electronic way from one country to another or to a central office or research institute. This new method of handling information is not only cost-effective in comparison with the classical way of transmitting information (publications of reports, etc.) but also more useful when actions (e.g. counter-measures) have to be taken in due time.

Interconnections of management systems can provide more and also better information. Consequently we can have more accurate actions.

4 Systems to be Coordinated

In the Road Transport management field we have - as mentioned - to combine database technologies, knowledge base technologies and communication technologies not only for one group of bundled elements e.g. Road Safety, but for all the groups to consider in a global Road Transport Management system (Figure 3).

This means that we have to install parts of a global management system on different places for which the coordination is to be realized (Figure 4) in a way that the different parts should ultimately fit into general Road Transport Environment Management System.

For different subenvironments (existing or new) the necessary systems (computer hardware and software) have to be provided. Interconnections for data and knowledge transfer (including graphics) have to be elaborated taking into account the necessity of an open system.

5 Standardization

Standardization work is needed. We have to do it step by step starting with particular standardization work on a small scale e.g. standardization of the links to be built between MISs (Management Information Systems); see Figure 5. Because of the fact that road transport is a worldwide activity, road transport management needs worldwide cooperation on standardization.

A big part of this work can be done in a profitable way in collaboration with offices/groups specialized in standardization e.g. for communication activities.

Standardization work has to provide practical solutions for people who are not experts. The transfer of data and knowledge, generally connected with graphics (diagrams, maps, etc.) must be kept simple.

Some part of the standardization work is to be done within the road transport management world itself. This is a task for international organizations in the transportation field.

6 Conclusions and Recommendations

To achieve the requirements of a Road Transport Management system - as was stated before - we need the combination of different technologies. Networking plays an important role in the achievement. The operability of the system to be developed depends for a major part of the standardization of protocols in the central network and in subnetworks of the management system.

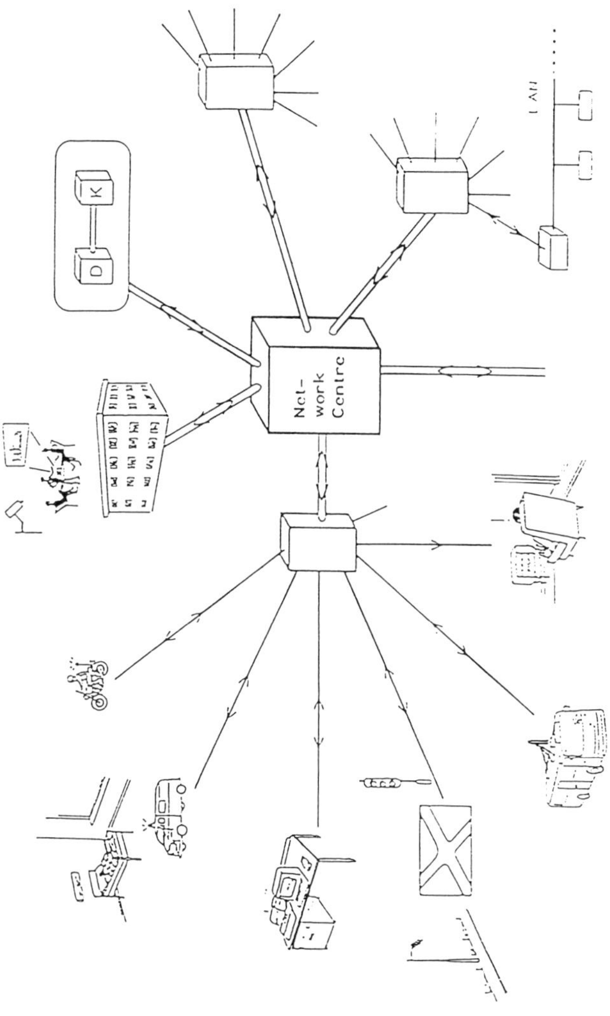

COMMUNICATION ( ) AND THE USE OF DATABASE AND KNOWLEDGE BASE (D K) TECHNOLOGIES

FIG. 2

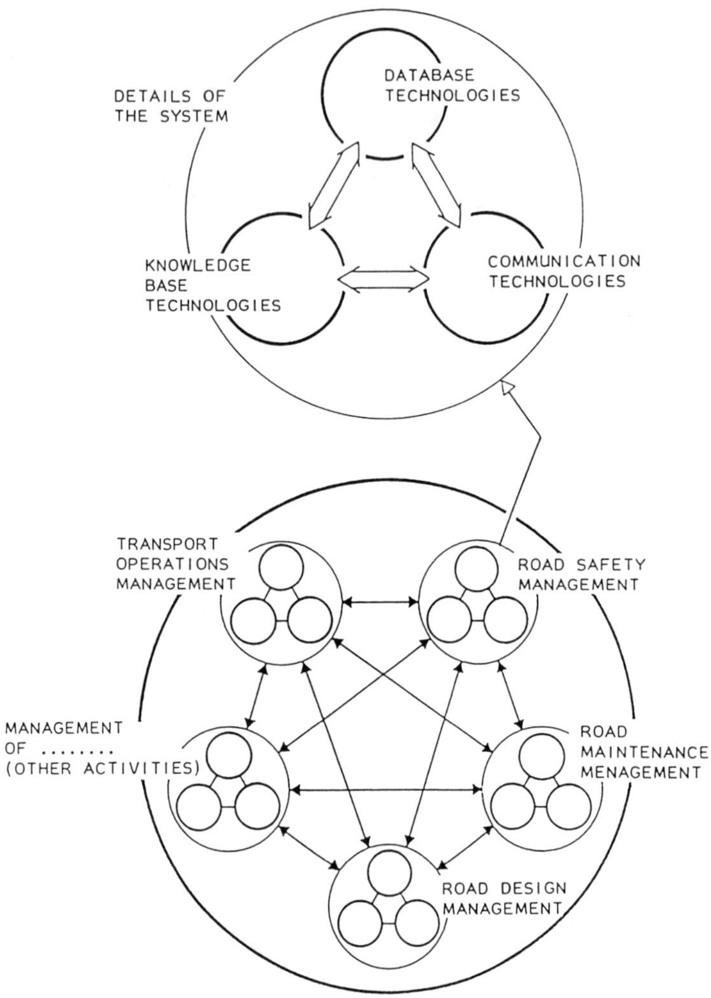

ELEMENTS OF THE DESIGN OF AN INTEGRATED ROAD TRANSPORT MANAGEMENT SYSTEM

FIG. 3

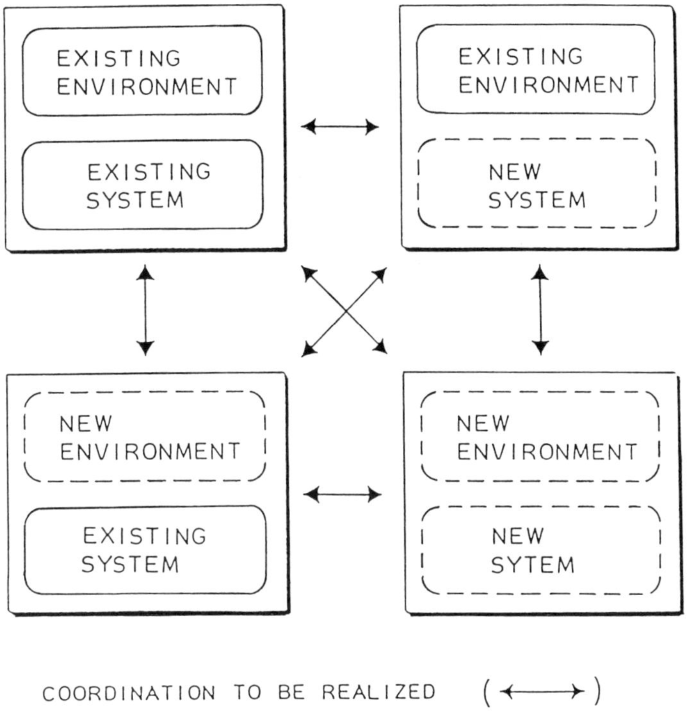
EXISTING ENVIRONMENT
EXISTING SYSTEM
EXISTING ENVIRONMENT
NEW SYSTEM
NEW ENVIRONMENT
EXISTING SYSTEM
NEW ENVIRONMENT
NEW SYTEM
COORDINATION TO BE REALIZED (⟷)

FIG. 4

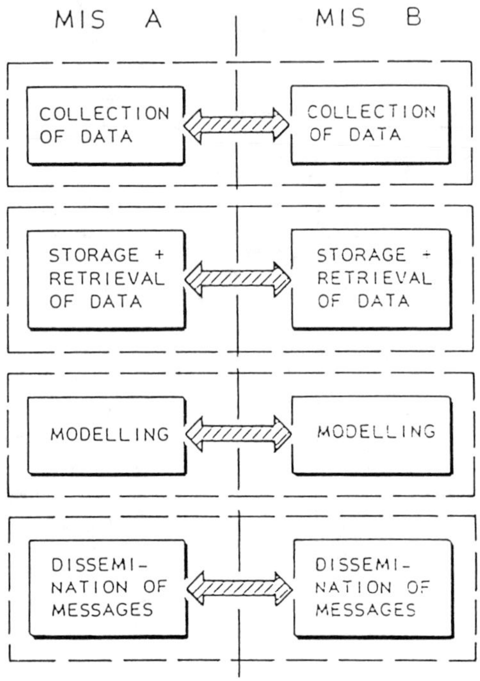

LINK BETWEEN SUBSYSTEMS OF TWO MISs.

FIG. 5

Special recommendations for sending graphical information from one system to another are to be provided.

For the specification of the characteristics of a global management system prototyping and field trials are necessary.

For the assessment of the operability of the systems and subsystems to be built, we have to take into account that the viewpoints of experienced and not experienced persons will be useful. A big number of tests will be necessary for a wide range of applications.

7 References

1. Commission of the European Communities, ''The DRIVE Programme in 1989. Project 1012: Road Safety Management combining Database and Knowledge Base Technologies (consortium: K.U. Leuven - SWOV - Dataport)'', EC-DG XIII-Telecommunications, Information Industries and Innovation, Brussels, 1989

2. Curtis, G., *Business Information Systems: Analysis, Design and Practice.* Addison-Wesley Publishing Company, Wokingham, U.K., 1989

3. Mortelmans, J.F., ''Standardization of Traffic and Transportation Information Systems'', *International Road and Traffic Conference, Berlin, Proceedings, Volume 1,* Forschungsgesellschaft fur Strassen- und Verkehrswesen, FGSV, Koln, 1988

4. Mortelmans, J.F., ''Managerial Aspects of Worldwide Cooperation on Road Safety'', *International Road Safety Conference,* Singapore, 1990

Chapter 14

PIC – A Metafile Format for Distributed Graphics Applications

W. D. Fellner, F. Kappe

Abstract

Currently, several standards for the exchange and storage of graphical data namely CGM (Computer Graphics Metafile), GKSM (GKS Metafile), and, to some extent, PHIGS CSS (PHIGS's Centralized Structure Store) are available to the graphics community. Nevertheless, in designing a specific graphics application, it could turn out that none of the above standards meets all the designer's requirements. This is what happened to us with the EDEN (short for EDitor ENvironment) project which is a generic concept for object-oriented graphics editing providing device independence at the workstation and graphics output level as well as an application independent file-format for the storage and exchange between different graphics applications.

As a consequence the PIC (short for Picture Interchange Coding) data format has been designed for, and is used in conjunction with, EDEN-based editors. It does not only provide a consistent way for the handling of *Closed Figures, Text*, and *Restricted Text* but introduces a hierarchical segment structure of local and global segments with formal parameters and generalizes bundles to variables. This paper presents an overview of the basic concepts and functionality of PIC, which has been defined in close relation to existing standards. PIC can be seen as a proposal for the extension of CGM to serve as a metafile format for distributed graphics applications.

Categories and Subject Descriptions: I.3.0 [**Computer Graphics**]: General — *metafile; standardization*; I.3.2 [**Computer Graphics**]: Graphics Systems — *distributed/network graphics*; I.3.4 [**Computer Graphics**]: Graphics Utilities — *graphics packages; software support*; I.3.6 [**Computer Graphics**]: Methodology and Techniques — *device independence; interaction techniques.*
General Terms: Distributed Graphics, Metafiles, Standardization
Additional Keywords and Phrases: Graphics Editors, CGM, CGI

---

*The support of this research by the Austrian Ministry of Science, grant 606.505, is gratefully acknowledged

1 Introduction

Due to the joint effort of industry, universities, and standardization organizations like ISO and ANSI several standards for the capturing of multiple, device-independent picture definitions as well as for the exchange and storage of graphical data are at the graphics community's disposal: CGM (Computer Graphics Metafile [12, 8]), GKSM (GKS Metafile [10]), and – as a guideline for the design of a graphical database – PHIGS CSS (PHIGS's Centralized Structure Store [14, 17]).

As this is a significant achievement we believe that these standards should be used whenever possible instead of re-inventing the wheel and defining its own (and incompatible) file format. Unfortunately, designing a distributed graphics application (especially one with an emphasis on structured graphical data or on digitized pictures), it could turn out that none of the above standards meets all the designer's requirements. Although we took into account current trends and standardization activities as well as those in the near future (eg. the last meeting of ISO JTC1/SC24 in Olinda, Brazil) this is what happened to us with the project EDEN started at the IIG[1] in 1987.

The EDitor ENvironment EDEN

Motivated by the increasing demand for programs allowing the creation and manipulation of graphical information by the user – so called *Graphics Editors* – EDEN is a generic concept for object-oriented graphics editing providing device independence at the workstation and graphics output level as well as an application independent file-format for the storage and exchange between different graphics applications [6, 7] .

EDEN supplies a common framework for graphics editing covering all the applications from Computer Aided Design (CAD) to Desk Top Publishing (DTP) or from Authoring Systems for Computer Aided Instruction (CAI) to the task of information providing for telematic services. Many different applications can be created using EDEN as their common nucleus or they can be custom-tailored on the basis of EDEN to meet their various requirements.

The Need for PIC

Obviously pictures and segments generated by EDEN-based applications have to be stored somehow. Usually there exists an application-specific file format for this purpose, but use of that format may have disadvantages (for instance, the hierarchical segment structure might be lost, the encode/decode process is slow etc.). Besides, an application-independent file format is desirable to interchange pictures across applications. Therefore EDEN supports both an application-independent file format called *Picture Interchange Coding (PIC)* and the encoder/decoder concept providing an interface to application-dependent file formats (see Figure 1).

Throughout the remaining document, the routine that writes PIC files will be called the *PIC Writer* and the routine that reads PIC files will be called the *PIC Reader*.

[1] Institutes for Information Processing, Graz University of Technology

Relation to CGM and PHIGS

The Computer Graphics Metafile (CGM) standardized by ISO [12] provides a file format suitable for the storage and retrieval of picture information in three different encodings. Unfortunately, CGM does not support the powerful segment concept of EDEN, and the extension of CGM for private purposes using the *Escape* and *Application Data* elements is somewhat clumsy, so the use of CGM for the application-independent interchange of EDEN picture data is not feasible.
However, PIC is closely related to CGM in the following sense:

- The graphic primitives and associated attributes of CGM are also found in profile '2D' of PIC.
- The actual encoding of PIC primitives is similar to the CGM binary encoding ([12, part 3]).

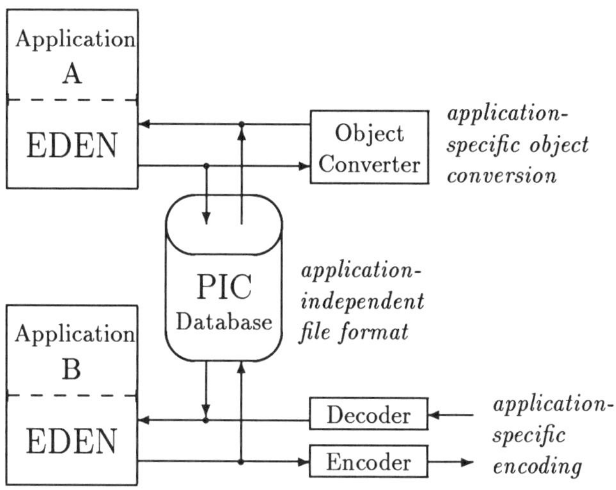

Figure 1. EDEN interfacing the World

Therefore, the conversion of CGM to PIC and vice versa can easily be done by the use of Encode/Decoder pairs (see Figure 1), although there are substantial coding differences:

- PIC supports more powerful concepts concerning segments (see Section 2.2) and attributes (see Section 2.3) in introducing a hierarchical structure of local and global segments with formal parameters and the generalization of bundles to variables.
- CGM allows a variety of selectable precisions, specification modes and representation modes that were avoided in PIC for the following reasons:
  - A large number of coding options would make the PIC Reader more complex and therefore slower, which is undesirable.
  - It introduces context-sensitivity, which is also undesirable. For instance, how could a segment using atoms with *Color Specification Mode = Indexed* be incorporated into a segment that uses *Color Specification Mode = Direct* instead?

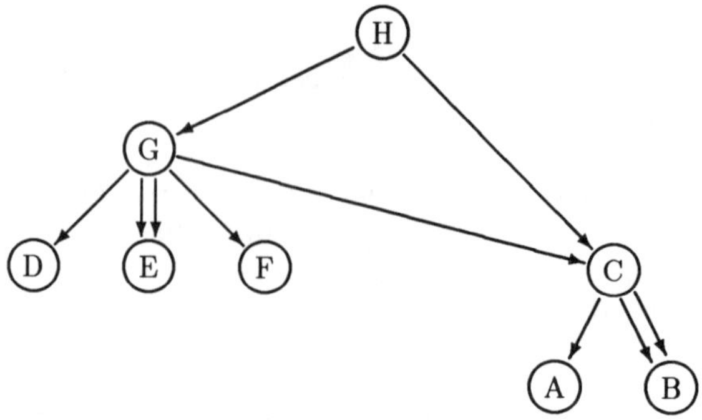

Figure 2. An EDEN segment network

The EDEN concept of composing hierarchically structured pictures is also found in the PHIGS standard proposed by ISO [14]. Segments (called *structures* in PHIGS notation) are organized as acyclic directed graphs, called *segment networks* (see Figure 2). A PIC file may contain one or more segment networks. However, the primitives of PHIGS are not part of profile '2D' of PIC.

PHIGS stores structure networks in the *Centralized Structure Store (CSS)*, that corresponds to the *PIC Filing System* discussed in Section 6.

Profiles

The main emphasis of PIC is the extensibility of the format. In particular, PIC adapts to the needs of different EDEN-based, special-purpose graphics editors. As easily as EDEN allows the extension of the set of supported objects, PIC allows the storage and retrieval of them.

Usually different EDEN-based graphics editors need different set of objects, attributes, and other capabilities. These sets are called *PIC profiles*. Profile '2D' defined in [16] is a 'foundation profile'. It contains the concepts, objects, and attributes of the EDEN-nucleus, that are automatically incorporated into every EDEN-based graphics editor. The '2D' profile supports static, two-dimensional pictures consisting of graphic primitives found in CGM together with CGM Addendum 1 ([12, 13]).

Other profiles, already defined or very likely to be defined in the future, are:

- A profile suitable for the storage of videotex images of different standards ([1, 3, 2]) is already defined.
- A profile for storage of Computer Aided Instruction (CAI) courseware ([9]).
- A '3D' profile.
- A profile suitable for handling of raster data.
- A profile for 2D- and 3D-animation.

Object converters (see Figure 1) are used to convert PIC files to different profiles (if possible, without loss of information).

2 Functional Specification

2.1 Atoms and Compound Objects

EDEN, and so does PIC, provides three different sets of objects, namely **Atoms, Compound Objects**, and **Segments.**

Atoms are the basic objects that all other objects consist of. The built-in atoms are the graphics primitives of CGI, also covered by CGM plus CGM Addendum 1. Profile '2D' of PIC supports storage and retrieval of the atoms listed in Table 1. A detailed specification of these atoms may be found in [11, part 3].

Compound Objects can be displayed using atoms and segments, but need more functionality than segments. Profile '2D' of PIC supports three compound objects: *Closed Figure, Compound Text,* and *Compound Restricted Text* as defined in [11, part 3] and [13].

PIC stores Atoms and Compound Objects with their attributes bound to them, in a way similar to the representation in the computer.

2.2 Segments

Segments are re-usable sub-images usually created interactively by the EDEN user. EDEN and PIC support two types of segments:

- **Global Segments** are stored like pictures. They may be referenced by any other picture. Modification of a global segments affects all pictures (or segments) referencing that segment. The PIC filing system is responsible for the integrity of the segment network (e.g. ensures that no global segment which is still referenced by other segments may be deleted).
- **Local Segments** are accessible only from the picture (segment) they are defined in. Local Segments are stored within that picture and are not accessible from the outside. As segments may be nested, a block structure similar to the nesting of functions in block-structured programming languages (like Algol68, Pascal) is created.

Figure 3 shows two ways of storing the segment network depicted in Figure 2. In Figure 3a only local segments are used. The picture H contains segments C and G, which in turn contain some other segments. Note two things:

- Segment C is referenced by segment G, but also by picture H. Therefore segment C must not be stored local to segment G.
- The PIC Writer ensures that all local segments are definded (stored) before they are referenced. In our example, segment C has to be stored prior to segment G, so G can reference C. Because the segment network is assumed to be an acyclic graph, such an order of segments always exists.

In Figure 3b segments C and G are stored as global segments (pictures), so they may be referenced by other pictures. C, G, and H may be stored in one file or in different files, the order within the PIC file is arbitrary. However, defining global instead of local segments introduces overhead to the PIC filing system.

Group	Atoms	Attributes
Line	Polyline	Line Type
	Disjoint Polyline	Line Width
	Circular Arc 3 Point	Line Color
	Circular Arc Center	
	Circular Arc Center Backwards	
	Elliptical Arc	
Marker	Polymarker	Marker Type
		Marker Size
		Marker Color
Fill Area	Polygon	Interior Style
	Polygon Set	Fill Color
	Rectangle	Hatch Index
	Circle	Pattern Index
	Circular Arc 3 Point Close	Fill Reference Point
	Circular Arc Center Close	Pattern Size
	Ellipse	Edge Type
	Elliptical Arc Close	Edge Width
		Edge Color
		Edge Visibility
Text	Simple Text	Text Font Index
	Simple Restricted Text	Text Precision
		Character Expansion Factor
		Character Spacing
		Text Color
Text		Character Height
		Character Orientation
		Text Path
		Text Alignment
		Character Set Index
		Alternate Character Set Index
Image	Cell Array	
	Pixel Array	

Table 1. Profile '2D' atoms and related attributes

2.3 Attributes

The attributes of EDEN objects may be bound directly to the object. In this case the attributes are said to be *individual*. PIC stores individual attributes together with the geometrical aspects of an object (in contrast to CGM, where *Set-Primitives* are used to set attributes affecting following display primitives).

EDEN (and therefore PIC) also supports *bundled* attributes. The *Aspect Source Flag (ASF)* determines whether an attribute is bundled or individual. When the ASF for an attribute is bundled, PIC stores the name of a *variable*, that holds the actual attribute value.

To realize this, PIC contains functions to set variables to a specific value of any type or to refer to another variable. The variable names are 32-bit entities, that could be viewed

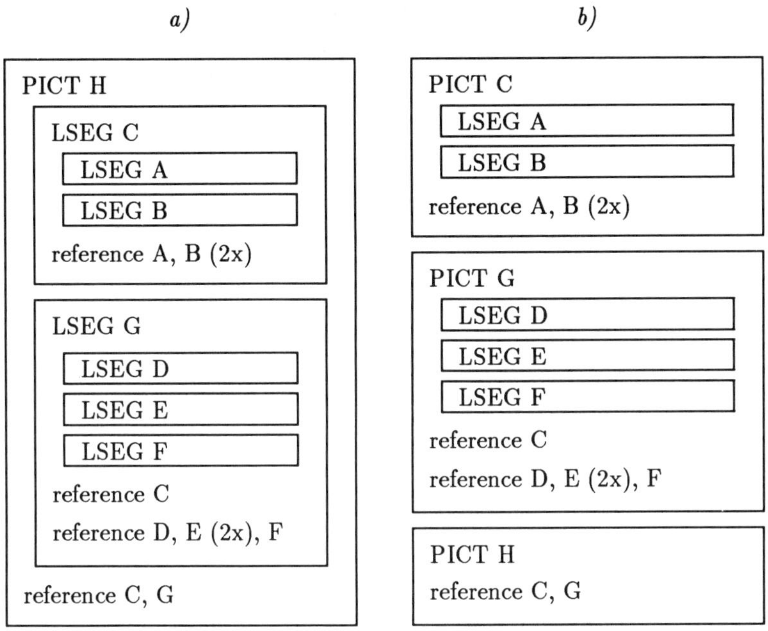

Figure 3. Storing the segment network of Figure 2 in different ways

as memory addresses, bundle table indices or 4-character names.
This *variable concept* allows the following features:

1. The *Bundle Table* concept of CGM/CGI, GKS [10] and PHIGS can be simulated, with a practically indefinite (2^{32}) number of bundle table entries.
2. The *Attribute Inheritance* concept of PHIGS and CGI can be simulated. A segment may, for instance, use a line color that was set in the referencing segment.
3. Segments may be parametrized. For instance, a segment might be referenced by something like

   ```
   Segment A (COL1=15, COL2=BLUE);
   ```

   where `COL1` and `COL2` are variables used by `Segment A`, and `BLUE` is another variable used by the referencing segment.

2.4 Coordinates

Coordinates are stored in *Virtual Device Coordinates (VDC)*, in a manner similar to CGM. The *VDC Extent* specifies the range of coordinates in a picture (or segment). Specification of values outside the VDC extent is permitted. It is intended that the visible portion of an image is contained within the VDC extent. For example, an EDEN application may display the bounding rectangle of a segment using the VDC extent of the

segment definition. An application may choose to describe pictures in coordinates that map directly to the Device Coordinates (DC) of a target device, but still are displayed correctly on other devices. Whether the mapping of VDC to DC is isotropic or not is implementation-dependent.
In order to keep PIC Readers simple (and fast), ther are differences when compared to CGM:

- In PIC, the direction of the positive x and positive y axis is fixed. The minimum x and y values of the VDC extent define the lower left corner and the maximum values the upper right corner of the drawing.
- All coordinates are stored as single-precision (32-bit), real values.

3 Overall Encoding Structure

A file format for encoding pictures can be designed with a number of different objectives:

1. *Compactness:* The encoding provides a highly compact file, suitable for systems with restricted storage capacity or transfer bandwidth (Example: CGM character encoding ([12, part 2]), CEPT videotex standards ([1, 3]).
2. *Processing Speed:* The encoding uses binary data formats similar to the representation used within the computer in order to minimize processing overhead in reading/writing the data file (Example: CGM binary encoding ([12, part 3]), PIC).
3. *Human Readability:* The representation of the data is easy to read, type and edit using a standard text editor (Example: CGM clear text encoding ([12, part 4]).
4. *Extensibility:* The encoding allows future growth in a natural way. The coded file should be sharable by a number of applications – even if they cannot process everything that is in the file (Example: PIC, TIFF ([5]).

The main design goals of the PIC file format were extensibility and processing speed.

3.1 Block Structure

The key feature of PIC-Files is that they may be generated by different applications that support different atoms and compound objects. This implies that an application has to ignore all data not related to the internal set of supported objects. All information stored in a PIC-File is contained inside so-called *blocks* of the following form:

ID	length	data	[0] [0] [0]
		length	

The ID is a 4-character (a 32-bit word) enumerate that identifies the type of the block. The length of the following data in bytes is also encoded as a 32-bit word. The meaning of the data following depends on the type of the block (the ID). In particular, it may contain other blocks, thus introducing a hierarchical file structure. Optional zero bytes (3 at maximum) are used to align blocks on 32-bit longword boundaries.
This block-oriented file structure has the following advantages:

1. The ID is a mnemonic name for the type of the block. When adding new blocks, name clashes have to be avoided. The length of the ID (4 characters) is a compromise between ease of adding new IDs and processing speed.
2. The PIC-Reader may easily skip over blocks with unknown IDs by using the length-of-data information. It is also possible to scan the file at high speed without interpreting the data.
3. The data field is fully transparent (any sequence of bytes may be stored here).
4. The smallest unit of processing is one byte. Blocks are longword-aligned, increasing the processing speed on most modern 32-bit processors.
5. Blocks can be nested. For instance, pictures may contain segments, the segments are composed of atoms. In addition, so-called *Property Blocks* may be used to define common properties of following blocks on the same level (Pascal-like scope rules).

The block ID is stored as a PIC enumerate and length is an unsigned 32-bit integer. Throughout the remaining document, a block with ID `'ABCD'` will be referred to as block `'ABCD'`.

3.2 General Form of PIC Files

A PIC-File may contain more than one picture. The individual pictures are stored sequentially in the PIC-File, each of this form:

[block 'CMNT']	block 'PICT'

The optional block `'CMNT'` is a comment block that may contain anything and is ignored by the PIC reader. The block `'PICT'` contains the actual picture. Observe:

1. As stated in clause 2 the PIC reader skips over encountered blocks of unknown type. The block `'PICT'` is currently the only defined block at the outer PIC file level that forces the PIC reader to inspect the block data. Therefore, any block other than the block `'PICT'` is ignored (like the block `'CMNT'`).
2. The block `'CMNT'`, however, is guaranteed to be ignored in future (extended) versions of PIC. Its use is to allow human-readable comments along with the pictures.

3.3 General Form of Pictures (Segments)

Pictures (segments) are stored in a block `'PICT'` containing the following data:

name	[block 'FILE']	block 'HEAD'	[block 'PICT']*	block 'BODY'

Name is a string of arbitrary length that holds the name of the segment. The string is terminated with one or more zero bytes (to align the next block on a longword boundary), so the segment name may contain any character except the character NUL[2].

The optional block `'FILE'` is intended for use by the PIC Filing System. Typically, information such as names of segments referencing that segment, use counts or names of segments referenced by that segment are stored in this block. A file system may pass this

[2] This representation of strings has been chosen to be compatible with C and UNIX.

information up to the PIC Reader or not. If the PIC Reader encounters a block 'FILE', it is ignored. Local segments contain no block 'FILE'.

The block 'HEAD' is the *Segment Header* and typically contains information concerning VDC extent, version, date and time of creation, etc. Values set in the segment header affect primitives stored in the corresponding picture body as well as in local segments defined in the corresponding block 'LSEG' (unless overridden by the segment header of the local segment). The exact layout of the segment header is described in Section 4.2.

A (possibly zero) number of blocks 'PICT' contain segments local to that segment (see Figure 3). Values set in the block 'HEAD' of the current picture (global segment) are automatically inherited into the local segments. The segment header of the local segment may redefine some of those values, not affecting other local segments or the segment body of the current picture (segment).

The block 'BODY' is the *Segment Body*. It contains graphical primitives such as atoms, compound objects (see Section 4.1) or references to segments (see Section 4.2.2).

In general, the structure of a PIC Segment is similar to the structure of a PASCAL procedure containing constants and parameter declarations, declarations of procedures local to that procedure and the executable code of the procedure itself.

4 Encoding of Compound Objects and Segments

For a detailed description of the encoding of the simple data types as well as the atoms and their attributes as specified in CGI the reader is referred to [16].

As we think that the consistent encoding of *Closed Figure, Text, and Restricted Text* and the encoding of *Segments* is either new or superior to existing formats we present them here in more detail.

As already mentioned PIC provides local and global segments with formal parameters. This feature makes the segment concept of PIC superior to all other segment concepts defined so far. Current segment concepts in computer graphics would, in case of nested segments, only provide means to change the size, position, and orientation of a referenced sub-segment. Introducing formal parameters, PIC not only gives full flexibility in using variable attributes (current concepts allow the control of attributes only in a very limited way) but even provides changes of the referenced sub-segment for different instances of the same segment. For example, the shape of a window (with the segment name 'WINDOW') in a segment called 'HOUSE' can be changed for every instance of this house by defining WINDOW as a formal parameter to the segment HOUSE.

Another new feature is the generalization of bundles to variables. This again gives PIC much more flexibility in the handling of graphical attributes than other graphics standards provide. PIC allows the usage of variables for all types of parameters like coordinates, strings, transformation matrices, and even for variable names themselves. But variables do not only enhance the bundle concept or the handling of attributes. Used for coordinates, they outperform transformation or modeling matrices which can only transform segments as a whole.

4.1 Encoding of Compound Objects

A compound object is stored as block 'COMP' (see Figure 4), very much like atoms. The first data longword specifies the ID of the compound object. CompoundIDs defined

31 . . 24	23 . . 16	15 . . 8	7 . . 0
enum='COMP'			
ulong:length			
enum:CompoundID			
data ⋮			

Figure 4. General Encoding of Compound Objects

for '2D' are listed in Table 2. As always, compound objects of unknown CompoundID are ignored by the PIC Reader. Note that **length** gives the size of the data plus 4 (the size of the enumerate specifying the compound ID) and that blocks are always aligned on longword boundaries.

ID	hex	Compound Object
'CFIG'	43464947	Closed Figure
'RTXT'	52545854	Compound Restricted Text
'TEXT'	54455854	Compound Text

Table 2. Profile '2D' CompoundIDs in alphabetical order

4.1.1 Encoding of Closed Figure

The storage format of a *Closed Figure* is shown in Figure 5. After the fill attributes a Segment Reference (a block 'LSEG' or block 'GSEG', see Section 4.2.2) follows. This segment stores the graphic primitives the closed figure consists of. During the display process, these primitives are rendered with respect to the following rules:

31 . . 24	23 . . 16	15 . . 8	7 . . 0
Header (Figure 4) length = ? CompoundID = 'CFIG'			
Fill Attributes			
Segment Reference (Figure 13)			

Figure 5. Encoding of Closed Figure

1. If the segment itself contains other segments, these sub-segments are treated as individual regions of the closed figure, realizing the *New Region* concept of CGM/CGI.
2. Any compound objects (including closed figures) in the segment or subsegment are ignored.

ID	Atom
'CELL'	Cell Array
'MARK'	Polymarker
'PIXL'	Pixel Array
'RTXT'	Restricted Text
'TEXT'	Text

Table 3. Atoms that cannot be part of a closed figure

3. Atoms found in Table 3 cannot be part of a closed figure and are ignored.
4. Other atoms (line and fill primitives) are rendered and the interior is filled using the given fill attributes.
5. The edge attributes *Edge Type* and *Edge Width* are local attributes, i.e. within the closed figure, line or fill primitives may specify their own (different) values for these attributes. *Edge Visibility* is also a local attribute and applies only to explicitly specified edges (see 4.2)
6. All other attributes are global attributes, i.e. they are applied as specified in the closed figure and the values associated with the atoms comprising the closed figure are ignored.
7. *Implicit Edge Visibility* is also a global attribute and affects the visibility of implicit edges. In the construction of closed figures, implicit edges are generated:
   (a) between the last point of one line primitive and the first point of the next, if the two points do not coincide.
   (b) between the last point of a line primitive and the current closure point, if the two points do not coincide, when a new region is started. A new region is started by a segment reference or a fill primitive. The current closure point is the first point of the first primitive of a region.
   (c) between all points $(2i + 2)$ and $(2i + 3)$, $i \geq 0$ of a disjoint polyline used to define a boundary.

In addition, all the features of segments apply:

- The atoms of the segment are subject to 2D transformation.
- The segment may contain sub-segments, the atoms of which form regions of the closed figure.
- The segment may be parametrized.
- The segment name itself may be a parameter.

This way, the user may create a commonly used shape (e.g. a rectangle with rounded corners) as a segment once and for all, and fill it (or not) with arbitrary fill attributes by referencing it in a closed figure. Segment transformation allows to display this shape in any desired size and orientation.

4.1.2 Encoding of Compound Text

The storage format of Compound Text is shown in Figure 6. The global text attributes apply to the whole compound object, while the local text attributes are given for every substring. Compound Text corresponds to the *Text* primitives of CGM/CGI with the *Final Flag* set to *not final* and subsequent *Append Text* primitives.

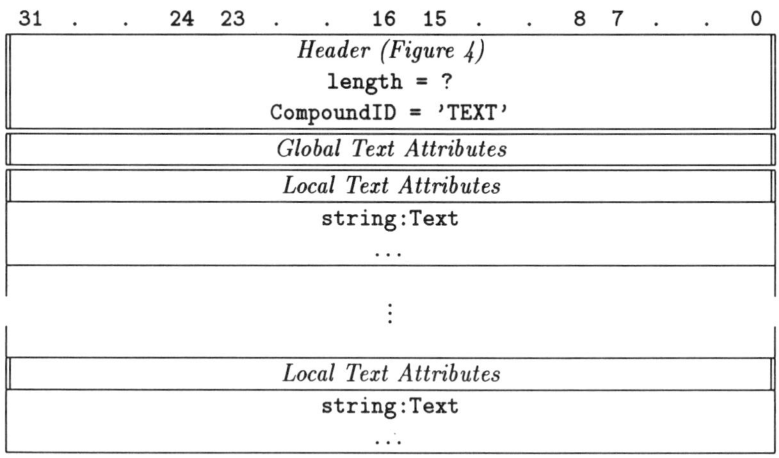

Figure 6. Encoding of Compound Text

After the text strings a number of pad bytes are inserted to align the next Local Text Attribute block on a longword boundary. The end of the strings can only be found by triggering on the terminating NUL-byte.

4.1.3 Encoding of Compound Restricted Text

The storage format of Compound Restricted Text is shown in Figure 7 and differs from the encoding of Compound Text only in the parameters *Extent Width* and *Extent Height* which apply to the whole compound object. Again, local text attributes are given for every substring. Compound Restricted Text corresponds to the *Restricted Text* primitive of CGM/CGI with the *Final Flag* set to *not final* and subsequent *Append Text* primitives.

4.2 Encoding of Segments

As outlined in Section 3.3, segments are stored just like pictures, i.e. pictures are segments. There are, however, global and local segments. While there is no substantial difference in the storage layout of global versus local segments the segment reference is different. In addition, the use of local instead of global segments reduces file system overhead and increases processing speed.

Segments (gobal or local) are stored in a block `'PICT'` as illustrated in Figure 8. `Name` is a string of arbitrary length that holds the name of the segment. The string is terminated with one or more zero bytes (to align the next block on longword boundary),

31 . . 24	23 . . 16	15 . . 8	7 . . 0
Header (Figure 4) length = ? CompoundID = 'RTXT'			
real:ExtentWidth			
real:ExtentHeight			
Global Text Attributes			
Local Text Attributes			
string:Text ...			
⋮			
Local Text Attributes			
string:Text ...			

Figure 7. Encoding of Compound Restricted Text

31 . . 24	23 . . 16	15 . . 8	7 . . 0
enum:blockID='PICT'			
ulong:length			
string:Name ...			
[block 'FILE']			
block 'HEAD'			
[block 'PICT']*			
block 'BODY'			

Figure 8. Encoding of Segments (Pictures)

so the segment name may contain any character except for the character NUL. Segment names are case-sensitive.

The optional block `'FILE'` is intended for use by the PIC Filing System (Section 6). Typically, information such as names of segments referencing that segment, use counts or names of segments referenced by that segment are stored in this block. A File System may pass this information up to the PIC Reader or not. If the PIC Reader encounters a block `'FILE'`, it is ignored. Local segments usually contain no block `'FILE'`.

The block `'HEAD'` is the *Segment Header* described in Section 4.2.1. Values set in the segment header affect primitives stored in the corresponding segment body as well as in local segments defined in the corresponding block `'LSEG'` (unless overridden by the segment header of the local segment).

A (possible zero) number of blocks `'PICT'` contain segments local to that segment (note that the definition of block `'PICT'` is recursive). Values set in the block `'HEAD'` of the current segment are inherited to the local segments. The segment header of the local segment may redefine some of these values, not affecting other local segments or the segment body of the current segment.

The block `'BODY'` is the *Segment Body*. It contains graphical primitives such as atoms, compound objects (Section 4.1) or references to segments (Section 4.2.2), i.e. a sequence of blocks `'ATOM'`, `'COMP'`, `'LSEG'`, and `'GSEG'`.

In contrast to CGM/CGI, no explicit *Segment Priority* is defined in PIC. However, display order implies a priority relation among objects (atoms, compound objects and segments) according to the *Painter's algorithm*: The segment with highest priority is displayed last. PIC reflects this priority scheme by defining objects in the block `'BODY'` in display order, which means that objects are sorted in ascending display priority indside the block `'BODY'`.

4.2.1 Encoding of Segment Header

The segment header contains a number of segment properties coded as *Segment Property Blocks* (Figure 9). These blocks are described in the following.

31 . . 24 23 . . 16 15 . . 8 7 . . 0
enum:blockID='HEAD'
ulong:length
[block 'TIME']*
[block 'VDCX']
[block 'PARM']*
[block 'SET ']*

Figure 9. Encoding of Segment Header

Encoding of Segment Property Block 'TIME': The encoding of block `'TIME'` is shown in Figure 10. Note:

- Multiple blocks `'TIME'` are allowed in a single block `'HEAD'` as long as they are distinguishable by their Version numbers. The EDEN application writing the file may choose to:
  - Write no block `'TIME'`. This option should not be used for global segments. Local segments of minor significance may be stored with no block `'TIME'` at all, as the version info is stored with the referencing global segment anyway.
  - Write a single block `'TIME'` corresponding to the last modification of the segment.
  - Write two blocks `'TIME'` corresponding to first creation and last modification of the segment. The block `'TIME'` with higher version number reflects last modification while the version number of first creation is usually 1.0.

– Write a new block `'TIME'` at every modification, not discarding the others. This way, the complete modification history of a segment is recorded and may be retrieved by sorting the stored blocks `'TIME'` by `Version` or `DateAndTime`.

31 . . 24 23 . . 16 15 . . 8 7 . . 0
enum:blockID='TIME'
ulong:length
real:Version
time:DateAndTime
string:Application ...
string:Author ...
string:Machine ...
string:Comment ...

Figure 10. Encoding of Segment Property Block `'TIME'`

- `Version` numbers are stored as reals, allowing major and minor version numbers (e.g. version 1.25). Version numbers smaller than 1.0 should not be used.
- `DateAndTime` is stored in UNIX-compatible fashion and reflects the Date and Time of segment creation/modification in GMT.
- The `Application` string tells the name of the program – usually an EDEN-based graphics editor or a code converter (Figure 1) – that created/ modified the segment (e.g. 'BTX/CEPT V1.2').
- `Author` holds the name of the person that created/modified the segement. If the author is known by real-world name, it is stored here. If only the login name is available, that name is used. If there is no author (e.g. segment is created by some decoder process), the user id of the process owner should be saved.
- `Machine` keeps the name of the machine on which the author created/modified the segment, preferable a logical node name like the one used for E-mail (or else the name of the organization and a machine name unique in that organization).
- `Comment` may be used to store an arbitrarily long comment on the purpose of the segment, limitations, reasons for modification etc. The string is intended to be interactively entered by the user and is not supposed to carry application-specific information (application-specific property blocks may be used for that purpose).
- All strings are aligned on byte boundaries. However, after the comment string a sufficient number of pad bytes is inserted to align the next block on a longword boundary.
- As strings are terminated by a NUL-byte, they may contain all other characters and are of arbitrary length. The empty string is a single NUL-byte.

Encoding of Segment Property Block 'VDCX': The *VDC Extent* (see Figure 11) specifies the range of coordinates in the segment. Specification of coordinates outside the VDC extent is permitted. Is is intended that the visible portion of the segment be contained within the VDC extent. For example, an EDEN application may display the bounding rectangle of a segment by using the VDC extent of the segment header.

31 . . 24 23 . . 16 15 . . 8 7 . . 0
`enum:blockID='VDCX'`
`ulong:length=16`
`real:MinX`
`real:MaxX`
`real:MinY`
`real:MaxY`

Figure 11. Encoding of Segment Property Block `'VDCX'`

An application may choose to describe pictures in coordinates that map directly to the Device Coordinates (DC) of a target device, but still are displayed correctly on other devices. Whether the mapping of VDC to DC is isotropic or not is implementation-dependent.

Only one block `'VDCX'`is allowed per segment header. If the block `'VDCX'` is missing, the default VDC extent is used.

Encoding of Segment Property Block 'SET ': The property block `'SET '` (see Figure 12) is used to set a variable (Section 2.3) to a value of a certain type.

31 . . 24 23 . . 16 15 . . 8 7 . . 0
`enum:blockID='SET '|'PARM'`
`ulong:length=8+length(value)`
`var:Name`
`enum:Type`
`Type:Value`   ...

Figure 12. Encoding of Segment Property Block `'SET '` and `'PARM'`

`Name` is the target variable name. `Type` indicates the type of the variable, according to Table 4.

If `Type` is not `'VAR '`, the actual value is stored in `Value` which is a value of the indicated type. The length of `Value` may be determined by the `length` field of the block `'SET '`.

If `Type` is `'VAR '`, `Value` stores the source variable name. Note:

- The evaluation of variables is not performed by the PIC Reader but by the display process.

ID	hex	Atom
'SI8 '	53493820	Signed integer at 8-bit precision
'SI16'	53493136	Signed integer at 16-bit precision
'SI32'	53493332	Signed integer at 32-bit precision
'UI8 '	55493820	Unsigned integer at 8-bit precision
'UI16'	55493136	Unsigned integer at 16-bit precision
'UI32'	55493332	Unsigned integer at 32-bit precision
'ENUM'	454E554D	Enumerate
'VAR '	56415220	Variable name
'REAL'	5245414C	Real number at 32-bit precision
'FLAG'	464C4147	Flag
'STRI'	53545249	String
'COLO'	434F4C4F	Color
'COOR'	434F4F52	Coordinate
'TMAT'	544D4154	Transformation matrix

Table 4. Profile '2D' data types

- Wherever a variable is supposed to store some value (e.g. attributes, segment name) the variable may also just hold the name of another variable, that eventually stores the desired value.
- As the source variable may also be set to another variable, variables may be indirected a number of times. This feature is used to pass parameters from upper-level segments down to lower-level segments (see Section 4.2.2).
- The value set by a block `'SET '` is only visible in the corresponding segment body and local segments defined in the segment containing the block `'SET '`. A local segment may override this value in its segment header, not affecting the other segments of same or higher level or the segment body of the current segment (Pascal-like scope rules).

The segment header may contain an arbitrary number of blocks `'SET '`.

Encoding of Segment Property Block 'PARM': The property block `'PARM'` is encoded like the block `'SET '` (Figure 12) but with a slightly different meaning. This block is used to declare the names of variables that are parameters of the segment, i.e. variables that may be used within the segment and assigned values to from outside the segment (by segment reference). The segment header may contain an arbitrary number of blocks `'PARM'`.

`Name` is the name and `Type` is the data type of the variable (= parameter). `Value` may be used to assign a default value to the parameter. The use of `Value` is optional (if not used, `length=8`).

The segment header of PIC might be compared to the procedure declaration part of a block-structured programming language (e.g. Pascal). The `'PARM'` blocks represent the declaration of formal parameters[3], while the `'SET '` blocks correspond to the declarations of local constants.

[3]It is not possible to assign default values to formal parameters in Pascal, but it is in C++ [18], for example.

4.2.2 Encoding of Segment Reference

There are in fact two different segment reference blocks:

1. block `'GSEG'` references a global segment. Usually the system will have to fetch the segment from secondary storage, e.g. the PIC Filing System (Section 6). There is a single name space for global segments, i.e. two different global segments must not have the same name.
2. block `'LSEG'` references a local segment. Usually the system manages to keep local segments in primary storage. To find the desired segment, the segment names defined in the blocks `'PICT'` of the current segment are scanned first. If the segment is not found there, the block `'PICT'` with the definition of the current segment is searched (as far as it is read in), and then the way up to the root segment, very much like Pascal scope rules.

31 . . 24	23 . . 16	15 . . 8	7 . . 0
enum:blockID='LSEG'|'GSEG'			
ulong:length			
f:NameASF	f:TransASF	(pad)	
var|string:Name ...			
trans:TMatrix			
[block 'SET ']*			

Figure 13. Encoding of Segment Reference

This distinction helps not only the system to find the segment, but – more important – the user of the system to define segments:

- When defining a global segment, the user does not need to care about existing local segments with the same name.
- When defining a local segment within a segment, no name clashes with global segments can occur.
- Also, name clashes with local segments defined within other global or local segments are resolved by the system.
- When incorporating a previously defined segment, possible name clashes with other segments already defined are automatically resolved.

The storage layout of block `'LSEG'` and block `'GSEG'` is shown in Figure 13. If `NameASF=false`, the segment name is stored directly in `Name` and no pad bytes are inserted before `Name`. If `NameASF=true`, however, the next longword stores the name of a variable, that stores the segment name. In conjunction with block `'SET '` and block `'PARM'`, this feature allows one to parametrize the name of a segment some other segment is to reference, just like passing function names as parameters to functions in a programming language.

`TMatrix` is the 2D transformation matrix that is to be applied to the referenced segment. `TransASF` allows bundling of the transformation matrix. If `TransASF=true`, the first longword of `TMatrix` (which is the x scale component) stores the name of the variable that contains the transformation matrix.

Zero or more blocks `'SET '` are part of the segment reference and set formal parameters of the referenced segment to actual values (or to the values of other variables or parameters).

5 Extension Guidelines

Profile '2D' corresponds to the minimum supported features of any EDEN-based graphics editor. Advanced EDEN applications very likely will need more functionality, that will be reflected in the PIC file format, for example:

- More atoms or compound objects (e.g. splines, 3D objects).
- Additional attributes (e.g. marker types).
- Additional segment features (e.g. 3D transformations, hidden-line/hidden-surface removal).
- More complex color model (e.g. shading, light sources).

In general, these additional features will be reflected in additional block types or other enumerates, that will be ignored or defaulted by the PIC Reader of other applications. The extended PIC profile will be compatible with profile '2D' and other profiles if it conforms with the general rules concerning the choice of the enumerate, byte order, and alignment.
In addition, the following criteria for design of new profiles apply[4]:

- *Completeness*: The profile should be complete in itself to handle a specific application.
- *Conciseness*: Redundant elements or parameters should be avoided.
- *Consistency*: Contradictory elements should be avoided.
- *Extensibility*: The ability to add new element and generality to profile '2D' should not be precluded.
- *Fidelity*: The minimal results and characteristics of elements should be well defined.
- *Orthogonality*: The elements of the profile should be independent of each other, context-sensitivity should be avoided.

6 The PIC Filing System

In general, PIC Files are not bound to a specific storage medium, operating system or filing system. However, the following problems may arise when storing arguments directly as files on operating-system level:

[4] List extracted and adapted from [12].

1. PIC segment names are of arbitrary length. Some operating systems (e.g. MS-DOS) are restricted to a certain length of filenames. This problem might be solved by computing 'Hash Filenames' from the segment name and storing segments with the same hash filename in a single file of that name (see Section 3.2)
2. PIC segment names are case-sensitive. If the operating system uses non-case-sensitive filenames, the solution to problem 1 will solve this problem, too.
3. When the user is able to delete a segment that is still referenced by another segment, file system integrity is violated. The integrity is best checked by use of a full-fledged data base system for segment storage.
4. In a multi-user environment, a user might modify a segment that another user is working with (or even modifying, too). In order to resolve that conflict the file system should take care that the segment is either locked for other users during modification or that another instance of that segment is being created. In addition, individual access rights may be used to prevent modification of certain segments by unauthorized users.
5. Instead of fetching every segment on every display process, the system might 'cache' segments in main memory. In this case, the segments will either have to be locked for other users or reloaded when modified by another user.

This documentation deliberately under-specifies the filing system and leaves the details to the implementation, so that PIC files may be used in various environments. The filing system is assigned a private block in the segment (block `'FILE'`, see Section 4.2) to store its information there. The exact layout of this block is also left to the implementation.

Acknowledgements

We would like to thank the many people who have contributed to EDEN. Our special thanks go to Hermann Maurer (department head of IICM) for the continuous support and to Keith Andrews, Klaus Rapatz, and Jodok Schäffler (all IICM) who have made significant contributions to the non-proprietary implementation of EDEN.

References

[1] CEPT: *Videotex Presentation Layer Data Syntax (Issue 1); Part 2 – Geometric Display*; T/CD 6.1, Innsbruck, Austria (May 1981).

[2] CEPT: *Videotex Presentation Layer Data Syntax (Issue 2); Part 1 – Alpha-Mosaic Display; Part 4-6 – Define DRCS, Colour, and Format; Part 8 – Reset*; Revision of T/CD 6.1, Cannes (Sept. 1983).

[3] CEPT: *Videotex Presentation Layer Data Syntax (Issue 2); Part 2 – Geometric Display*; T/CD 6.2, (Nov. 1987).

[4] COMMODORE BUSINESS MACHINES: Amiga ROM Kernel Reference Manual: EXEC; Amiga Technical Reference Series; Addison-Wesley (1985).

[5] DAVENPORT T., VELLON, M.: *Tag Image File Format (TIFF) – Rev. 4.0*; Aldus Corp. & Microsoft Corp. (April 1987).

[6] FELLNER W.D., KAPPE F.: *EDEN – an Editor Environment for object-oriented Graphics Editing*; to appear in EUROGRAPHICS '90, Elsevier Science Publishers.

[7] FELLNER W.D., KAPPE F.: *EDEN – A General-Purpose Graphics Editor Environment*; Report 262, IICM, IIG, Graz University of Technology (Nov. 1988).

[8] HENDERSON L., JOURNEY M., OSLAND C.: *The Computer Graphics Metafile*; IEEE Computer Graphics & Applications, Vol. 6, No. 8 (Aug. 1986) pp 24-32.

[9] HOLWEG G.: *Ein komfortables Editiersystem für CUU*; Master's Thesis, IIG, Graz University of Technology, Austria (May 1988).

[10] ISO: *Information Processing Systems – Computer Graphics – Graphical Kernel System (GKS) – Functional Description*; ISO IS 7942 (1985).

[11] ISO: *Information Processing Systems – Computer Graphics – Interfacing techniques for dialogues with graphical devices (CGI), Part 1-6*, ISO DIS 9636 (Dec. 1989).

[12] ISO: *Information Processing Systems – Computer Graphics – Metafile for the Storage and Transfer of Picture Description Information (CGM)*; ISO IS 8632 (Aug. 1987).

[13] ISO: *Information Processing Systems – Computer Graphics – Metafile for the Storage and Transfer of Picture Description Information (CGM), Draft Addendum 1*; ISO 8632/DAD1 (Dec. 1988).

[14] ISO: *Information Processing Systems – Computer Graphics – Programmer's Hierarchical Interactive Graphics System (PHIGS)*; ISO DIS 9592 (Oct. 1987).

[15] KAPPE F.: *Design und Implementierung eines EDEN-basierenden Bildschirmtext-Editors*; Master's Thesis, IIG, Graz University of Technology, Austria (Feb. 1988).

[16] KAPPE F.: *Picture Interchange Coding (PIC); Functional Specification and Encoding of Profile '2D'*; Report 266, IIG, Graz University of Technology (Feb. 1989).

[17] SHUEY D., BAILEY D., MORRISSEY T.P.: *PHIGS: A Standard, Dynamic, Interactive Graphics Interface*; IEEE Computer Graphics & Applications, Vol. 6, No. 8 (Aug. 1986) pp 50-57.

[18] STROUSTRUP B.: *The C++ Programming Language* Addison-Wesley; (1986).

Chapter 15

An Overview of the FTAM Standard and its Application to CGM File Transfer

Paolo Artico, Fabio Dilonardo, Michele Re

1 Abstract

The technology trend of computer systems advances the usage of distributed applications in opposition to centralized systems. The international standards are the means for supporting this process. Standards are available for the communication between eterogeneous systems (OSI standards) and for graphical applications. One of the aims accomplished by the work presented in this paper is the liaison between these standards. This paper describes the FTAM OSI standard and its possible application to the distribution of computer graphics applications. The first part of the paper is a tutorial on FTAM, reporting the services and the facilities offered; the second part is an attempt to define the extensions needed by FTAM in order to allow the transfer of CGM files.

2 Introduction

Today's computer technology offers a wide variety of systems, differing for models, features, complexity, etc.; all such systems, owing to the dramatic advances in semiconductor technology in the last ten years, have the common characteristic to give very high performances at low cost.

Such situation pushes every day the distribution of computing resources, at department and individual level, offering to the users the possibility to run on their personal system, applications more and more complicated (i.e. applications requiring many computing resources or applications managing large data bases); such applications just a few years ago could be processed only by large and expensive computing systems.

Another relevant factor for the computer system user is the availability of communication services both at local and geographical level.

The combination of these elements increases the distribution of the applications among different eterogeneous systems.

Two conditions are needed to allow eterogeneous systems to communicate: the first is the overcoming of the variety of conventions used by different systems for representing and processing information and for communicating; the second is the possibility for the users to run the same application on systems of different manufacturers avoiding the costs for the duplication of software, whose development is now the main factor in computing system costs.

The International Standards and in particular the OSI standards have the specific objectives to enable the communication and the interworking between applications running on eterogeneous systems regardless of their characteristics.

The OSI Reference Model [1] provides a layered architecture in which framework the standards needed to solve all the problems of the communication and the interworking of eterogeneous systems have been specified. The lower layers of the architecture (Physical, Data Link, Network) address all the problems related to the physical transport of data over communication networks. The upper layers address all the application needs in terms of synchronization of dialog between applications, presentation of data and processing of user data.

The standards are now pretty stable; and there are many products, offered by the same computer manufacturers or by specialized software houses.

In particular the offering of standardized products, rather than the underlying layers, is concentrated on two applications: MHS concerning the exchange of messages and FTAM concerning the exchange of files. These are the two first applications standardized by the international bodies.

But an interesting thing is the possibility offered by these two standards to develop customized distributed applications on top of them avoiding all the problems related to the communication on different interworking systems.

This is what is happening in the field of EDI (Electronic Data Interchange); where the OSI X.400 (MHS) standard supports document exchange. Also in the field of computer graphics, the communication between distributed applications could be supported by OSI standards; this paper is an overview of a possible use of FTAM as communication support for exchange of graphic files.

3 File Transfer Access and Management

3.1 Introduction

The File Transfer Access and Management (FTAM) OSI application is defined in the ISO 8571 [2] standard. ISO 8571 specifies the transfer of and access to files stored in the filestores of two end systems, including management of these files. One end system acts in the *Initiator* role and requests access to the file, the other end system acts in the *Responder* role and provides access to the file in the Virtual Filestore.

The model used is one of two end systems establishing an association and accessing files of the Responder's Virtual Filestore as shown in figure 1.

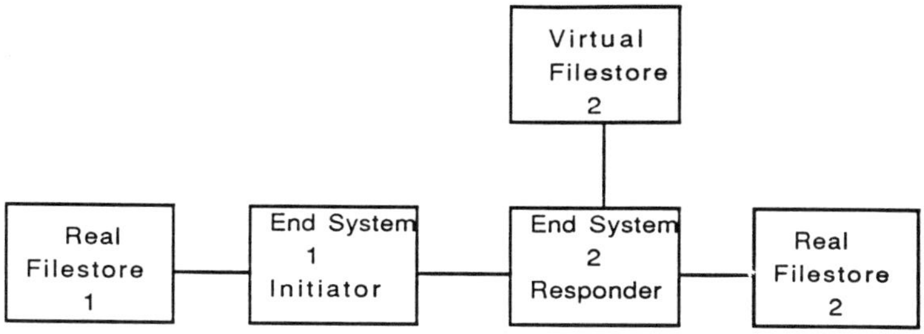

Fig. 1

3.2 The Basic Concepts of the Filestore Model

The ways in which real filestores are implemented vary considerably among existing real systems. Different real systems have a wide range of styles for describing the storage of data and the means by which it can be accessed. A common model for use in describing files and their attributes is needed before services, protocols and procedures for file transfer, access and management can be used in the *Open Systems Interconnection Environment*

This model is called the *Virtual Filestore*. Such a filestore definition is very powerful, because it allows the differences in style and specification to be absorbed into a *mapping function* from the open system onto the *real open system*, and any particular real open system can then interwork with other different real open systems in terms which can be mutually understood.

The definition of the Virtual Filestore forms a schema for the description of filed information, where a file is an entity having:

- a single *filename*, that allows it to be referenced without ambiguity;
- other descriptive file attributes which express properties of the file such as accounting information, history, etc.;
- file attributes expressing the actions capable of being performed on the file;
- file attributes describing the logical structure and dimensions of the data stored in the file;
- any file access data unit forming the contents of this file.

These are all aspects of the file which can be observed by any authorized initiator. If two observers make the same enquiry about these aspects of a single file, they will obtain the same information about its properties, provided that no modification took place between the enquiries. These properties are called *file attributes*.

3.3 File Service Overview

The file service is concerned with creating, in a series of stages, a working environment in which the initiator's desired activities can take place.
The dialogue, in turn:

- allows the initiator and the responder (filestore) to establish information about each other; including their respective identities in terms of their application entity titles; the related service primitives include F-INITIALIZE, F-TERMINATE, F-ABORT;
- identifies the file which is needed; the related service primitives include F-CREATE, F-SELECT, F-DESELECT, F-DELETE;
- establishes the attributes describing the file and the bulk data transfer which is to take place in this activity; the related service primitives include F-OPEN, F-CLOSE;
- engages file management; the related service primitives are F-READ-ATTRIBUTES, F-CHANGE-ATTRIBUTES;
- locates the position in the file access structure of the FADUs to be accessed; the related service primitives are F-LOCATE, F-ERASE;
- inserts, replaces, extends or erases one or more complete FADUs; the related service primitives are F-WRITE, F-READ, F-DATA, F-DATA-END, F-TRANSFER-END.

These steps build up various parts of a set of file contexts. The period for which some part of the common state held by the service users is valid is called *regime*. As progressively more shared state is established, a nest of corresponding regimes is built up.
Four types of file service regime are defined:

- the FTAM regime which exists while the application association is used for the FTAM protocol;
- the file selection regime during which a particular file is associated with the FTAM regime;
- the file open regime during which a particular set of processing mode, presentation contexts and concurrency controls is in operation;
- the data transfer regime during which a particular bulk data transfer specification and direction of transfer are in force.

There is at most one instance of each type of regime at any one time.

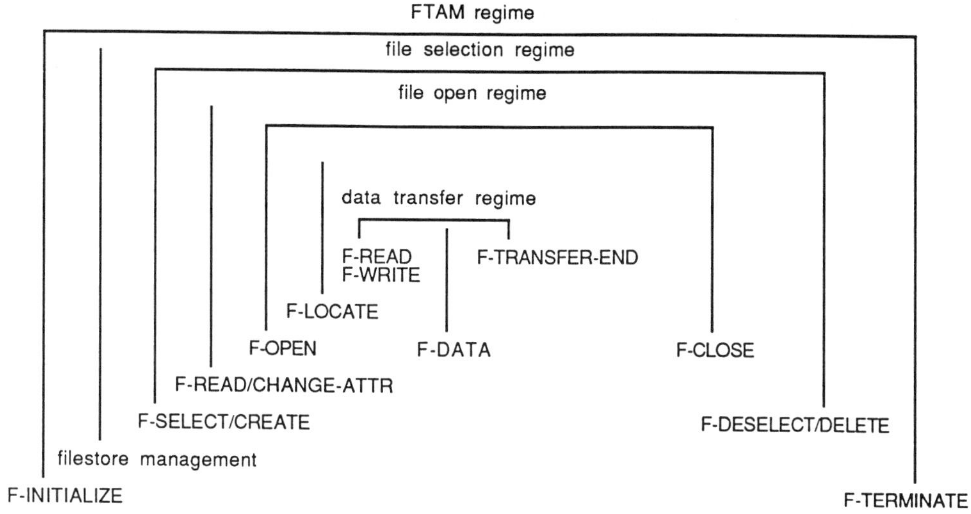

Fig. 2

The file service provides for:

- a sequence of file selection regimes in an FTAM regime;
- a sequence of file open regimes in a file selection regime;
- a sequence of data transfer regimes within a file open regime; the data transfer regimes may each be for either read or write data transfer. Write data transfer permits the operations insert, replace or extends.

Termination of a regime implies termination of all regimes nested within that regime. The nesting of regimes is shown in figure 2.

3.4 Functional Units and Service Classes

The FTAM protocol and service is very rich in function. A wide range of types of application can be supported, but the cost of implementing all parts of the protocol on all occasions would be correspondingly high.

If implementers were given arbitrary choice as to which of the function were to be provided, there would, on the other hand, be little chance that similar choices would be made, and so little probability of communication.

To avoid these problems, the FTAM service defines two types of functional selection. At the most basic level, the functions defined are grouped into *functional units*. An implementation must support a functional unit either completely or not at all; the number of choices to be made are thus limited. Mechanisms are defined which allow negotiation of functional units when the FTAM regime is initialized, and these allow the two communicating entities to reach a common understanding of the set of functional units available.

This in itself reduces variety, but still leaves considerable freedom. Further convergence is achieved by defining *service classes*, each of which support broad categories of use. These classes are:

- the *transfer class*, which allows for the movement of files or parts of files between systems, placing emphasis on simple operation with a minimum of protocol overhead before and after the data transfer;
- the *management class*, which allows control of the virtual filestore by a series of independent confirmed service exchanges, but does not include file transfer mechanism;
- the *transfer and management class*, which combines the features of the transfer class and the management class;
- the *access class*, which allows the initiating entity to perform a sequence of operations on the file access data units, providing for the manipulation of remote data;
- the *unconstrained class*, which leaves the selection of functional units to the designer of the distributed application, giving full flexibility for optimization, but no guarantee of a common functional kernel.

The classes of service which are needed are negotiated when the FTAM regime is initialized.

3.5 Overview of the File Protocol

The file protocol supports the file service using the Access Control Service Element (ACSE) Services ISO 8649 and 8650 [3,4] and Presentation Services ISO 8822 and 8823 [5,6]. It supports the following functions:

- representation of the file service primitives as a sequence of protocol data units for transmission by the ACSE and Presentation Services;
- grouping, when appropriate, of the representations of logically separate service primitives as distinct data values in a single P-DATA-request service primitive;
- ensuring the progress of the protocol.

In abstract, the operation of the protocol is modelled by the interaction of two file protocol machines (FPMs). The two FPMs communicate by means of the services available at their lower boundary (ACSE and Presentation), in such a way as to provide the services required at their upper boundary (FTAM services). These concepts are illustrated in figure 3.

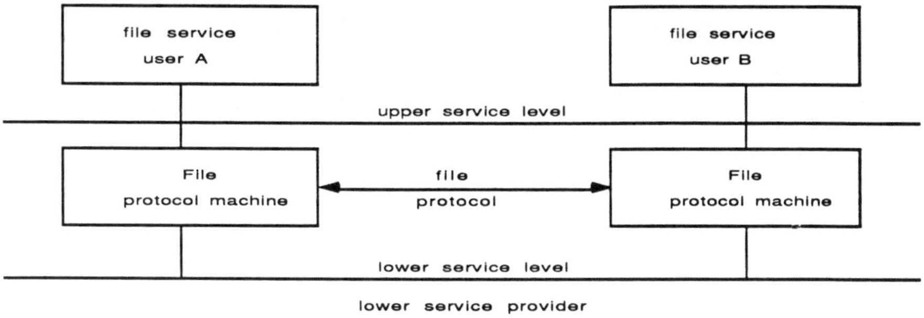

Fig. 3

The file service is defined asymmetrically with the file service user "A" being the initiator and the file service user "B" being the responder. The behaviour of each FPM is defined in terms of:

- the actions it takes;
- the stimuli it receives;
- the information available.

3.6 File Protocol Data Units

The file PDUs are complex data types defined by an abstract syntax definition given in Abstract Syntax Notation 1 (ASN.1) ISO 8824, 8825 [7,8].

For information which is always required default values are defined to avoid unnecessary overhead. The transfer syntax of these data types is negotiated and encoding performed by the presentation service provider.

The PDUs are transmitted as data values, either on a P-DATA primitive or in the user information of an ACSE primitive or in the user data of a Presentation Service primitive.

4 Representation of File Structures

In the following we will try to illustrate one of the main issues in the FTAM standard, i.e. which is the structure of a virtual file and its relationship with real files. Even though it is not the purpose of this paper going into the details of the FTAM standard, we will try to clarify some basic concepts related with the structure of a file.

FTAM defines a virtual file as "*an unambiguously named collection of structured information having a common set of attributes*". The first thing that should be clear in mind is that the standard defines four different kind of information regarding the structure of a file:

- The *file access structure*, describing which are the basic access units of the file and their relationships.

- The *presentation structure*, describing the relationships between data elements, data units, and file contents.
- The *transfer structure*, describing which is the ordering of file access data units (FADU) when transferring the file.
- The *identification structure*, describing in which way the nodes of the file access structure are named and how the FADUs are identified.

4.1 File Access Structure

The file access structure is a tree structure that describes the file in terms of the units which can be accessed separately (FADUs). The structure is a hierarchy of these units, as can be seen in an example shown in Fig. 4.

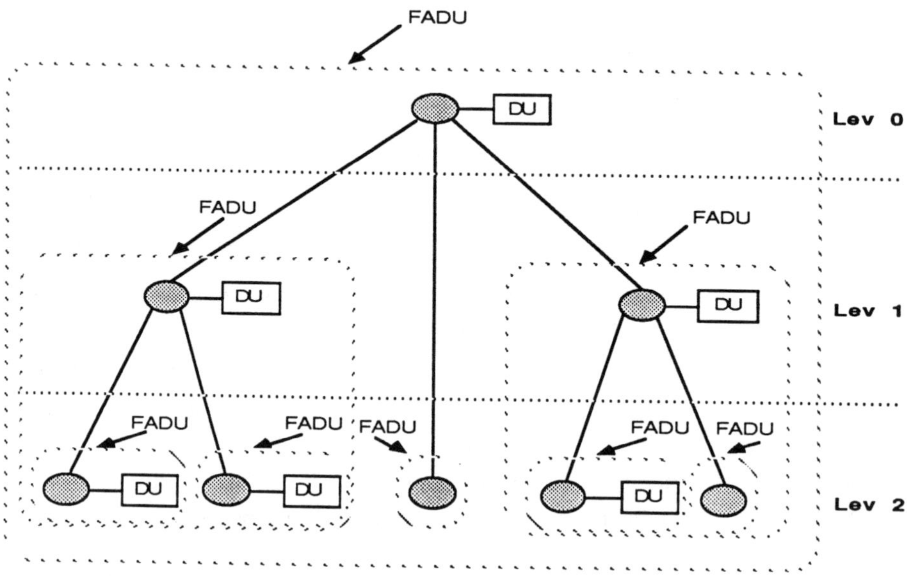

Fig. 4

The file access structure is described using ASN.1 and must conform the following rules:

- it is an ordered tree;
- zero or one data unit are associated to each node;
- each node within the structure is a structural element and doesn't contain any data element, but gives access to its subtree. The access unit (that is, the subtree) is a FADU and is comprised of the structural nodes of the subtree and the data units contained within the subtree. The root node of the tree gives access to the entire file;
- optionally a node has a name assigned to it;

- the number of levels, the arc lengths and the number of arcs originating from each node are not restricted.

A FADU is then the minimal access unit and is a subtree of the hierarchical file (FADUs are recursively nested); the actual data units are associated with the nodes of the tree, and can be identified by their relative node name. This is a general hierarchical structure which can be used to represent a wide range of real file structures, from unstructured to very complex ones.

The determination of the appropriate file access structure is a fundamental step in the process of mapping real files to virtual ones. We will see in the following how restrictions of the general file access structure just described are necessary in order to realize this mapping in an efficient way.

4.2 Presentation Structure

The presentation structure indicates how the record structure of the real file can be mapped onto the FTAM file structure, and how the presentation data values (PDV) are mapped to P_DATA primitives. An example regarding an unstructured text file is illustrated in Fig. 5.

4.3 Transfer Structure

The transfer structure states that the nodes, and then the data elements, are transferred in the order in which they appear in the preorder traversal sequence. There are four types of data elements: Node-Descriptor-Data-Element, Enter-Subtree-Data-Element, Exit-Subtree-Data-Element, and File-Contents-Data-Element.

It depends on the real file to be transferred and then on its access structure, which of the above information makes sense to be transferred. For this purpose, the standard defines the concept of *access context*, providing a restricted view of the data elements involved during communication. The defined access contexts are: Hierarchical All Data Units (HA), Hierarchical No Data Units (HN), Flat All Data Units (FA), Flat One Level Data Units (FL), Flat Single Data Unit (FS), Unstructured All Data Units (UA), and Unstructured Single Data Unit (US). As you can notice, the choice of the right access context depends on the file access structure. When the access context is selected, both the ordering of FADUs (contained in the subtree of the transferred FADU) and the information transferred for each of these FADUs is determined.

4.4 Identification Structure

The last structural information listed above, i.e. the identification structure, permits to identify a FADU by means of some defined operators called: first, last, previous, current, next, begin, end, Node_Name, Sequence of Node_Names, Node number.

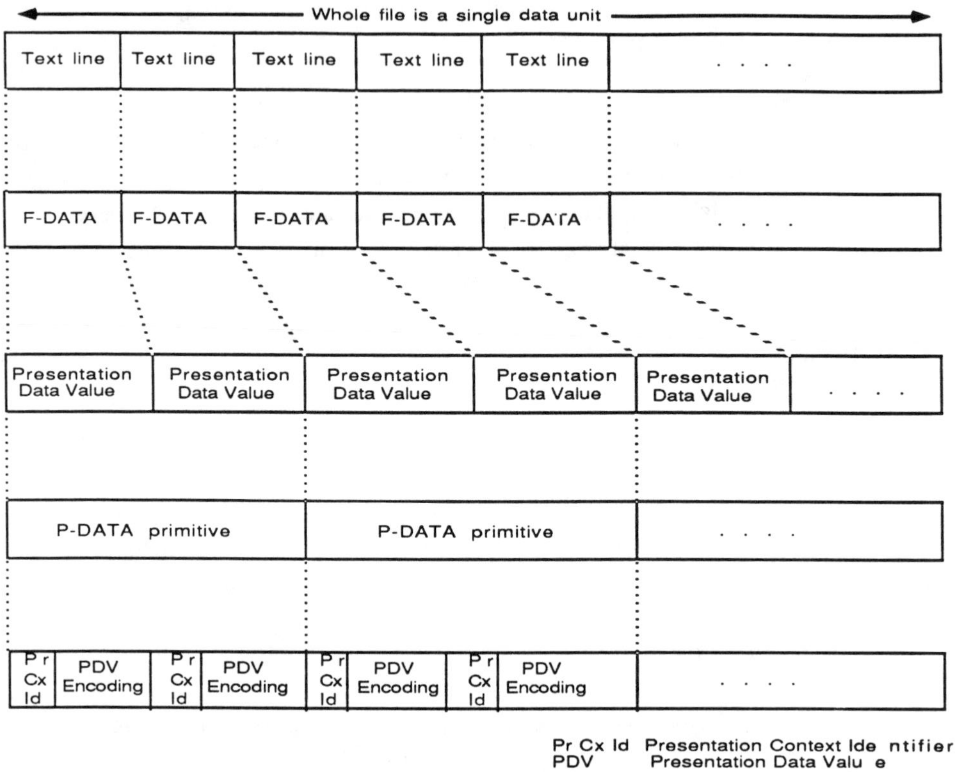

Fig. 5

The set of structures and associated parameters that we have defined till now can be combined one to the other and together with other parameters, and usually some restrictions are necessary on the general structure in order to fit the real file structure.

4.5 Constraint Set

Because of the negotiation nature of the FTAM communication, it would not be easy to specify all these parameters one by one. For this reason the standard provides the concept of *constraint set*. A constraint set defines a set of restrictions and refinements of the general file model, thus specifying a less general model tailored to the needs of a particular class of applications. A constraint set can be addressed by means of a single constraint set identifier, in order to simplify the process of negotiation.

Lets us see some of the information specified in the definition of a constraint set:

- field of application, i.e. the set of files to which the constraint set can be applied;
- basic constraints, related to node names, to the set of qualified actions and available access contexts; they also define which is the FADU located after the file open action, which is the beginning of the file, how to read or write the whole file, etc.

- structural constraints concerning node names, the association between data units and node names, arc lenghts, etc.
- action constraints, i.e. restrictions on the possible actions;
- identity constraints, stating for each identity the set of actions that can be performed.

The standard defines the following constraint sets: Unstructured, Sequential Flat, Ordered Flat, Ordered Flat with Unique Names, Ordered Hierarchical, General Hierarchical, General Hierarchical with Unique Names. Other constraint sets can be defined and registered; we will see in the following, when dealing with our case study of CGM files, how this is an actual need for defining file structures different from the ones already defined by the standard.

4.6 Document Type

As we have seen, the definition of the virtual file structure is a potentially complex process because of the large amount of parameters that need to be specified in order to unambiguously define which is the structure of the file, the independent units which can be accessed as a whole, how the data elements are grouped, which information is transferred, and so on. For this reason the standard provides another useful tool which permits to specify in a simple way all the parameters needed to identify a class of files with a sufficiently precise structure: this is called the *document type* mechanism. A document type specifies:

- the file contents;
- the file access structure;
- the constraint set;
- the transfer syntax;
- the document semantics;
- the abstract syntax.

The standard defines the following document types:

- Unstructured Text (FTAM-1), based on unstructured constraint set. The file consists of one FADU with zero, one, or more character strings;
- Sequential Text (FTAM-2), based on sequential flat constraint set. The file consists of zero, one, or more file FADUs, each of which consists of zero, one, or more character strings;
- Unstructured Binary (FTAM-3), based on unstructured constraint set. The file consists of one FADU with zero, one, or more binary strings;
- Sequential Binary (FTAM-4), based on sequential flat constraint set. The file consists of zero, one, or more FADUs, each of which consists of zero, one, or more binary strings;

- Simple Hierarchical (FTAM-5), based on the general hierarchical file model as specified by FTAM. The FADUs are named by unique string identifiers.

Other document types can be defined and registered by an international and national authority. The document type is then the most practical and efficient way to specify a virtual file. The idea is that a number of new document types should be defined and registered in order to obtain a more efficient and logical management of files. The present implementations of the FTAM standard usually provide only access to Unstructured and Sequential files, with a consequent poor behaviour of the applications dealing with files with a more complicated structure. The problem is particularly important with interactive applications dealing with large files but usually interested only in parts of them. For example in the case of unstructured files, an application that needs to read a single word of a remote dictionary requires the transfer of the whole dictionary!

On the other side we don't know of any FTAM implementation providing access to Simple Hierarchical files. This is due partly to the fact that the standard is relatively new and partly to the fact that a Simple Hierarchical file has a structure that is usually too general to be effectively used in an OSI environment. We will explain a bit more this concept when dealing with the case of CGM files.

What should be clear at the end of this description is the fact that several document types are required in order to obtain more efficiency, flexibility, and simplicity in FTAM applications.

5 Transfer of CGM Files

We have seen in the previous chapters how the FTAM standard defines a virtual file. The concepts introduced are general and in fact it is not part of the standard to show which is the mapping of real files onto virtual files. The standard only gives guide-lines for specifying the semantics and the abstract view of the file contents. The annex B to part 2 of the standard, which defines the 5 document types above mentioned, is the only part of the standard document giving some information on this matter.

What we want to show now is how these concepts can be applied to real situations. The real file structure that we will consider is the structure of Computer Graphics Metafile (CGM) files.

5.1 Computer Graphics Metafile (CGM)

CGM is an ISO standard [9] defining the format of files containing the description of pictures as sequences of primitives and related attributes.

The description is device and application independent and is then well suited to be used in an OSI environment. Its use is intended as a mechanism of picture capture, thus providing snapshots of the graphics screen. The standard only defines the structure of the file and the allowed encodings, but it doesn't consider the problem of implementing a generator or an interpreter of this file (only guide-lines are provided at this purpose).

Let's shortly summarize the main characteristics of this standard. A file CGM is a sequential file with the structure shown in Fig. 6. The following rules apply:

- more than one metafile may be present in the same CGM file;
- zero or more pictures may be present in each metafile;
- each picture is independent by each other;
- the Metafile Descriptor contains global information for the metafile which are necessary to display each single picture.

A file CGM is composed of elements of 8 different kinds:

- Delimiter Elements, acting only as delimiters of the main structures (Metafile and Picture);
- Metafile Descriptor Element, providing global information on the metafile;
- Picture Descriptor Elements, defining the way the picture attributes must be interpreted;
- Control Elements, permitting to modify values previously set;
- Graphical Primitive Elements, describing the output primitives of a picture;
- Attribute elements, defining the attributes of the output primitives;
- Escape Elements, giving access to device-dependent and application-dependent features;
- External Elements, containing information useful to the application but not to the display of pictures.

For simplicity we will not consider the addenda of the standard, which mainly adds 3D capabilities and segmentation. The standard also specifies which are the permitted encodings for a CGM file:

- Character encoding, using 7 bits encoding techniques;
- Binary encoding, using binary numbers;
- Clear Text encoding, using only the 94 printable characters from the 7 bit ISO 646 code table.

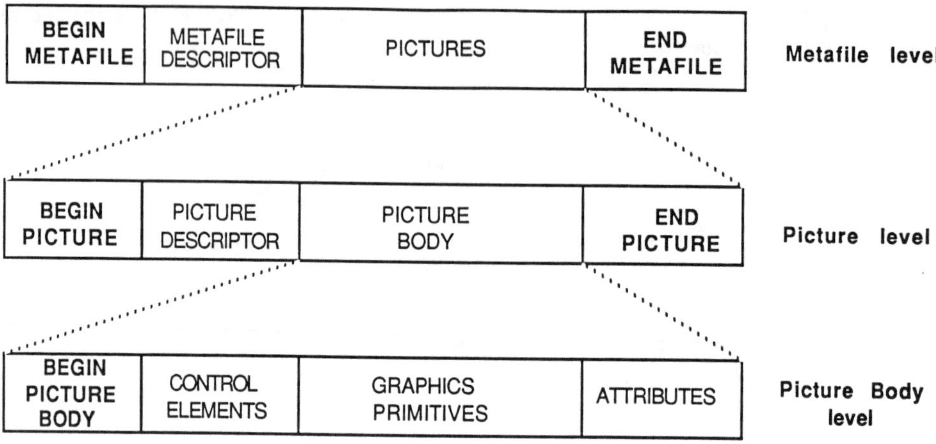

Fig. 6

This is essentially the structure and the semantics of a CGM file. Because FTAM doesn't impose any constraint on the contents of the files that are actually transferred, it is a reasonable approach the use of FTAM for transferring CGM files. As we said in the previous chapters, in order to establish communication, the initiator and the responder of an FTAM activity must agree on a certain number of parameters; most of them are specified by the document type parameter. What we want to investigate now is the mapping between an existing or a new document type and the structure of a CGM file. Please notice that the structure of the CGM file is well suited for FTAM because is virtually a hierarchy even if physically the CGM file is a sequential file.

5.2 User Requirements

In order to individuate the best mapping, we must have clear in mind which are the requirements of the graphics user in the utilization of CGM files. By previous investigations [10,11] and by the results of some meetings that we had on this subject inside the consortium of the ESPRIT II 2463 ARGOSI project, the graphics user requirements can be summarized by listing which are the CGM elements that need to be accessed and transferred separately:

- the whole file
- each metafile
- each metafile descriptor
- each picture.

5.3 Mapping with Existing Document Types

The first choice for a document type and the most simple to realize, is the use of unstructured files. This is in principle a possible choice but it has the inconvenient to be too expensive in the case of large CGM files containing more than one metafile. In this case the only unit which can be accessed and transferred is the whole file, and the application cannot efficiently manage the display of a single picture inside the file, for example. Only the first of the 4 requirements that we have just listed is satisfied by this solution.

A step further is accomplished by the use of sequential files. In this case, thinking of assigning a metafile for each FADU, we have reached only the first two goals prefixed: even if access to single metafiles is obtained, this solution doesn't give us the granularity that we want to access the single pictures and metafile descriptors individually.

Another choice that could come in mind is the use of a simple hierarchical document type; unfortunately this is not convenient. Let us suppose to have, in an OSI environment, two users located in different countries, running different applications but both using standard CGM and FTAM implementations. If they want to manage CGM files as simple hierarchical files, they won't be able to easily access a single picture. This is because they can't assume to have structured the CGM files in the same way. For example user A could be interested in accessing

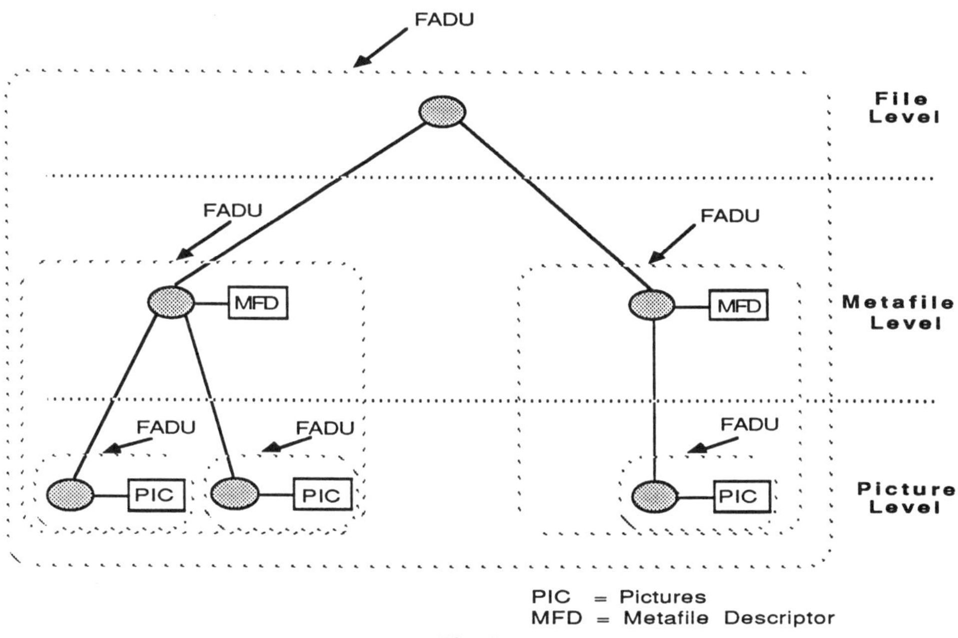

Fig. 7

the single pictures, while user B is only interested in accessing the single metafiles contained in the same CGM file; their FTAM implementations will structure the relative CGM files consequently. In this case the two users have a different view of the same standard object, because they use an FTAM virtual file structure not sufficiently precise for the goal of their activity.

5.4 The "CGM binary" Document Type

The only way to reach our goals intended to provide an efficient file transfer, is through the definition of a new constraint set and document type [12-14]. This approach would permit to have an uniform view of CGM files in an OSI environment, independent of the applications involved. In Fig. 7 is depicted the file access structure of the new document type called "CGM binary" (FTAM-6); by comparing it with the real structure of CGM files shown in Fig. 8 we can see how the logical structure is the same. The structure of the file is then a *two level depth hierarchical file*, where the FADUs at the first level correspond to CGM metafiles and the FADUs at the second level correspond to CGM pictures; the requirements previously listed are so satisfied:

- the file is accessed through the root FADU (level 0); a request of transferring the root FADU with FA or HA access context will transfer the whole file contents;
- each metafile is accessed through the FADUs at level 1; a request of transferring a FADU at the metafile level with FA or HA access context will transfer all the pictures with the related metafile descriptor;
- the metafile descriptors are the data units associated with each node at level 1; a request of transferring a FADU at the metafile level with US access context will transfer a single metafile descriptor; by specifying the FL access context applied at level 1 all the metafile descriptors are transferred with a single request;
- each picture is accessed through the FADUs at level 2; a request of transferring a FADU at the picture level with UA or US access context will transfer a single picture.

Please note that in principle we could have gone one step further and have in the access structure another level containing the single graphics primitives and control elements. This would provide a better resolution but would introduce a considerable overhead for the protocol: for each graphics primitive or attribute or control element, FTAM should provide a subtree!

An example of mapping of a CGM file into the CGM binary document type is provided in Fig. 8.

Table 1 shows the basic constraints defined in the two levels depth hierarchical constraint set with unique names. This constraint set has been defined in order to address issues like the fact that the root node has no data unit or node name associated with it, the arc lenghts must be one, the beginning of file is the root node, etc. Table 2 shows the identity constraints for the above constraint set.

Table 3 shows the information objects of the CGM binary document type as it is at the current stage.The document semantics of the CGM binary document type states, among the other things, that each FADU consists of zero, one or more binary strings; the order of these elements is significant.

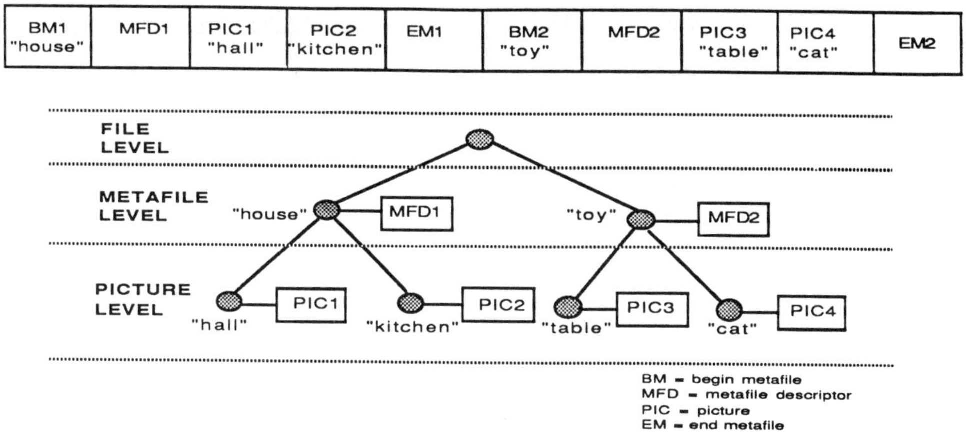

Fig. 8

Table 1 - Basic constraints in the two levels depth hierarchical constraint set with unique names

Constraint set identifier	{iso standard 8571 constraint-set (4) two-levels-depth-hierarchical-unique-names (8)}
Node name	All names shall be of the same type; the names of the children of any particular parent shall be unique
File access actions	Locate, Read, Insert, Replace, Extend, Erase
Qualified actions	Insert: normal action "insert as a sister"; qualified action "insert as a child"
Available access contexts	HA, HN, FA, FL, FS, UA, US
Creation state	Root node without an associated data unit
Location after open	Beginning of file
Beginning of file	No node selected; next gives the first node in the traversal sequence (the root node); current and previous give an error
End of file	No node selected; previous gives the last node in the traversal sequence; current and next give an error
Read whole file	Read in access context HA with FADU identity consisting of an empty sequence of node names
Write whole file	Transfer the FADU as the sequence of data-elements which would be generated by reading the file in access context HA: perform the transfer with a FADU identity consisting of node names and a file access action of replace

Please note that there is a relationship between the chosen CGM encoding technique and the "CGM_encoding" parameter value. If binary encoding is used, then the CGM_encoding parameter shall have the value "binary". If character encoding is used (please note that the CGM character encoding is not, despite its name, a character encoding but an octet encoding: 7 bits encoding techniques are used and not IA5Strings), then the CGM_encoding parameter shall have the value "character".

Table 2 - Identity constraints in the two levels depth hierarchical constraint set with unique names

Action	Begin	End	Current	Next	Previous	NodeName	NodeSeq
Locate	valid	valid	valid	valid	valid	valid	valid
Read			valid	valid	valid	valid	valid (note[1])
Insert			valid	valid	valid	valid	valid
Replace			valid	valid	valid	valid	valid (note[1])
Extend			valid	valid	valid	valid	valid
Erase			valid	valid	valid	valid	valid (note[1])

[1]An empty sequence of node names is used to address the root node when performing actions on the whole file.

Table 3 - Information Objects in the CGM binary document type

document type	{iso standard 8571 document type (5) CGM binary (6)} "ISO FTAM CGM binary"
abstract syntax names a) name for asname1 b) name for asname2	 {iso standard 8571 abstract syntax (2) unstructured binary (4)} "FTAM unstructured binary abstract syntax" {iso standard 8571 abstract syntax (2) ftam-fadu (2) "FTAM FADU"
Transfer syntax names	{joint-iso-ccitt asn1 (1) basic encoding (1)} "Basic encoding of a single ASN.1 type"
Parameter syntax	PARAMETERS ::= SEQUENCE { maximum-string-length [0] IMPLICIT INTEGER OPTIONAL, string-significance [1] IMPLICIT INTEGER {variable (0), fixed (1), not-significant (2)} OPTIONAL, CGM_encoding [2] IMPLICIT INTEGER {binary (0), character (1)} OPTIONAL}
file model	{iso standard 8571 file model (3) hierarchical (1)} "FTAM hierarchical file model"
constraint set	{iso standard 8571 constraint set (4) two-levels-depth-hierarchical-unique-names (8)} "FTAM two levels depth hierarchical constraint set with unique names"
File contents Datatype1 ::= Datatype2 ::= CHOICE	 OCTET STRING {Node-Descriptor-Data-Element, Enter-Subtree-Data-Element, Exit-Subtree-Data-Element}

As far as regards CGM clear text encoding, the character switching techniques available for text elements, makes translation into other character sets almost impossible. Use of clear text encoding CGM files is essentially local and for debugging purposes. This is why, following a recommendation provided by the ISO Computer Graphics Device Interfaces and Metafile Secretariat [14], we decided to provide no document type definition for the transfer of clear text CGM files [13]. The proposed solution is presently under development. It shows how a suitable document type can be defined for a particular file structure.

However an open issue of this proposal is the overhead introduced by FTAM for managing the above structure. The encoding of the structuring information could in fact virtually produce an overhead that could vanish the benefits of the flexibility provided by the structuring itself.

6 Conclusion

An overview of the FTAM standard with particular attention to the definition of virtual file, file attributes and file structure has been presented. However the real objective of this paper was to show how these general concepts can be adapted to real situations.

The transfer of graphic files in an OSI environment is a problem which is going to get more attention than before. This is due to a real need of this kind of capabilities. In this paper we have investigated the particular case of the CGM file, which is well suited to be transferred by FTAM because of its logical hierarchical structure. The approach of defining a new document type has been presented and must be considered as a general approach, when existing document types or access contexts and constraint sets don't permit a good mapping with the given real structure.

The process of document type definition has been started following the ISO procedures: an FTAM liaison to Graphics has been established in November 1989; moreover a draft proposal of a particular document type for CGM files has been submitted to ISO in the same date. The evolution of this proposal has seen some changes and the last version numbered 1.3 has been submitted to ISO in November 1990. The final goal of this work is the registration of such document type by the ISO registration authority and we believe this will contribute to the development of OSI applications.

7 References

1. *Basic Reference Model*, ISO 7498 - Information Processing Systems - Open Systems Interconnection.
2. *File Transfer, Access and Management*, (FTAM) ISO 8571 Parts 1 through 4 - Information Processing Systems - Open Systems Interconnection, 1988.
3. *Service Definition for the Association Control Service Element*, (ACSE) ISO 8649 - Information Processing Systems - Open Systems Interconnection, 1988.
4. *Protocol Specification for the Association Control Service Element*, (ACSE) ISO 8650 - Information Processing Systems - Open Systems Interconnection, 1988.
5. *Connection Oriented Presentation Service Definition,* ISO 8822 - Information Processing Systems - Open Systems Interconnection, 1988.
6. *Connection Oriented Presentation Protocol Service Definition,* ISO 8823 - Information Processing Systems - Open Systems Interconnection, 1988.
7. *Specification of Abstract Syntax Notation One,* (ASN.1) ISO 8824 - Information Processing Systems - Open Systems Interconnection, 1987.
8. *Basic Encoding Rules for Abstract Syntax Notation One,* (ASN.1) ISO 8825 - Information Processing Systems - Open Systems Interconnection, 1987.
9. *Computer Graphics Metafile for the Storage and transfer of Picture Description Information* (CGM), ISO 8632 Parts 1 through 4, 1987.
10. *FTAM support for CGM*, ISO/TC97/SC21/WG2 n. 507, Sept. 1986.
11. *FTAM support for CGM*, ISO/TC97/SC21/WG2 n. 508, Sept. 1986.
12. *Proposed FTAM document type to support CGM*, ISO/IEC JTC1/SC21/WG5 FIRENZE 1989 n. 86, Nov. 1989.
13. *FTAM constraint set and document type for CGM Version 1.4* EWOS/EGFT/91-05, Dec. 1990.
14. *Liaison statement from SC24/WG3 to SC21/WG5*, ISO/IEC JTC1/SC24/WG3 n. 136, Nov. 1990.

Chapter 16

Application Profiles and the CGM

Anne M. Mumford

1 Introduction

The Computer Graphics Metafile (CGM) standard was published in 1987. It is concerned with defining the functional specification and 3 encodings for storing pictures on computers. It has been the subject of some extensions work within ISO/SC24. Amendment 1 is now completed and includes some extra features for GKS support and to parallel the work on the Computer Graphics Interface (CGI) as well as some static segment capabilities. Amendment 2 will simply note the new parts being developed for 3D extensions of CGM. Amendment 3 is now at Draft International Standard stage and adds capabilities for finer drawing control, user defined hatches and lines and raster capabilities.

CGM has become a well used standard. Is has been adopted by a wide range of graphics software suppliers. It has been a standard that has received good promotion via demonstrations of exchange of pictures between different companies (NCGA, Eurographics-UK, Computer Graphics Show). It has also been taken on as part of the US CALS initiative which is a major factor in its acceptance in the market place and which indicates the need of a standard in this area.

The use within CALS (and also in the MAP/TOP communities) is via the definition of a profile for that application community. This paper reviews the need for profiles for CGM and the profiles which have been defined to date. It then goes on to look at the development of International Standardised Profiles in ISO. The paper concludes with some suggestions as to what the ARGOSI project could do to use CGM within the project and also how the ARGOSI project might help promote the development of a CGM profile (or profiles) within ISO.

2 Subsets of Standards

Standards tend to be very complete specifications. This is true for a wide range of standards in the information technology area. There is no problem with this in theory as long as the standard is self consistent. In an ideal world all implementations of the standards would implement all possible options and there would be no problems in exchanging implementations and files.

The real world is never quite like this and there are good reasons why an implementor may not wish to include all possible options available in the standard. Some of these reasons are:

- that the implementor has limited time in which to implement the standard;
- that the machine on which the implementation is being carried out has limited memory and thus compact code is important;
- that the applications of using the CGM interface cannot make use of some of the features of the standard.

The implementor has to decide on a reasonable subset of the standard. Someone generating a metafile might, for example, choose to use just default values thus saving on code and metafile size. There are no problems in the metafile generators choosing to use a subset of the metafile elements and options. The problem which can occur comes when the interpreter of the metafile also chooses a subset of elements but a different subset from the one chosen by the generator software.

There is no assistance in the standard towards finding a solution. The standard makes some suggestions about minimum capabilities but there is no requirement for this.

The problem is not new in graphics standards however. When GKS was being developed the problems outlined above were appreciated by the developers of the standard. They were concerned that it should not be necessary to implement all features of GKS in order to have a correct GKS system. In GKS there are a number of levels defined which have increasing functionality. Thus an implementation can be implemented to a particular level of the standard. Defining subsets of the available functionality was not addressed in the CGM standard at all. The CGI standard is however addressing this by including profiles as part of the standard and for conformance.

The use of GKS levels allows an implementor to implement a subset of the features of GKS in a controlled way. It is clear that people need some assistance in implementing other standards in a similar way.

There are two solutions to the problem we have identified here:

- have simpler standards which can be fully implemented;
- create standard subsets of elements

The standards world is moving towards the latter of these options. The definition of subsets of a wide range of standards is becoming appreciated as a useful, and necessary in some cases, aid for implementors. One of the features seen with current GKS implementations is that they have focused in on just 2 or 3 of the 9 GKS levels available. This probably suggests that some of the levels were not useful in practice even if the division into so many levels was a good one in theory.

The use of subsets of the standards by implementors of the CGM and the need to guarantee final results, led to a more formal consideration by user groups of the use of profiles. These moves are described in the next section.

3 The Concept of Application Profiles

The problem of defining subsets of standards to ensure interworking has gained momentum in the general area of Open Systems Interconnection (OSI) which includes the graphics standards. The standards in this area are designed, in theory, to ensure interworking between machines, sites and applications. The standards do tend to be complex and offer a wide range of options. There is a great deal of potential for implementations which agree with the standard to have little possibility of working together. For this reason a number of groups of users have come together to define subsets of the standards which they will work to. These subsets of the standards have become known as application profiles.

Why do we need application profiles? We need them for a number of reasons which include:

- standards are often semantically incomplete;
- standards offer too many options for some applications;
- standards offer too few options for some applications;
- standards (unfortunately) have errors.

An application profile may do some or all of the following:

- complete the semantics to 'plug the holes' in the standard;
- specify the behaviour or the required software, for example, the behaviour of a CGM generator and interpreter;
- define minimum and maximum support requirements;
- correct errors;
- define extensions to the standard;
- define useful subsets of the standard.

To date there have been initiatives in this area from three groups who are moving together now towards forming standard subsets which can be approved within the international standards community. The initiatives have come from:

- the MAP and TOP working groups
- the US Department of Defense CALS Project

Work in this area has been carried out most notably by the MAP and TOP working groups and by the CALS Project for the US Department of Defense. The Manufacturing Automation Protocol (MAP) and the Technical and Office Protocols (TOP) have been developed to increase communications between equipment and between applications. The groundwork and impetus for these was carried out by General Motors for MAP and by Boeing for TOP. The protocols used are based on the OSI standards. Despite being aimed at different communication environments, the specifications for MAP and TOP are the same above the Network Layer in the OSI 7 layer model. Where appropriate the two committees work together to produce the same agreements as to the use of OSI protocols. Although the work started out in private industry the specifications are now being developed in the ISO arena.

The CGM is included in the MAP and TOP specifications. An Application Profile for the CGM had been developed at the McDonnell Douglas Corporation where there was a considerable interest in the storage of text and graphics. This was used as the basis for discussions leading to the production of profile specification.

The Application Profile defines conformance for the MAP/TOP users. All generators must generate metafiles that are within the Application Profile specification. Interpreters must be able to interpret any metafile to the Application Profile specification. In this way the Application Profile definition is a minimum requirement for an interpreter and a maximum specification for a generating system.

The Computer-aided Acquisition and Logistics Support (CALS) programme is an initiative within the U.S. Department of Defense to solve the problems arising from its current paper-intensive logistics process. CALS, through the National Institute of Standards and Technology (NIST - formerly the National Bureau of Standards), has made a major effort to identify and incorporate national and international standards for data and application interfaces. Graphics standards have been seen as playing a useful role in the automation of the logistics information. The CGM is seen as being a major method used for the storage of the large amounts of graphical information required.

The CALS environment is a multi-system environment. It is involved in a wide range of applications. To avoid the use of standards in an incompatible way it has been decided to specify a CGM application profile for CALS to ensure that graphical data can be transferred. It is also designed to increase the conformance requirement to guarantee final results when pictures are drawn.

It is also worth noting at this stage that the ODA standard for the Office Document Architecture includes a subset of the CGM standard as its Graphics Content Architecture. The subset chosen is very close to the MAP/TOP Profile.

4 The MAP/TOP Profile

The MAP/TOP profile is designed to:

- limit private elements or values. For example: the LINE TYPE element may not appear with any negative values, which indicate private line types, and GDP elements may not appear at all.

- limit useless values of elements. For example: 16-bit and 32-bit integers are allowed, but 24-bit are not.

- limit unusual element values (where CGM has no standard values defined). For example: character sets are limited to two that together provide a fairly full Latin alphabet.

- define resource limits, maxima for generators and minima for interpreters. For example: polylines may have at most 1024 points.

- define defaults where CGM has not done so. For example: the contents of the predefined colour table and attribute bundles are defined for interpreters.

- specify how to transfer the CGM datastream. The profile discusses both how to use the File Transfer Access and Management (FTAM) standard and how to write a metafile onto magnetic tape. It limited conforming interchange to the Binary Encoding of CGM.

The MAP/TOP profile contains relatively few of some of the other specification categories noted above, specifically:

- there is not much in the way of completing the semantics of CGM, i.e., defining the behaviour of interpreters. The specifications of CGM annex D are required, but even these are not complete. For example, nowhere in CGM is it stated that interpreters shall maintain dashed line types across the vertices of POLYLINES, and neither does the profile.

- the profile does not extend the functionality of CGM significantly. There are two ESCAPE definitions that allow viewporting and composition of pictures.

- the profile does not correct known errors in the CGM standard.

As the first application profile MAP/TOP was valuable in recognizing and publicizing that such specifications were required to supplement the CGM, if predictability of picture interchange is to be assured. It was formulated at a time when there were very few CGM implementations and not much experience with the problems of metafile interchange. As far as it goes it is a successful specification and was the basis for a MAP/TOP interoperability demonstration, the Enterprise '88 event.

5 The CALS Profile

The MAP/TOP Profile provided the foundation for the CALS application profile, which used the springboard of MAP/TOP and the lessons learned from another year of technology development to attempt to improve profile specification.

The specification categories that CALS recognizes are similar to MAP/TOP but go somewhat further in some cases in that it:

- defines two interpreter conformance levels;
- limits metafiles to the Basic Set (restricting the use of private, unusual, and useless values);
- defines resource maxima and minima for generators and for interpreters;
- defines defaults;
- limits encodings to binary, but contains only part of the file format specification of MAP/TOP;
- goes further in specifying interpreter behaviour;
- extends functionality with line types, hatch styles;
- tackles a common (in practice) indeterminancy in CGM colour usage;
- corrects known errors in the CGM standard;
- allows metrically equivalent fonts to be substituted for Hershey.

One can extract a large number of individual implementation requirements from the CALS profile. The text below highlights some of the main features of the profile.

The first sections define conformance criteria for metafiles, generators, and interpreters, very much like those we we discussed earlier for MAP/TOP. CALS defines two conformance levels for interpreters: Draft and Publication. The names are suggestive of their intent. In Publication level, the interpreter must do everything accurately and predictably. In Draft level some time and cost saving shortcuts may be taken that will result in picture renditions that are approximate, but acceptable, in the draft stage of document production.

There are some further sections of general specifications. Some care is taken in specifying the colour to black-and-white mapping for monochrome environments. Details of how and when to apply the fallback actions of CGM annex D are given. The encoding is limited to the Binary encoding. File formats in terms of 80-byte records are specified (this point is contentious and will almost certainly have to be revisited). Known errors in the relevant parts of the CGM are listed.

The profile then goes into specifics, starting with the definition of the Basic Set by metafile element class. This material is largely identical to the MAP/TOP profile. For most elements that have a set of standardized values in CGM the profile limits elements to those values or a subset of them. For example INTEGER PRECISION is limited to 16 and 32; MARKER TYPE is limited to the 5 standard values 1-5 (dot, plus, asterisk, circle, cross). LINE TYPE and HATCH STYLE are exceptions to this pattern. For those elements where CGM does not define a fixed set of standard values, this section of the profile limits the permited values. For example, character set are limited to a pair defining most of the Latin alphabet, and fonts are limited to the Hershey set.

One of the areas where CALS goes further than MAP/TOP is in restrictions on colour usage: it is required that either all colour indices have their representations defined or none do. This is really a conformance requirement on generators, but does lead to a conformance test on metafiles themselves. Implementations have been encountered that define some but not all colours that are used. The worst case of this is when foreground is defined but background is assumed (or vice versa): if foreground is white it looks fine on a dark terminal screen but not so good on a sheet of white paper!

The engineering line types and hatch styles that are added to the CALS Basic Set are defined and given private (negative) indices pending their completion of the Graphical Registration process (which is expected soon). A number of ambiguities are removed, for example: clipping behaviour; clearing the view surface; line type continuation.

Like MAP/TOP, the Hershey font set is specified for support. This was done in both cases because no other public domain fonts were identified, and there was a reluctance to mandate copyrighted or trademarked material. This is one of the weakest areas of both the CGM and the profiles. Work is proceeding in both arenas to remedy the lack of predictable and adequate font support.

CALS specifies the viewporting ESCAPEs as does MAP/TOP. CALS also specifies an "Implicit Colour Table" ESCAPE which, combined with the other colour specifications, intends to solve the colour problems which were seen in practice.

The specifications of the remainder of the profile are largely concerned with establishing resource maxima and minima for generators and interpreters -- polylines are limited to 1024 points, colour tables limited to 256 entries, etc. These are the same as MAP/TOP, except that strings are limited to 254 characters instead of 256 (254 is the limit of the Binary Encoding short form string).

6 International Standardized Profiles

The ISO technical group for information technology is JTC1. They have set up a Special Group on Functional Standardization to look at the use of IT standards. This section of the paper looks at how this work has progressed and leads into the next section which addresses how the current work on application profiles might be brought into the ISO arena.

One of the tasks of this special group has been to define a framework within which profiles of standards could be defined. This work is described in the technical report on the Framework and Taxonomy of International Standardized Profiles (ISP). This work describes how profiles at different layers in the OSI model should be defined. The relevant profile class for the CGM standard is the F-Profile type which is defined as being for the Interchange Format and Representation Profile. The technical report reserves the name FCG for CGM class profiles.

An ISP is defined as providing the following:

- it restricts the choice of the options in the standard to the extent necessary to maximise the probability of interworking between systems implementing the Profile
- it does not specify any requirements that would contradict or cause non-conformance to the standard
- it may contain conformance requirements which are more specific and limited in scope than those of the standard
- it may exclude some valid optional capabilities and optional behaviour permitted in the standard

7 What should ARGOSI do?

One of the major practical problems with the takeup of CGM is the problem caused by suppliers supporting different subsets of the standard. Many are also developing their own extra features which results in interworking being almost impossible. The CGM also has far too many implementation dependent features which make the predictable drawing of the final picture almost impossible.

There is a need for application groups to agree subsets of the standard to be used if suppliers are not going to implement all the standard. The development of too many profiles could however be the complete undoing of the standard. The use of a strong pressure group like CALS is a major step forward. There are some (recognised) problems with the current CALS profile. The use of the disable clear escape may well be against the intent of the CGM standard. The use of 80 character records is at best quaint. The hatch and line styles have now been registered and should be recognised as such. The CGM Amendments also need to be taken account of and it is expected that features of Amendment 3 in particular will become part of a CALS profile revision. It is however a good basis from which to start.

I would like to suggest that a small number of well defined profiles within the ISO arena would help writers of CGM software. They also make CGM testing possible if conformance to the CGM standard is a requirement for a purchase. Predictable interchange also needs a specification of the interpreter action and any acceptable fallbacks. One advantage of developing a profile is the need to develop tighter conformance requirements against which products can be measured.

Part 2 of the Technical Report recognises that CGM is an area for study to develop ISPs. I would like to suggest that this work should be carried out within ISO and that a European based initiative is made within SC24. The ARGOSI project could be the initiator of this work within ISO. The work should be based on the CALS profile but should also take into account the CGM amendment work. The strength of the CALS work should not be underestimated. It is to this that many people will be writing software. However, there are flaws in it and these could be sorted out. Work which improves on the CALS profile, takes account of the Amendments and which conforms to the ISP specification will be welcomed in ISO.

The work will need to be realistic in its aims and not be seen as a challenge to the US work if it is to gain the necessary widespread acceptance. The consideration of a wider range of users would be a useful addition. The CALS profile concerns itself with the needs of engineers. The development of profiles which recognise the needs of users with a requirement for picture exchange is needed. The ARGOSI project has collected information via its survey which may assist in the specification of application areas which need (possibly) different Profiles.

I would like to recommend that the ARGOSI project considers developing a CGM profile for its own use which conforms to the ISP definition produced by JTC1 and that it considers widening this to make it a more general proposal.

Acknowledgement

Thanks are due to Lofton Henderson for contributing to this paper. The ideas presented have been developed through discussions with Lofton particularly whilst writing our CGM book.

References

Henderson, L.R., Mumford,A.M., The Computer Graphics Metafile, Butterworths, 1990, ISBN 0-408-02680-4

ISO/IEC 8632 (Parts 1-4 and Amendments 1-3) Information Processing Systems - Computer Graphics - Metafile for the storage and transfer of picture descriptive information

ISO/IEC/TR 10000-1:1990, Information Technology - Framework and Taxonomy of International Standadized Profiles - Part 1: Framework

ISO/IEC/TR 10000-2:1990, Information Technology - Framework and Taxonomy of International Standadized Profiles - Part 2: Taxonomy

ISO/IEC JTC1/SGFS N100 rev 1, Information Processing Systems - International Standardized Profiles - Directory of ISPs and Profiles contained therein

ISO/IEC JTC1/SGFS N201, Information Processing Systems - International Standardized Profiles - Taxonomy Update, ISP Approval and Maintenance Process

MIL-D-28003, Military Specification, Digital Representation for Communication of Illustrated Data: CGM Application Profile, US Department of Defense, 1988, available from the National Institute of Standards and Technology, Gaithersburg, MD

Chapter 17

Access to Segments in a Version 2 CGM Metafile

André Ducrot

Abstract: CGM Addendum 1 has introduced the possibility of including segments into a metafile. In this paper, we will study what are the possible uses of this new functionality and show the interest for accessing the global segments independently from each other. In order to be able to do that, a subclass of CGM Version 2 possible metafiles will be defined. This will provide also new requirements for defining profiles in CGM.

CGM (ISO 8632)

CGM introduces a set of basic elements to describe and transport static pictures. The structure of a metafile is shown in Figure 1.

BEGIN METAFILE xxxx

Metafile Descriptor

METAFILE VERSION 1

Optionals Default replacements and other parameters

Picture Descriptor

BEGIN PICTURE

Optional modes and attributes

Picture Body

BEGIN PICTURE BODY

Optional attribute settings and primitives

END PICTURE

Several Pictures composed of Picture Descriptor and Picture Body

END METAFILE

Figure 1 Structure of a CGM Version 1 Metafile

A CGM metafile is composed of one Metafile Descriptor followed by one or several pictures (in fact, a metafile with no pictures at all is allowed but has more limited interest). Each picture is composed of a Picture Descriptor and a Picture Body.

The Metafile Descriptor contains elements which are valid for the whole metafile. An element indicating the version of CGM which has been used, an element which identifies the metafile and an element indicating which is the set of elements possibly used by this metafile are mandatory. Then, follows optional elements which applies to all following elements and pictures. These elements define in particular coordinates type (integer or real), colour characteristics, fonts and character sets, encoding parameters and default attributes to be used at the beginning of each picture. Graphical primitives cannot belong to the Metafile Descriptor.

A Picture Descriptor contains all elements needed to interpret a picture which differ from those defined in the Metafile Descriptor. It is possible to redefine some encoding parameters and attributes. Still, graphical primitives cannot belong to a Picture Descriptor.

A Picture Body is composed of primitives and attribute settings. It is a static picture in the sense that no attribute element can have retroactive effect on previous primitive elements in the picture which result either in a visual change or a redraw of the picture.[1]

CGM Amendment 1

CGM amendment 1 introduces the possibility to store segments in a CGM metafile. To distinguish between metafiles requiring these new facility and "old" metafiles, the metafile version is 1 for basic CGM and 2 for metafiles including segment facilities.

A segment is a collection of primitives and associated attributes. There are some fundamental differences between CGI (or GKS) segments and CGM segments. A CGM segment is not a dynamic entity. In particular, resetting segment attributes such as segment transformation, highlighting, visibility is not allowed after segment definition. No redrawing of a picture results from segment operation in CGM. On the opposite, CGI and GKS use segments essentially for dynamic effects (i.e. for producing a set of pictures in the CGM sense). The major element in common between CGM and CGI (GKS) is the capability to use segments to compose pictures. A segment in CGM can be included in the Metafile descriptor, it is called "global" in this case, or in the picture body, it is then called "local". A global segment does not belong to any picture. It can only be used in conjunction with the COPY SEGMENT element to build primitives in a picture or in another segment. COPY SEGMENT allows to transform primitives of the segment to be copied and to change the setting of attributes within these primitives according to the value of the INHERITANCE FILTER. This mechanism allows to construct pictures from a set of already stored "picture parts".

Another interesting difference between CGI (GKS) segment model and CGM is that what CGM provides is not a set of "flat" independent segments but a structure store à la PHIGS. A segment

[1] Note: In order to insure that this is true with all interpreters, we will make the assumption that COLOUR TABLE elements are not present in any picture body.

can itself include a COPY SEGMENT element. Exploitation of this property in conjunction with 3D extension (CGM Amendment 2) could be done to provide a standard PHIGS archive facility. CGI and GKS segments are composed of primitives with their bounded attributes and are complete in the sense that all information needed to draw them is within the segment. A CGM segment is the collection of primitive and attribute setting elements which has been used to construct the segment, but in order to use it, it is necessary for the interpreter to rebuild the state list at the time the segment was created. A CGM segment is not independent from the context it was created. This fact prevents access to a particular segment within the Metafile Descriptor for example.

What should be the interest of accessing segments independently?

If it was possible to access segment independently from each other within the Metafile Descriptor, or even within the picture body, this would prevent needs to store different segments by the interpreter. Actually, a context-independent segment needs to be build from each CGM segment by the interpreter and it is this segment which is used and not the original one. The interpreter needs to rebuild a structure that most of the generators have already if they are using segments (for example, CGI and GKS are able to provide context-independent segments since it is exactly the concept they use).

With the appropriate file structure, it would be even possible to use the Metafile itself as a segment store, thus avoiding duplication of information and needs for an important software development.

Other interesting concepts such as segment libraries shared by several metafiles could be easily build as an extension of the actual facility. This is a more powerful concept than the symbol facility introduced in Amendment 3 because such a segment library could be exchanged as a CGM metafile; the content and the format of a symbol library is not defined by CGM amendment 3.

How to insure segment independence in a CGM Version 2 Metafile?

If CGM amendment 1 does not force segments to be independent[2] , it is easy to build conforming metafiles with this property. A segment in which all needed attributes for all primitives it contains are included has this property (this is equivalent to the CGI/GKS segment model where attributes are bound to the primitives).

Furthermore, from any CGM Version 2 metafile, it is possible to construct an "equivalent" Version 2 metafile in which segments are independent. The algorithm is quite simple. A translator composed of an interpreter part and a generator part reads the metafile and produces a new metafile.

[2] Note: Independence of segments means that there is no need to know the context in which it was defined (i.e. the state list) to interpret it.

The interpreter maintains an attribute state-list for all primitives and when it encounters a primitive within a segment, for all attributes for this primitive that have not been sent after CREATE SEGMENT, it sends to the generator before the primitive element an additional attribute element. The generator receives all elements from the original metafile and new attribute elements inserted by the interpreter and produces a new metafile. There are, of course, some optimization possibilities in order to insure that the expansion between the original and the new metafile is not too important.

Additional problems to be addressed when converting a metafile:

Some other elements may create problems and prohibit segment access in a metafile. The translator defined above can remove them and replace them by a more appropriate action. The most simple one is the inclusion of SAVE/RESTORE ATTRIBUTE CONTEXT elements which introduces another level of dependencies not only possibly between segments but also between pictures. A replacement of RESTORE by the appropriate sequence of attribute setting elements solves the problem. The other and more complex to address is the problem related to default replacement elements. In a version 2 metafile, it is possible to include such elements inside the Metafile Descriptor between segments. These elements affect both the following segments and the default values when starting the picture. They do not affect already defined segments.

```
BEGIN METAFILE
DEFAULT REPLACEMENT
CREATE SEGMENT 1
 LINE COLOUR BLUE
POLYLINE                                      * blue polyline
END SEGMENT
DEFAULT REPLACEMENT LINE COLOUR RED
CREATE SEGMENT 2
POLYLINE                                      *  red polyline
LINE COLOUR YELLOW
POLYLINE                                      * yellow polyline
END SEGMENT
BEGIN PICTURE
BEGIN PICTURE BODY
POLYLINE                                      * red polyline
INHERITANCE FILTER (LINE COLOUR, SEGMENT)
COPY SEGMENT 1                                * keeps colour as defined (blue)
COPY SEGMENT 2                                * keeps colour as defined (red, yellow)
LINE COLOUR GREEN
POLYLINE                                      * green polyline
INHERITANCE FILTER (LINE COLOUR, STATE LIST)
COPY SEGMENT 1                                * inherits green colour for polylines
```

Figure 2 Examples of attribute settings in a CGM Version 2 metafile

There are several ways to remove this problem. The simplest is to keep a different state list in which all default replacements are done and to pass these default replacements to the generator after the last segment in the metafile descriptor.

This operation is equivalent to a restriction of valid metafiles to a subset of those indicated within the actual formal grammar.

```
cd dxrn
<metafile descriptor>     ::=   <identification> <characteristics>;
<identification>          ::=    <version> <element list>;
<characteristics>         ::=   <optional descript. elm>* <default replacement>* &lt;segment&gt;*
                            |   <optional descript. elm>* &lt;segment&gt;*  <default replacement>*;
<optional descript. elm>  ::=   <description>
                            |   <vdc type>
                            |   <colour extent and max index>
                            |   <font and character lists and announcer>
                            |   <max vdc extent>
                            |   &lt;segment priority extent&gt;;
```

This is an example of syntax restrictions which may be part of a profile for a particular class of CGM metafiles.

CGM Profiles: the needs for a definition in the standard.

In this paper, we have shown that a particular subclass of CGM Version 2 metafiles have interesting properties. A natural idea is to define a profile which characterize this class. At the moment, in CGM, there is only one way of creating a subset of all valid metafiles : the METAFILE ELEMENT LIST element which give the list of elements that may be encountered in the metafile. Here, we impose other restrictions such as

- the metafile follows stricter syntactic rules,
- no segment dependency as defined above.

These restrictions are not requirements from the generator to the interpreter (the list of elements is such a requirement), but a definition of the properties of generated metafiles.

CGM Amendment 3:

CGM amendment 3 has introduced new concepts. In particular, the concept of geometric pattern which uses a segment to describe the pattern to fill a fill area is an interesting one. At this occasion, it was discovered that local segments belonging to the picture was insufficient and that there is a need for "invisible" local segments. The appropriate way to introduce such segments should have been to authorize them in the picture descriptor. Unfortunately, it was preferred to add an attribute visibility and to leave them only into the picture body.

Conclusions:

In my opinion, CGM should follow more strictly the Computer Graphics Reference Model and be a static picture capture metafile as it claims to be. A revision of CGM should remove from picture body any element which does not contribute directly to the picture and authorize them only in the picture descriptor or in the metafile descriptor. Examples of such elements are COLOUR TABLE, invisible segments, user-defined hatch and linetypes. That will solve the problem of elements which are defined as if they have dynamic effects but where static interpretation is required. Elements which are only relevant in a programming interface such as SAVE and RESTORE PRIMITIVE CONCEPTS should be removed. It is not clear that segments should be maintained in the picture body. COPY SEGMENT is sufficient to build the picture from a segment store. A more strict syntax should be adopted. The evolution of the syntax from ISO 8632 to Amendment 1 has obscured the concepts without providing any advantage. There is not enough guidance to the generator about which syntactically correct metafiles are valid from interpretation point of view. Putting more constraints on the generator is easier than asking the interpreter to solve problems resulting from a badly designed metafile. There is clearly a need for such an annex in the CGM document.

References:

ISO 8632 Information Processing - Computer Graphics - Metafile for the storage and transfer of picture descriptive information (CGM) (1987)

ISO/IEC 8632 Information Processing - Computer Graphics - Metafile for the storage and transfer of picture descriptive information - Amendment 1 (1990)

ISO/IEC 8632 Information Processing - Computer Graphics - Metafile for the storage and transfer of picture descriptive information - Committee Draft Amendment 3 (1990)

ISO 7942 Information Processing Systems - Computer Graphics - Functional Specification of the Graphical Kernel System (GKS) (1985)

ISO 9592 Information Processing Systems - Computer Graphics - Functional Specification of the Programmer's Hierarchical Interface to Graphics (PHIGS) (1988)

ISO/IEC DIS 9636 Information Processing Systems - Computer Graphics - Interfacing techniques for dialogues with graphical devices (CGI) (1990)

ISO/IEC CD 11072 Information Processing Systems - Computer Graphics - Computer Graphics Reference Model (1990)

L. R. Henderson, A. M. Mumford The Computer Graphics Metafile - Butterworths (1990)

Chapter 18

X Windows over OSI

John Dyer

1 Background

There is a growing user community that has access to a windowing environment, either exclusively on their own machine or to other machines on a local network. Amongst the reasons that this has come about are the users' desire for higher functionality and the widespread availability of freely distributed software. A prime example of a system that is becoming widely used in this way is the X Windows System.

In general it is in the computer users' interest to adopt a solution that adheres to a specification that is maintained in the public domain. The reason for this is that it should prevent any one organisation changing the technical specification under the feet of implementors.

A windowing system should be capable of being supported over communication networks in a network independent way so that it may be carried over the diverse networking technologies that are being developed world-wide.

The Joint Network Team of the United Kingdom Academic Community (JNT) operates a Wide Area Network called JANET based on X.25. This connects most UK University, Polytechnic and Research Council Sites. At the majority of these sites the X.25 network is connected to a variety of Ethernets and in some cases Token Rings. The aim of the JNT is to offer JANET users X Windows access from their workstation to remote hosts. Initially this will be to the users of the Supercomputers at Rutherford Appleton Laboratory and at The University of London Computer Centre. It is the intention to offer this X Windows Service over an OSI stack that is compatible with the Open Network service that is already operated by the JNT on JANET.

It is important that any standardisation process that is to be undertaken is completed before the major users become entrenched in the use of non-standard (and non-interworking) alternatives.

The purpose of this paper is to discuss the alternatives that have been considered, the evaluation that took place and the standards work currently underway.

2 The Alternatives

There are a wide variety of Windowing environments available, particularly at the PC end of the market. These include Presentation Manager, MS-DOS Windows, GEM, DeskView and Apple Finder. Some of these work only on standalone systems. All are proprietary and are therefore unable to meet the criteria needed for becoming an International Standard. They are not discussed further in this paper.

In the Unix market, SunView, NeWS and the X Window System are examples of systems that are available.

Of the Unix solutions only NeWS and the X Window System come close to meeting the criteria needed for adoption as an International Standard solution.

News was developed by SUN Microsystems. It is network independent and reasonably network efficient as it uses display postscript to transmit images. The problem is that although the published specification for NeWS is in the public domain, and freely available to implementors, change control rests with SUN Microsystems. SUN are therefore free to change the specification at will. It seems not unreasonable for other manufacturers not to wish to implement NeWS on a widescale basis under these conditions. SUN seem unwilling to relinquish control of the specification and allow international and independent control in order to permit the specification becoming an International Standard. It has not therefore been possible to suggest progressing NeWS as an International Standard.

The X Window System was in a similar position to NeWS. It was originally developed by The Massachusetts Institute of Technology (MIT) in 1984 having been based on the earlier W system. MIT chose to set up a consortium to regulate changes to the specification. Furthermore, they allowed the American National Standards Institute (ANSI) to take a version of the standard with a view to progressing it to become an American National Standard. The ANSI committee X3H3.6 started work on the standardisation of X11 Release 3 in 1988. During the process, which is nearly complete, ANSI have been encouraged to progress the standard to become an International Standard upon completion of national standardisation. It is expected that work on the international standardisation will commence in 1991, becoming complete in 1992. It also became clear that if the X Window System was to be successfully accepted by ISO, it would need to be accompanied by a standard mapping onto a supporting ISO communications stack.

The formal X Window System specification that is being considered for standardisation consists of the original three parts:

Part 1 — The Functional Specification
Part 2 — Data stream Encoding
Part 3 — KEYSYM
plus the new: Part 4 — Mapping to OSI.

Initially two alternative mapping of the X Window System were proposed. These were from Digital Equipment and the Joint Network Team and are discussed below.

3 ISO Standards

3.1 Reference Model

The International Standards Organisation (ISO) defined a reference model in standard ISO7498. The definition is for a stack of layered functionality comprising 7 layers, each building on the layer below. In brief the functions of each layer are as follows:

Layer 1: The Physical Layer (the lowest layer) — provides the definition of the interface for computer systems to the physical medium that provides the transmission of data bits.

Layer 2: The Data Link Layer — provides the definition framework for the detection and correction of errors at the bit level.

Layer 3: The Network Layer — this is the primary level for the undertaking routing. It also permits routing through intermediate computer systems (for gateways and relays).

Layers 1 to 3 co-operate to provide raw data transmission. The Network Layer provides at its upper boundary a reliable service to the layers above. (Some network technologies eg. X.25 are capable of delivering a more reliable service than others eg. Datagram based networks — the reliability is network technology dependent).

Layer 4: The Transport Layer — defined as one of 5 protocol classes the complexity and functionality of which are chosen to bring the service delivered by the layers below up to the same standard. By this means the Transport level delivers a consistent level of service to the layers above, independent of the quality of service delivered by layers 1–3 below.

Layer 5: The Session Layer — provides management and control of data flow between the end systems eg insertion of synchronisation points, provision of tokens to convert the full duplex communication provided by the lower layers into two way alternate.

Layer 6: The Presentation Layer — establishes a common representation of application data between the two co-operating end-systems. For example, one computer may represent data internally by the EBCDIC format, the other by ASCII. The presentation layer ensures that an appropriate transformation is performed on the information.

Layer 7: The Application Layer — contains the high level system- independent functionality. The most well known application ISO Applications that have been defined include the following:

Virtual Terminals
Message Handling Service — electronic mail
Directory Service
File Transfer
Job Transfer and Manipulation

It is in the Application Layer that The X Window System will reside.

ISO are also working on other application level standards. The emerging Terminal Management Standards (ISO 10184) are of note in respect of this discussion along with ISO Virtual Terminals (ISO 9040 and ISO 9041) which has already been ratified.

3.2 ISO Virtual Terminals

These comprise of two standards ISO 9040 Basic Class VT Service and ISO 9041 Basic Class VT Protocol. They cannot in themselves be implemented to deliver a fully functional product without a VT Profile or functional standard. The European Workshop for Open Systems (EWOS) has completed work on a suitable profile for use in Europe. It has been ratified as European functional standards ENV 41208 and ENV 41209 (S-Mode Forms Functional Standard). The other two equivalent regional workshops (NIST-OIW in the US and AOW in the Pacific Basin have also undertaken some standardisation work in this area). Virtual Terminals provide Full Screen access over ISO networks. They do not provide a Windowing environment in the traditional sense however. ISO VT does not demand the high bandwidth requirements that are imposed by applications such as X. ISO VT will therefore be useful over long distance communication links where transit delays may be high and the bandwidth limited. It is my contention the X and VT are complementary rather than competitors.

3.3 ISO Terminal Management

This standard is still in the definition phase. When complete it will be a three part standard; Model, Service and Protocol. The Model has reached the Draft Proposal Stage and is currently out for ballot. The Service is a Working Draft and should go out for its first ballot after the next Working Group meeting in May 1991. It is not expected that work on these standards will be complete until 1992. Terminal Management is being designed with integration into the ISO OSI environment as prime consideration. It will be very much more general than X, providing functionality to allow dialogue splitting, merging, multiplexing and synchronisation. Like X it will have the ability to utilise externally (user) supplied window managers to give flexibility. It is not the intention to provide an ISO standard window manager.

The ISO community regard the X Windows System to be a first generation windowing environment and therefore regard it as interim in nature. Terminal Management is regarded by most of the ISO world as being the strategic direction for windowing within the medium future. However, this view is not held by all, particularly not by some of the ANSI committee.

4 Choice of Mapping

The ISO reference model was specified with the intention that all seven layers would need to be present in a system to support an ISO application. This decision was based on the premise that the supporting stack would only be used to support applications specifically written for the ISO communications environment. Unfortunately The X Window System was not written with the ISO environment in mind, and as a consequence, does not fit well into the application layer of the ISO model. One of the reasons is that X duplicates some of the functionality of the ISO Session and Presentation layers (for example the support of big or little end machines). It should be noted that the ISO reference model does not preclude the duplication of functionality in this way, but it can lead to loss of performance in the implementations.

This situation lead to the independent development of two approaches to the support of the X Window System in the ISO environment, both of which were proposed to the September 1989 meeting of the ANSI Committee X3H3.6.

Digital Equipment proposed that X be regarded as any other ISO application and run over the full seven layer stack.

The Joint Network Team proposed that in the interest of permitting performant implementations of Xosi it should be run over a short stack consisting of layers 1-4 (eg up to the Transport Layer).

To evaluate the performance advantage in using the Transport Stack, and to aid the ANSI committee in coming to a decision, the JNT undertook to get pilot implementations of both X over a full ASCE stack and X over a Transport stack. This pilot work was carried out by the communications group of Edinburgh University. Additional work was undertaken by the University of London Department of Computer Science and The University of Nottingham. In parallel the Mitre Corporation in the United States undertook a similar development independently.

5 Evaluation of Results

Very early in the pilot, Edinburgh University was able to demonstrate that it was feasible to run the X Window System over a wide area X.25 network such as JANET. Cursor Tracking and other simple actions require the transmission of about 5 Packets per second (which represents up to 15 KBits of data per second). More complex actions such as freehand drawing or menu manipulation require slightly high data transmission rates 25 packets per second (25 KBits per second). Continuous drawing of points generates up to 60 packets of data per second (221 Kbits per second).

It is thought from these figures that a group of users who were on average able to utilise 20 KBits of bandwidth each would receive a satisfactory response. This does not mean a single user with a 19.6k line would always receive a satisfactory response because his peak demand may in some instances be way in excess of that which could be provided and degraded performance would then be seen. What it does mean is that 200k bits of bandwidth could support 10 users.

Having established the viability of the concept, attention was turned to the investigating the effect of using various supporting stacks.

Four different stacks were evaluated.

X11 over TCP/IP	
X11 over Pink Book	(X11/TP0/X.25/LLC2 - non ISODE)
X11 over TP0	(X11/TP0/TCP/IP - ISODE)
X11 over ACSE	(X11/ACSE/Presentation/Session/TP0/TCP/IP)

The following tests were run over each of the stacks.

Muncher: In this test the client draws points to the server. The program was modified so that the client always output 1.7 Mbytes of data. The average data transfer rates were then calculated. The test was run on a single SUN 3 in loopback and between two SUN3 machines one client, one server to avoid CPU bottlenecks. The percentage CPU utilisation is given in brackets after each throughput.

Stack	*Single Machine*		*Between Two Machines*	
TCP/IP	72 KBytes/sec	(100%)	72KBytes/sec	(C 42, S 82)
X Pink Book	60 KBytes/sec	(100%)	70KBytes/sec	(C 42, S 78)
ISO Transport	44 KBytes/sec	(100%)	48KBytes/sec	
ISO ACSE	24 KBytes/sec		25KBytes/sec	

Opening an Xterm Window:	TCP/IP	2.1 seconds
	X Pink Book	2.1 seconds
	ISO Transport	2.6 seconds
	ISO ACSE	3.8 seconds
	TCP/IP X Terminal	4.0 seconds
	IP Tunnel	5.0 to 7.0 seconds
Character Echo:	TCP/IP	10.0 msec
	ISO Transport	15.5 msec
	ISO ACSE	26.0 msec

As mentioned above the Mitre Corporation in the United States of America also undertook some development and evaluation. It should be noted that they used the same hardware and software packages as Edinburgh to develop their implementation. It is not surprising that their results were very similar. Their ACSE solution being capable of providing about 50% of the throughput of the Transport solution.

6 Selection of Stacks for Standardisation

The Joint Network Team runs a Special Interest Group made up of many commercial and academic members worldwide. Discussion is conducted on an email distribution list:

iso-xwindows@uk.ac.rutherford (JANET)

It meets about four times a year, usually around London at which the predominance of attendees are from the UK. In the past we have had delegates from the USA and Europe. The group is open to ALL interested parties who think they may be able to contribute. The SIG has become the major discussion forum for all the UK input to the standards making process in this area. It has been given a remit by the British Standards Institute (BSI) and UK GOSIP to undertake technical work on their behalf. Any decisions are then passed back to the relevant committees for their ratification so that they may become the national view. At present the SIG is working on the production of an EWOS Technical Guide (ETG).

It is the view of this committee that from the users point of view, the most acceptable supporting stack for Xosi would be based on an ISO Transport solution. Unfortunately from a political perspective it would be unreasonable for this to be adopted as an ISO standard solution. It is a fairly widely held view that implementations of full ISO stacks will become sufficiently performant in the future so as to provide reasonable support for Xosi. In the meantime there would be the need for an intercept based on the transport solution. The SIG supports the development of a full mapping to ACSE to be progressed through ISO as the strategic target for Xosi. In the meantime they wish to pursue an intercept that will support the users in the interim period until the ACSE solution becomes available.

7 Development of an Intercept Mapping

In July 1990, ANSI held a joint meeting with the JNT X Windows SIG in Reading, UK. At that meeting it was suggested that the contents of the ISO Session and ISO Presentation headers would remain essentially constant. In this case the Presentation and Session headers could be generated by a fairly simple piece of software and used to encapsulate the X Windows data stream. This avoids the need for the full functionality of the Session and Presentation software being present in each end system. It has been the inefficiency of the Presentation and Session layer that has been the major contributor to loss of performance in the implementations that have been evaluated to date.

The system would however mimic the behaviour of a system in which all the functionality was present. In fact to a protocol analyser sitting on the communications line the protocol would be conformant. It therefore follows that provided the authors of the intercept take sufficient care to align the contents of their document with the ANSI work on the full ACSE mapping, the two solutions will interwork.

The exact specification of the octet stream to be generated has not yet been finalised. It is to be defined in parallel with some prototyping work that is to be carried out by the University of London Computer Centre. The prototyping will evaluate the performance and check for interoperability with existing full stack implementations.

It was also agreed at the Reading meeting that rather than encode the X Window System in ISO Abstract Syntax Notation (ASN.1), it would be preferable to use the existing encoding as specified in Part 2 (Data Stream Encoding) of X Window Standards. This specifies the syntax for X Window System requests, replies, events and errors. It should be noted that there are two transfer syntax specified in the X Windows specifications, one for big endian and one for little endian connections.

As it is not possible to publish the specification as a formal standard. It is the intention to publish as an EWOS technical guide.

8 Status of Activities

The ANSI committee have sent the Parts 1–3 of the X Window System out for public review. It is expect that it will become an American National Standard by the end of 1990.

ANSI X3H3.6 decided at its August interim meeting that the mapping document that had been out for postal ballot needed such substantial changes that it should be re-written and balloted again. It is expected that this process will be complete by the end of 1990. Part 4 will then be balloted as an American National Standard.

When internal American Standardisation is complete, all four parts will be submitted to ISO for fast track standardisation by the International Community. It is thought that Parts 1–3 of the standard are well known and understood Internationally, and are therefore likely to be accepted. ANSI has taken care to ensure they have given Part 4 sufficient international exposure, so as to ensure its success also.

The intercept mapping is being progressed by the European Workshop for Open Systems Expert Group on Virtual Terminals (EWOS VT/EG). This is a functional standardisation group which has particular expertise in the area of full screen terminal access communications. They are working on a draft of an EWOS Technical Guide. It was discussed at the October 1990 meeting with a view to being ratified by the EWOS Technical Assembly in January 1991.

Chapter 19

CGI Profiles for Use with X

Graham J. Reynolds, David B. Arnold

1 Introduction

The idea of a CGI (Computer Graphics Interface [3]) extension to X [4,17] has recently been recognised within certain USA communities as a viable way of securing some portion of the computer graphics marketplace for the CGI, and for continuing the lifetime of existing CGI software, whilst providing a network independent windowing environment. This possibility was noted in [2] and is undoubtedly equally plausible in the European marketplace as well. In this paper, an approach for promoting the CGI / X relationship in the form of specifications of CGI profiles for two of the architectural configurations discussed in our earlier papers is presented.

It is important to face the question of motivation for this work – why should anyone want to achieve a CGI to X mapping or vice versa, and why are CGI profiles an appropriate method for prompting implementations of these mappings?

It is our opinion that, sooner rather than later, the use of graphics standards in a networked environment will lead to both the desire to send a CGI data stream around a network to a device running X11, and to 'plug in' a CGI device into a network where applications are being run with X11 and producing X protocol over the network. If the implications of both of these situations can be understood then we will be in a much better situation to revise and extend both proposals in directions which will assist compatibility, and manufacturers will be in a better position to design products which support the operations required for compatibility. In practical terms, the amount of change required to implement greater X compatibility in the CGI and the time that this would inevitably take would delay the standard's publication unacceptably and, if only for this reason, the pragmatic decision must be to try and understand how to achieve maximum support for the graphics capabilities of X within the constraints of the standardisation process. It is extremely unlikely that any changes to achieve greater compatibility with X could be incorporated within the first release of CGI and it is therefore most likely that the suggestions which arise from an exercise such as this would take the form of suggestions for registration of ESCAPE's and possible scope for amendments. The CGI profile mechanism provides a means of bringing together a set of CGI functions and resource requirements perceived to be necessary for a specific user constituency and furthermore, CGI profiles can also be registered. A profile can require the provision of a number of registered ESCAPE's thus providing a standardised way of extending the functionality of the basic standard in a constrained manner to satisfy the needs of a particular user constituency.

2 An Overview of the Architectural Relationships Between CGI and X

In [1-2] three arrangements of a CGI Virtual Device within a window managed environment provided by X windows were described, and can be summarised as follows:

(1) A CGI Client interfaces to a CGI Virtual Device, which is in turn implemented as an X client. The specific method of implementation may vary, for example, it may be an application built on top of Xlib[5] and Xt[6], or it may be implemented as an X toolkit which matches a CGI language binding. The protocol that is communicated to the X server is entirely part of the X protocol.

(2) A CGI Client interfaces to a CGI Virtual Device, which is implemented by an X extension to an X server, specifically providing a protocol for CGI functionality (this need not conform to any of the CGI standardised encodings). The X server provides the necessary support of the CGI-Extension protocol. This has been the approach adopted to provide the PEX definition [9], which is an extension of the X protocol for support of PHIGS (and PHIGS PLUS).

(3) A CGI Virtual Device is used to implement some (or all) of the capabilities of an X Server, for example, the graphics components of the server. This type of configuration is not explicitly included in the CGI standard, but of course is not prohibited. Currently, several firmware implementations of CGI include windowing support in a similar way to this.

Figure 1 illustrates the architectural arrangement numbered 1 above. It shows an X server with two clients connected, one is an unknown category of X client, the other is a CGI client / CGI interpreter combination. Other X clients could also connect to the X server without any (functional) impact on this arrangement. The CGI interpreter is shown as a layer of software between the CGI client program and the combined procedural libraries of the X intrinsics (Xt) and the X library (Xlib). The interface between the CGI client and the CGI interpreter may either be a procedural library binding or a data stream encoding, in the figure it is shown as a procedural binding. The CGI interpreter performs two major tasks in this arrangement, namely, it maps those CGI functions that have a direct or semi-direct translation to X functions by appropriate parameter encoding and function conversion, and it emulates those features of the CGI virtual device for which there are no acceptable mappings to X functions. The figure shows the X server as an unaugmented system, however, there is no particular reason why the server cannot include extensions such as the PEX extension, etc.

The second arrangement proposed above is illustrated in figure 2. This shows a single CGI client connected to an X server that includes a CGI interpreter extension. The CGI client is shown interfaced to a CGI procedural language binding which provides the equivalent of a CGI data stream generator. However, the data stream produced by this generator will need to use the encoding conventions of the X protocol to encapsulate CGI function representations and hence will be a so-called private CGI binary encoding. The CGI client can also access the normal set of X functions through a procedural interface to the libraries Xt and Xlib. As a consequence of this, the protocol communicated between the client and server is a merged core X protocol and X/CGI-Extension protocol.

On the server side of this arrangement, the merged protocol is received by a connection component of the basic X server and each request is dispatched accordingly. X requests are dispatched to the appropriate routines within the basic X server, CGI requests are dispatched to the CGI extension component. The CGI extension can make use of all of the facilities of the basic X system where necessary. For example, it can use X graphics contexts to support CGI attributes. Both the basic X and CGI extension components are divided into device independent and device dependent portions to ease the development and maintenance of the server, and for portability and efficiency reasons. Input events and solicited information are collected together by a central distributor component that determines which clients are to receive the data and passes data to those clients via the appropriate connection component.

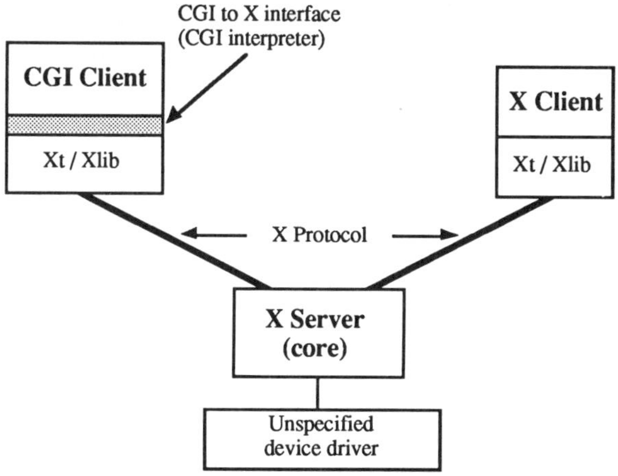

Figure 1. Arrangement 1 – CGI interpreter implemented above an X server

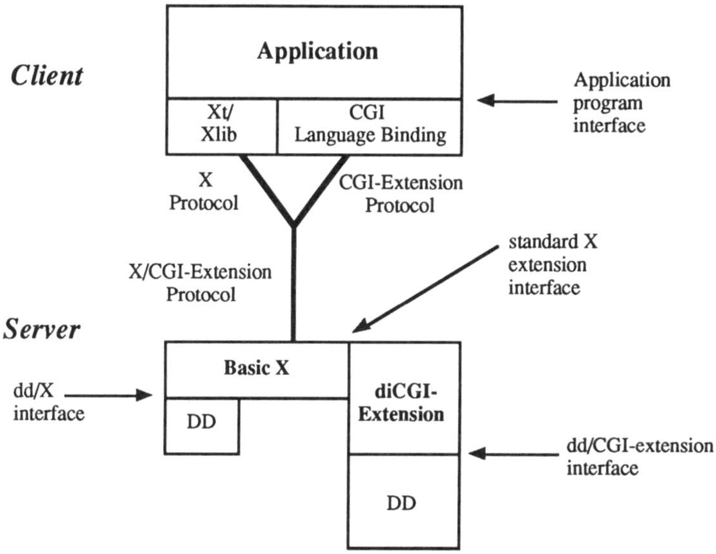

Figure 2. Arrangement 2 – a CGI interpreter implemented as an X server extension

The final arrangement is shown in figure 3. This arrangement is significantly different from the other two in that there is no CGI client involved at an application level. However, the combined X server / CGI generator is a CGI client to the underlying CGI virtual device. The front-end portion of the X server will be no different from an X server implemented without the support of the CGI virtual device. The back-end portion of the server provides an emulation of any graphics features of X which cannot be supported by the CGI virtual device and invokes the appropriate CGI functions for all other X graphics requests.

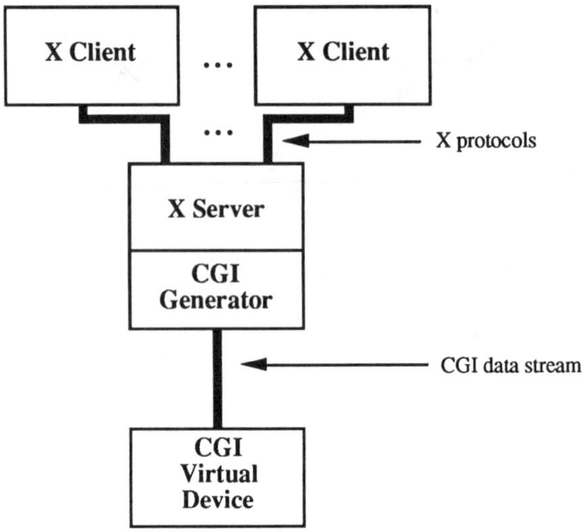

Figure 3. Arrangement 3 – a CGI virtual device used to support an X server implementation

The structure of the rest of this paper is as follows. In the next section, we compare, in brief, the major functional areas of the CGI with those relevant areas of X (i.e. its graphics facilities). A more detailed comparison is beyond the scope of this paper, but can be found in [2]. Here, we aim to provide enough information on the two specifications so that the profiles defined subsequently have a satisfactory context. We assume that the reader is in general familiar with the basic concepts of primitives, attributes, input methods and raster operations found within the CGI and also familiar with the graphics concepts found within X.

Section 4 begins by describing the profile concept of the CGI and then defines two draft CGI profiles that address two of the three architectural arrangements discussed in section 2. Section 5 considers some of the issues raised in defining these profiles, and section 6 provides a summary.

3 A Brief Comparison of CGI and X Functionality

To give a brief comparison of the relevant functional capabilities of both CGI and X, each of the major functional areas of the CGI is examined and the most significant aspects of their overlap and difference with X's graphics facilities are considered. The major areas to be considered include: device management, coordinate systems and clipping, output primitives and attributes, segments, input, and raster. The other areas of X which are concerned with window management and sharing of resources between multiple clients have been excluded from this comparison, primarily because the CGI has no counterpart for these facilities.

Device Management: The CGI view of its device is one of complete control. It assumes that it has complete control over the total display space and device resources, such as the colour map, input devices, etc. In the managed environment on top of X windows, this view of the device is reversed and the assumption (made by the X server) is that X now has complete control of the device and device resources. The usual approach to solving this conflict is to treat the CGI display surface as a single X window, the CGI device colour map becomes a logical X window colour map, the physical input devices used to implement the CGI logical input devices are shared between X clients, etc. (How other resources are mapped to equivalent X resources – and *vice versa* – will largely depend on more specific requirements.)

The link between a CGI client and CGI interpreter is specified to be a single serial synchronous connection. Whether asynchronous processing occurs below this connection is not directly relevant to the CGI client. This differs from the X client to X server connection, which is an asynchronous network link over which protocol packets can pass in either direction.

The CGI defines two separate queues of returned data from the interpreter for error and event input handling. Access to this queued information by the CGI client is synchronous, in-line with the synchronous connection. In X, this information is all contained in a single queue, i.e. errors are considered as just another type of event.

Coordinate Systems and Clipping: The CGI defines two separate abstract device independent coordinate spaces, termed Virtual Device Coordinates and Device Coordinates. The data type and precision of the coordinate systems can be selected according to either application requirements or specific device requirements. Clipping of graphic output can be controlled in both the VDC space and DC space through appropriate clipping rectangles. Clipping is limited to convex regions (normally rectangular) but can be controlled on a primitive by primitive basis.

In X, the coordinate system is window specific and hence there is no coordinate system transformation, as in the CGI's VDC-to-Device Mapping. The window coordinate system is specified in device specific pixels and has a fixed type and precision. Clipping is specified in the windows coordinate space and may be either a list of clip rectangles or a bitmap clipping mask. (The list of clip rectangles is used by the server to produce a suitable bitmap clipping mask.)

X provides a single coordinate system for each window and all coordinate data is specified with respect to the windows coordinate system. The origin of the window is always the top left hand inside corner pixel with increasing x-coordinates left to right and increasing y-coordinates top to bottom. This situation does not correspond to either the default VDC extent or default device viewport of the CGI. Provision is made in the CGI to indicate whether spontaneous change to the display surface (e.g. user initiated change of the X window) is possible and entries in a description table are provided to record any such change.

The CGI distinguishes between two types of clipping and refers to these as *Locus* clip and *Shape* clip. Locus clipping is applied to the mathematical definition of the primitive before application of attributes associated with the primitive, whereas Shape clipping is applied to the rendered area covered by the primitive, i.e. after any associated attributes have been applied. *Attributes* here specifically includes those which affect the area covered by the primitive – for example line width or marker type. Two separately specified clip regions are provided, both of which are restricted in their specification to rectangular regions aligned with the relevant coordinate system axes. One clip rectangle is specified in VDC, the other is specified in device viewport coordinates. The VDC clip can be controlled as to whether it is applied to the Locus, the Shape, or both Locus and Shape, for lines, markers, and edges of fill primitives. This corresponds conceptually to clipping being applied at distinct positions in the CGI graphics output pipeline. The VDC clip applied to the interior of fill primitives, cell arrays and gdp's is a clip of the rendered shape. VDC clipping applied to text can effectively be specified to be either Locus or Shape clipping although the control of this is somewhat different. Note that VDC clip rectangles can be transformed and intersected in some circumstances and hence form a convex polygonal region. The second clip rectangle provides an additional Shape clip to a region of the device viewport and is termed the drawing surface clip.

X provides the equivalent of Shape clipping, specified by a clip mask, which basically determines the pixels of the rendered primitive that are to be included in the drawable (i.e. window or pixmap) and those that are not. The clip mask can, however, specify arbitrarily complex shapes for use in the clip operation.

Output Primitives and Attributes: The CGI provides several device independent 2-D geometric graphic primitives with their appearance controlled by associated attributes. These output primitives range from relatively simple connected (and disjoint) sequences of line segments, sets of marker symbols positioned at defining points, cell array's, and various polygonal regions, through to more complex primitives that include circular and elliptical arcs and regions, and text. In addition, the CGI incorporates two types of so-called compound object, which allow more complex regions to be drawn consisting of a combination of curved and polygonal shapes, and which allow portions of text to be composed together with a variety of alignments. The attributes that control the *geometric* and *cosmetic* appearance of these primitives are divided into groups for lines/edges, markers, filled areas, and text. For lines and edges, the attributes are used to determine line width and style including control over the transformability of line width, line colour, and control over the kind of clipping to be performed on the primitive. Similar attributes exist for markers. For filled areas, the attributes are used to determine fill colour and interior style. Text has a number of attributes that control the height and width of characters, orientation and writing direction, and the alignment of the text to a specified reference position.

The CGI also defines attributes that apply globally across primitive classes. These include transparency and drawing mode. Transparency can be used to control the appearance of those parts of a primitive that represent 'holes' or 'gaps' in its definition; these can either be opaque and hence drawn with a defined auxiliary colour, or transparent. The drawing mode attribute is relevant to raster devices and controls the method of combining pixels during the drawing operation. Three types of combination of pixel values are allowed for: the commonly encountered boolean operations, arithmetic operations, and comparison operations.

X provides a number of 2-D device dependent raster based primitives with their appearance controlled via *graphics contexts*. Graphics contexts are basically collections of primitive attributes organised in a structure that closely models hardware mechanisms found in modern display controllers. The range of primitives is similar to that of CGI, although the parameterisations often differ. For example, X provides only one parameterisation of its arc drawing primitive, compared to four different forms in the CGI. X does not provide polymarker or cell array primitives, nor does it provide the more complex compound objects defined in the CGI. The attributes that X defines allow detailed control over the appearance of its primitives and can be grouped into three categories: line attributes, fill attributes and text attributes. Line attributes provide control of the line width and line style and the cap and join style for the ends of line segments. Fill attributes provide control of the interior fill style of filled primitives. The control of text font attributes is significantly different from the text and character attributes of the CGI, and provides a method of selecting a collection of text font properties associated with each X font. Control over character orientation and alignment is not directly supported.

X also defines global attributes that may apply to all primitive types. These include foreground and background colour, pixel level clipping information including a plane mask, and the equivalent of a pixel combining function. The combining function only allows for boolean operations between pixel values.

Segments: The CGI provides graphic data storage in the form of linear segments, (i.e. non-hierarchical), and supports a number of manipulation facilities of such data storage objects. Segments may contain any of the graphics primitives mentioned above and each primitive held in a segment conceptually has an associated set of attributes. Displayed graphical information can be regenerated from the stored graphics data.

In contrast, X does not define any graphic data storage mechanism of this kind. Pixel data storage is provided for storage of rendered graphical information, in the form of bitmaps and pixmaps. Manipulation of such data is restricted to raster type operations and re-display is dependent upon whether the pixmap or bitmap is mapped to a visible window.

Input: CGI provides a complete Logical Input Device model with an extensive input methodology. CGI clients can use eight classes of logical input device in Request, Sample and Event modes of input. Event input processing is under client control.

X provides a much simpler input device model centred around a logical pointing device and keyboard. Its input methodology is essentially asynchronous event handling, however, the X client must still take responsibility for implementing an event loop (this can be provided by an X-toolkit). Of the eight CGI input classes, Locator , Choice and String correspond reasonably closely to those of X. Locator and Choice correspond approximately to the pointer device with associated buttons. String can be considered the analog of the X keyboard device, however, this assumes that triggering of String input can occur on both key press and key release actions. The other CGI input classes, namely: Stroke, Valuator, Pick, Raster, and General, provide for the input of more abstract data types than simple points, button, and key actions.

Raster: The CGI Raster part defines functionality very close to the eventual physical device. It is thus rather separate to the rest of the abstract virtual graphics defined in the standard, although it attempts to relate the physical device characteristics to the virtual device space in such a way as to describe a usable facility which can be made independent of particular devices with judicious use of inquiry functions.

X raster functions, in contrast to those of the CGI are unashamedly rooted in the physical device, and to map from virtual pixels of the CGI to the physical pixels of the X raster functionality would require a CGI interpreter to transform data a step beyond the CGI's coordinate systems to implement, for example, isotropic drawing. Both CGI and X provide a similar set of raster functions, although once again their parameterisations differ. These include the BitBlt function which supports, in addition to a straight copy, tiling and stippling operations. They also both provide functions for drawing and retrieving image data into and from pixmaps.

4 CGI Profiles

4.1 An Overview of the CGI Profile Concept

Profiles in the CGI provide a mechanism of allowing conforming CGI implementations to have different functional scope that is specifically designed to suit a range of user communities. As such a profile represents a minimal level of capability that a CGI virtual device must provide to satisfy the user constituency for which the profile has been defined. Conversely, a profile represents a maximum level of capability that a client program can expect when using a CGI virtual device that conforms to a particular profile. This relationship reflects the dynamic resource allocation of certain CGI resources whereby it becomes almost meaningless to specify maximal levels of capability for the virtual device.

A CGI profile is organised into a block of information that is required and a block of information that is optional which can be used to provide useful or in some cases critical information to a user of the profile. The required information of a profile consists of an introduction describing the constituency the profile serves, a list of required CGI functions, and a list of required ESCAPE, GET ESCAPE and GDP functions. The optional information which may be included consists of a statement of minimum resource requirements, a statement of any restrictions on the behaviour of functions, and a statement as to the initial values of state list entries (that must be established by a client program) where they need to differ from the CGI default values.

A single virtual device implementation is not restricted to supporting only one profile. In fact, all registered profiles have to be a superset of at least one of the CGI's predefined foundation profiles. The profiles that have been used as a basis for the following draft proposed constituency profiles are TWO-WAY OUTPUT, LOCATOR INPUT, CHOICE INPUT, and STRING INPUT foundation profiles. The TWO-WAY OUTPUT profile provides a minimal set of functions for an output virtual device using a two-way communications link (i.e. a limited line and text output capability). The LOCATOR, CHOICE, and STRING INPUT profiles provide minimal logical input device control and support the request input method. All of these profiles also allow inquiry of the virtual device's description table and state list information.

4.2 Profile 1 — A CGI Profile for Supporting an X Server

4.2.1 Introduction to the Constituency

This profile is primarily directed to manufacturers of device level hardware and firmware that have developed or will develop CGI conforming devices and to software developers who provide an implementation of the X server on a range of devices. It describes the minimal level of functions and resource requirements necessary to support an implementation of the X window system server on top of the CGI, see figure 3. Such a profile can provide the following benefits to members of its constituency:

(1) it can simplify the development and implementation of X servers and X server extensions on a (potentially) wide range of graphics devices;

(2) it can lower the cost of transporting X server implementations between installations that use CGI devices;

(3) it can reduce the device dependence of X server implementations through the use of a standard CGI device independent interface;

(4) it can enable users, manufacturers and vendors to take advantage of low cost graphic hardware designs.

In addition, the benefits listed in part 1 of the CGI may also be applicable, particularly for example at a site which may require the use of the same graphic hardware systems in non-window managed environments. Typical reasons for this are, an existing software base, performance and efficiency, safety in safety critical systems, security, etc.

A certain amount of processing is required by an X server implementation in transforming X protocol requests into suitable CGI functions. This profile is designed with the goal of minimizing this layer of processing and, in consequence, the functions included in the profile reflect design choices made about the structure and operation of an X server implementation.

(It probably should be stated that no guarantee can be given that this profile represents an optimal profile as this would depend on other external factors.)

4.2.2 List of Required Functions

Note that this is a superset of the 2-WAY OUTPUT, LOCATOR INPUT, CHOICE INPUT, and STRING INPUT foundation profiles of the CGI. Underlined functions and resource requirements indicate those functions that are from these foundation profiles.

The list of inquiry functions assumes that all significant state information needed by the X server implementation will be maintained above the CGI information except for necessary information obtained from the description tables and any default state list values.

Virtual device management:

INITIALIZE	TERMINATE
EXECUTE DEFERRED ACTIONS	PREPARE DRAWING SURFACE
END PAGE	ESCAPE
GET ESCAPE	

Coordinate space control:

VDC EXTENT	DEVICE VIEWPORT

Primitives:

POLYLINE	DISJOINT POLYLINE
POLYMARKER	TEXT
APPEND TEXT	CIRCULAR ARC CENTRE
ELLIPTICAL ARC	RECTANGLE
POLYGON SET	CIRCULAR ARC CENTRE CLOSE
ELLIPTICAL ARC CLOSE	

Attributes:

LINE TYPE	LINE WIDTH
LINE COLOUR	MARKER TYPE
MARKER COLOUR	CHARACTER HEIGHT
TEXT FONT INDEX	TEXT COLOUR
CHARACTER CODING ANNOUNCER	INTERIOR STYLE
FILL COLOUR	FILL REFERENCE POINT

General attributes and output control:

CLIP INDICATOR	CLIP RECTANGLE
AUXILIARY COLOUR	TRANSPARENCY
COLOUR TABLE	FONT LIST
SAVE PRIMITIVE ATTRIBUTES	RESTORE PRIMITIVE ATTRIBUTES
DELETE PRIMITIVE ATTRIBUTES SAVE SET	

Input control:

INITIALIZE LOGICAL INPUT DEVICE	RELEASE LOGICAL INPUT DEVICE
ECHO CONTROLS	PUT CURRENT LOCATOR MEASURE
ECHO DATA	LOCATOR DEVICE DATA
CHOICE DEVICE DATA	STRING DEVICE DATA
ASSOCIATE TRIGGERS	INITIALIZE EVENT QUEUE
RELEASE EVENT QUEUE	ENABLE EVENTS
DISABLE EVENTS	EVENT QUEUE BLOCK CONTROL
FLUSH EVENTS	FLUSH DEVICE EVENTS

Request and sample:

REQUEST LOCATOR	REQUEST CHOICE

- REQUEST STRING
- SAMPLING STATE
- SAMPLE LOCATOR
- SAMPLE CHOICE
- SAMPLE STRING

Event:

- AWAIT EVENT
- DEQUEUE LOCATOR EVENT
- DEQUEUE CHOICE EVENT
- EVENT QUEUE TRANSFER

Raster operations:

- PIXEL ARRAY
- GET PIXEL ARRAY
- GET PIXEL ARRAY DIMENSIONS
- SOURCE DESTINATION BITBLT
- TILE THREE OPERAND BITBLT

Raster control:

- GET NEW BITMAP IDENTIFIER
- CREATE BITMAP
- DELETE BITMAP
- DRAWING BITMAP
- DISPLAY BITMAP
- TRANSPARENT COLOUR
- MAPPED BITMAP FOREGROUND COLOUR
- MAPPED BITMAP BACKGROUND COLOUR

Raster attributes:

- DRAWING MODE
- FILL BITMAP

Device identity description table:

- INQUIRE DEVICE IDENTIFICATION
- INQUIRE DEVICE DESCRIPTION

Function and profile support description table:

- LOOKUP FUNCTION SUPPORT
- LOOKUP PROFILE SUPPORT

Control description table:

- INQUIRE DEVICE CONTROL CAPABILITY
- LOOKUP ESCAPE SUPPORT
- LOOKUP GET ESCAPE SUPPORT

Primitive support description table:

- INQUIRE PRIMITIVE SUPPORT LEVELS

Line description table:

- INQUIRE LINE CAPABILITY
- INQUIRE LIST OF AVAILABLE LINETYPES
- INQUIRE LIST OF AVAILABLE SCALED LINE WIDTHS

Marker description table:

- INQUIRE MARKER CAPABILITY
- INQUIRE LIST OF AVAILABLE MARKERTYPES
- INQUIRE LIST OF AVAILABLE SCALED MARKER SIZES

Text description table:

- INQUIRE TEXT CAPABILITY
- INQUIRE FONT CAPABILITIES
- INQUIRE LIST OF AVAILABLE TEXT FONTS
- INQUIRE LIST OF AVAILABLE CHARACTER SETS
- INQUIRE LIST OF AVAILABLE CHARACTER HEIGHTS

Fill description table:

- INQUIRE FILL CAPABILITY

Output control description table:

- INQUIRE COLOUR CAPABILITIES
- INQUIRE MAXIMUM NUMBER OF SIMULTANEOUSLY SAVED ATTRIBUTE SETS
- INQUIRE ARRAY OF SUPPORTED CHARACTER CODING ANNOUNCERS

Input description table:

- INQUIRE INPUT CAPABILITY
- INQUIRE LIST OF AVAILABLE INPUT DEVICES

Class-independent LID description table:

- INQUIRE COMMON INPUT DEVICE PROPERTIES

INQUIRE LIST OF SUPPORTED ECHO TYPES

INQUIRE LIST OF SUPPORTED PROMPT TYPES

INQUIRE LIST OF SUPPORTED ACKNOWLEDGEMENT TYPES

INQUIRE LIST OF ASSOCIABLE TRIGGERS

Class-specific LID description table:

INQUIRE LOCATOR CAPABILITIES INQUIRE CHOICE CAPABILITIES

INQUIRE STRING CAPABILITIES

Raster description table:

INQUIRE RASTER CAPABILITY

INQUIRE LIST OF SUPPORTED DRAWING-MODE/TRANSPARENCY PAIRS

INQUIRE LIST OF SUPPORTED DRAWING-MODE-3/TRANSPARENCY PAIRS

General attributes and output control state list:

INQUIRE OBJECT CLIPPING INQUIRE COLOUR STATE

INQUIRE LIST OF COLOUR TABLE ENTRIES

Class-independent LID state list:

INQUIRE COMMON LOGICAL INPUT DEVICE STATE

INQUIRE LIST OF ASSOCIATED TRIGGERS

INQUIRE ECHO DATA RECORD INQUIRE INPUT DEVICE DATA RECORD

Class-specific LID state list:

INQUIRE LOCATOR STATE

Event input state list:

INQUIRE EVENT INPUT STATE

Raster state list:

INQUIRE RASTER STATE

INQUIRE LIST OF NON-DISPLAYABLE BITMAP IDENTIFIERS

INQUIRE LIST OF DISPLAYABLE BITMAP IDENTIFIERS

Bitmap state list:

INQUIRE BITMAP STATE

4.2.3 List of ESCAPE, GDP and GET ESCAPE Functions Required

These would usually be listed by referring to the entry in the register maintained by the appropriate registration authority.

Escapes functions:

1. An escape to set the pixel location relative to coordinates to “centred on coordinates”. Note, the CGI preferred default is “between coordinates”, hence this has to be altered using an escape.
2. An escape function to set the plane mask.
3. An escape to set the line cap and join style.
4. An escape to set the line style dash pattern and dash offset.
5. An escape to select the fill bitmap to be applied during the rendering of line primitives.
6. An escape to define the drawing surface clip region by a clip mask.
7. An escape to select the *winding* interior fill-rule.
8. An escape to load new fonts into the CGI virtual device and an accompanying get escape function to obtain ISO 9541 font descriptions.
9. Escape and get escape functions to provide the X concept of a screen saver, to provide control of the keyboard, and to provide control of the pointing device.

4.2.4 Resource Requirements

Note, only those resources which are extended beyond the default resource requirements or where no specific default value is required by the CGI are listed. For example, the minimum requirement for number of available indexed colours would be 2, but this is the minimum required by the CGI and so is not shown here.

Output resource requirements:

List of available line types	[solid] note, other dash patterns are set using the required escape function.
List of available line widths	[ ] i.e. a continuous range given in physical device coordinates
Array of available line clipping modes	(SHAPE)
List of available marker types	[dot, asterisk]
List of available marker sizes	[1] i.e. in physical device coordinates
Array of available marker clipping modes	(SHAPE)
List of available interior styles	[HOLLOW, SOLID, BITMAP]
Background colour capability	[INDEX-0]
Colour realization	ADDITIVE
Array of available character coding announcers	(BASIC 7-BIT, BASIC 8-BIT, PRIVATE) PRIVATE for use with 16 bit character encoding
List of available character sets	???

Input resource requirements:

List of available LOCATOR device indices	[1] corresponding to the pointer device
List of available CHOICE device indices	[1] corresponding to the button device
List of available STRING device indices	[1] corresponding to the keyboard device
For the locator device:	
Sample support	YES, needed for X query pointer function
Event support	YES
Put current measure effective	YES, needed for X warp pointer function
List of associable triggers	[1] trigger operates on δx and δy displacement
List of supported echo types	[1, 2] echo type 1 is implementation dependent, echo type 2 should be used to indicate a bitmap for use as a cursor. The echo data record should provide the additional data for cursor colour.
For the string device:	
Sample support	YES, needed for X query pointer function
Event support	YES
List of associable triggers	[1, 2] triggers 1 and 2 provide key press and key release.
Maximum number of string alternatives	(256) note this assumes 256 is sufficient for the keyboard.
For the choice device:	
Sample support	YES, needed for X query pointer function
Event support	YES
List of associable triggers	[3, 4] triggers 3 and 4 provide button press and button release.

Maximum string buffer size	(1) i.e. only one character at a time.
Raster resource requirements:	
Number of predefined displayable bitmaps	1
Displayable bitmap creation supported	YES (see below)
Source bitmap truncation support	TRUNCATION, however, note that X requires those regions in the destination that correspond to truncated regions of the source to be tiled with the background colour
Drawing mode/transparency support	ALL
List of drawing mode/transparency values	all boolean operations (0 through 15) are required, each of which shall provide OPAQUE and TRANSPARENT support.
Drawing mode-3/transparency support	ALL
List of drawing mode-3/transparency values	all boolean operations are required, each of which shall provide OPAQUE and TRANSPARENT support. Note, this may be a bit extreme !

4.2.5 Definition of Restrictions and Recommendations

The relationship between pixel location and coordinates should be set such that pixels lie centred on physical device coordinates using the registered escape function.

The VDC extent should be set such that the aspect ratio of the defining rectangle exactly matches the aspect ratio of the default display surface, that the first defining point corresponds to the upper left of the display surface and the second defining point corresponds to the lower right of the display surface. Likewise, the device viewport should be set in the same manner. This ensures that the sense of the coordinate systems used in the VDC-to-Device mapping correctly match that expected by X (i.e. origin at top left, increasing X from left to right, increasing Y from top to bottom).

A displayable bitmap should be created following the establishment of the VDC-to-Device mapping and its bitmap extent should be chosen to match that of the VDC extent. This is necessary because the state lists of any predefined displayable bitmaps will have been initialised at CGI initialisation time to the default VDC-to-Device mapping, which of course can differ from that required because an isotropic mapping will be forced. The created displayable bitmap should be selected as the current display bitmap.

The default for the clip indicator should be set to OFF since this form of clipping is not required by the X server.

The CGI uses colour table index 0 for background colour, whereas X uses index 0 for foreground colour and index 1 for background. The X server implementation will have to correctly reverse this relationship when defining colours on the CGI virtual device.

The default marker type of the CGI differs from that of an X server, thus it is necessary to initialise the marker type to CGI marker type 1, corresponding to dot drawn at maximum device resolution.

The default interior style for an X server is SOLID, not HOLLOW as in the CGI.

The locator and choice LIDs should be initialised using INITIALIZE LOGICAL INPUT DEVICE. The event queue should be initialised and event input enabled for the locator and choice LIDs. Similarly, sampling should be enabled for these LIDs to support the X request QueryPointer.

Prompt and acknowledgement control should both be disabled using the ECHO CONTROLS function as these are not required, echoing for the locator device should remain enabled as this is to be used to provide a cursor indicating the current locator position.

4.3 Profile 2 — A Minimal CGI Profile for use with a CGI Interpreter Incorporated as an Extension to an X Server

4.3.1 Introduction to the Constituency

This profile is primarily directed to developers of software products that utilize a subset of the standard device independent CGI interface and that, in addition, require their software products to execute safely and consistently within the X window system environment. The profile defines access to as much of the X window system graphics functionality through a standard CGI interface as possible. It is restricted to those components of the CGI that map onto the graphics subset of the X window system functions and additional ESCAPE's and GET ESCAPE's are specified where there is no obvious direct or indirect mapping.

The CGI display surface is mapped to a single X window and all graphic objects and raster operations that are rendered by the X server are transformed to the window's coordinate system. This transformation conceptually takes place below the level of the CGI's device coordinates. If the window is resized (by an external agent) the CGI extension will record this change in the output device description table as a change to the device bottom-left and upper-right corners and display surface height and width. The profile does not require any additional behaviour in this event, such as maintaining a backing store image of the window or scaling/clipping policies for regenerating the contents of the display surface.

Some of the functions listed have no obvious X counterpart. This is sometimes where a function is included because it is part of one of the foundation profiles. Support of these functions has to be provided by the CGI extension component of the server. In other cases, the CGI interpreter will need to perform a transformation of the CGI request into an appropriate sequence of X functions or routines (within the X server). For example, the CGI function TEXT FONT INDEX has no obvious X counterpart, but could be transformed into setting an appropriate *font* entry in a graphics context to the desired font within the basic X component of the server.

4.3.2 List of Required Functions

This profile is a superset of the 2-WAY OUTPUT, LOCATOR INPUT, CHOICE INPUT, and STRING INPUT foundation profiles of the CGI. Underlined functions and resource requirements indicate those functions that are from these foundation profiles.

(For the sake of brevity, the necessary inquiry functions have been omitted.)

Virtual device management:

- INITIALIZE
- TERMINATE
- EXECUTE DEFERRED ACTIONS
- PREPARE DRAWING SURFACE
- END PAGE
- ESCAPE

Coordinate space control:

- VDC EXTENT
- DEVICE VIEWPORT
- DEVICE VIEWPORT SPECIFICATION MODE
- DEVICE VIEWPORT MAPPING
- DRAWING SURFACE CLIP
- DRAWING SURFACE CLIP INDICATOR

Errors:

- DEQUEUE ERROR REPORTS
- ERROR HANDLING CONTROL

Primitives:

- POLYLINE
- DISJOINT POLYLINE
- POLYMARKER
- TEXT
- APPEND TEXT
- CIRCULAR ARC CENTRE
- ELLIPTICAL ARC
- RECTANGLE
- POLYGON SET
- CIRCULAR ARC CENTRE CLOSE
- ELLIPTICAL ARC CLOSE

Attributes:

- LINE TYPE
- LINE WIDTH
- LINE COLOUR
- MARKER TYPE
- MARKER COLOUR
- CHARACTER HEIGHT
- TEXT FONT INDEX
- TEXT COLOUR
- CHARACTER CODING ANNOUNCER
- INTERIOR STYLE
- FILL COLOUR
- FILL REFERENCE POINT

General attributes and output control:

- CLIP INDICATOR
- CLIP RECTANGLE
- AUXILIARY COLOUR
- TRANSPARENCY
- BACKGROUND COLOUR
- COLOUR TABLE
- FONT LIST
- SAVE PRIMITIVE ATTRIBUTES
- RESTORE PRIMITIVE ATTRIBUTES
- DELETE PRIMITIVE ATTRIBUTES SAVE SET

Input control:

- INITIALIZE LOGICAL INPUT DEVICE
- RELEASE LOGICAL INPUT DEVICE
- ECHO CONTROLS
- PUT CURRENT LOCATOR MEASURE
- ECHO DATA
- LOCATOR DEVICE DATA
- CHOICE DEVICE DATA
- STRING DEVICE DATA
- ASSOCIATE TRIGGERS
- INITIALIZE EVENT QUEUE
- RELEASE EVENT QUEUE
- ENABLE EVENTS
- DISABLE EVENTS
- EVENT QUEUE BLOCK CONTROL
- FLUSH EVENTS
- FLUSH DEVICE EVENTS

Request and sample:

- REQUEST LOCATOR
- REQUEST CHOICE
- REQUEST STRING
- SAMPLING STATE
- SAMPLE LOCATOR
- SAMPLE CHOICE
- SAMPLE STRING

Event:

- AWAIT EVENT
- DEQUEUE LOCATOR EVENT
- DEQUEUE CHOICE EVENT
- EVENT QUEUE TRANSFER

Raster operations:

- PIXEL ARRAY
- GET PIXEL ARRAY
- GET PIXEL ARRAY DIMENSIONS
- SOURCE DESTINATION BITBLT
- TILE THREE OPERAND BITBLT

Raster control:

- CREATE BITMAP
- DELETE BITMAP
- DRAWING BITMAP
- DISPLAY BITMAP
- TRANSPARENT COLOUR
- MAPPED BITMAP FOREGROUND COLOUR
- MAPPED BITMAP BACKGROUND COLOUR

Raster attributes:

- DRAWING MODE
- FILL BITMAP

4.3.3 List of ESCAPE, GDP and GET ESCAPE Functions Required

An escape to set the pixel location relative to coordinates to "centred on coordinates". Note, the CGI preferred default is "between coordinates", hence this has to be altered using an escape. This escape is needed by a CGI client in order to ensure correct rendering of any CGI graphical output. Any CGI client which doesn't invoke this escape will be liable to unexpected rendering effects.

4.3.4 Resource Requirements

Control resources:	
List of supported device viewport specification modes	[FRACTION OF DRAWING SURFACE, PHYSICAL DEVICE COORDINATES]
Output resource requirements:	
List of available line types	[solid] note, other dash patterns are set using the required escape function.
List of available line widths	[ ] i.e. a continuous range given in physical
Array of available line clipping modes	(SHAPE)
List of available marker types	[dot, asterisk]
List of available marker sizes	[1] i.e. in physical device coordinates
Array of available marker clipping modes	(SHAPE)
List of available interior styles	[HOLLOW, SOLID, BITMAP], note that X does not provide HATCH or PATTERN fill as such, and cannot support transformable patterns or hatches.
Background colour capability	[INDEX-0]
Colour realization	ADDITIVE
Array of available character coding announcers	(BASIC 7-BIT, BASIC 8-BIT, PRIVATE) PRIVATE for use with 16 bit character encoding
List of available character sets	???
Input resource requirements:	
List of available LOCATOR device indices	[1] corresponding to the pointer device
List of available CHOICE device indices	[1] corresponding to the keyboard devices
For the locator device:	
Sample support	YES, used for X query pointer function
Event support	YES
Put current measure effective	YES, used for X warp pointer function
List of associable triggers	[1] trigger operates on δx and δy displacement
List of supported echo types	[1, 2] echo type 1 is implementation dependent, echo type 2 should be used to indicate a bitmap for use as a cursor. The echo data record should provide the additional data for cursor colour.
For the choice devices:	
Sample support	YES, needed for X query pointer function
Event support	YES

List of associable triggers	[3, 4] triggers 3 and 4 provide button press and button release.
Maximum number of choice alternatives	(3) note this assumes 3 buttons
For the string devices:	
Sample support	YES, needed for X query pointer function
Event support	YES
List of associable triggers	[1, 2] triggers 1 and 2 provide key press and key release.
Maximum string buffer size	(1) i.e. only one character at a time.
Raster resource requirements:	
Number of predefined displayable bitmaps	1
Displayable bitmap creation supported	YES (see below)
Source bitmap truncation support	TRUNCATION
Drawing mode/transparency support	ALL
List of drawing mode/transparency values	all boolean operations (0 through 15) are required, each of which shall provide OPAQUE and TRANSPARENT support.
Drawing mode-3/transparency support	ALL
List of drawing mode-3/transparency values	all boolean operations are required, each of which shall provide OPAQUE and TRANSPARENT support. Note, this may be a bit extreme !

4.3.5 Definition of Restrictions and Recommendations

Of those default CGI state list values that differ from the X graphics context defaults, we assume that the CGI extension will, at initialisation time (on receipt of the CGI INITIALISE function) establish appropriate default X values in the graphics contexts that it is using.

The relationship between pixel location and physical device coordinates should be set such that pixels lie centred on physical device coordinates using the registered escape function. Although CGI clients that do not alter this aspect of the CGI virtual device may produce rendered output that is acceptable to them, in other cases this may produce unforseen effects that are not acceptable.

The CGI uses colour table index 0 for background colour, whereas X uses index 0 for foreground colour and index 1 for background. The CGI extension will have to correctly reverse this relationship when defining colours to be used by the basic X component of the server.

5 Some Comments on these Profiles

5.1 Comments on Profile-1

Perhaps not surprisingly this profile is more complex than one might initially think. A number of design choices have been taken that assume a particular X server implementation strategy and this inevitably has lead to a particular set of functions and corresponding resource requirements in the profile. A simpler approach in this situation would be to include all conceivably useful CGI functions in the profile and avoid an attempt to minimize the profile size. A considerable amount of the complexity in this profile arises from the different methods taken in the two specifications for identifying minimal resources required for conformance reasons and default values of these resources. This is particularly difficult with the X data stream definition [17], partly because any defaults and minimal resource requirements that are specified are distributed throughout clause 7 of the document, and partly because the conformance requirements for some areas of X appear to be quite weak. Related to this second point are the various implementation and device dependences.

The other aspect which produces considerable complexity in the profile is related to the CGI's profile conformance requirements. Specifically, when defaults are allowed to be specified in the profile and when they have to be achieved through the use of escape functions. In general, allowed latitude in the behaviour of a function or variance in a supported feature can only be required in the profile if the CGI has not specified a preferred behaviour or if the CGI does not specify that it is implementation dependent. If, however, these conditions do not hold then the required default or behaviour has to be achieved using escapes. An additional requirement states that only registered escapes are allowed to be included in a profile.

The escapes listed in the profile serve to highlight the most significant differences between the two specifications at the level in which we are interested. Obviously, there are many other differences, however the majority of these can be dealt with using suitable sequences of CGI functions. Perhaps the most important difference is that of font information. This is an area where other international standardisation work has been progressing for some time [16] and which has significance not only on the relationship between the CGI and X, but with other international standards that use *text* as well. The CGM with amendment 3 is one particular example where provision for using the minimal set of ISO 9541 font properties has been included. An X server implementation which does provide access to standardised font information will clearly be that much more able to provide satisfactory support to clients (such as a CGM interpreter) expecting such facilities. (A font service MIT consortium standard is apparently under development, but unfortunately, we are unaware of the goals and content of this document.) Provision in an X server for the use of standardised font descriptions may impact the underlying graphics interface, such as that described by this profile. (The CGI in fact only does a passing job of referencing ISO 9541 as the approved place for obtaining font descriptions.)

5.2 Comments on Profile-2

Probably the most interesting comment on this profile is the difficulty encountered in trying to limit its scope to only providing a close match between the CGI's graphics capabilities and X's. Some obvious areas where it is relatively straightforward to support CGI functionality using X are for example: edge control on fill primitives, bundle representations, additional marker types and fill styles, some additional text attributes, etc. These features have not been incorporated as they are not directly available from X and would require the extension component to implement them, albeit in a straightforward manner.

Such a restriction in scope is not very useful to a CGI community. This approach means that, in general, only a limited set of CGI clients could make use of an extended X server of this type. This falls short of our stated motivation of being able to send a CGI data stream across a network to a device running X and have the CGI function representations interpreted correctly. A much better profile and a much better product would provide extensive CGI support and hence serve a large variety of CGI clients.

6 Summary

This paper has presented an approach to addressing the viability of the CGI as a useful and persistent international standard. The CGI has been accused by some over the last two years of being a non-starting entry in the standards race (predominantly by US workstation manufacturers). Their reasons are centred around the belief that the CGI's window of opportunity has passed and that this is primarily because the standard has taken too long to develop, is too large and complex, and addresses too many variations in device capability. This is of course not the whole truth and probably a more significant reason has been the development and emergence of the X window system as a de-facto standard. The CGI and X in a sense became competitors, both in the market place and for development resources; both of them define device level graphics facilities (the CGI facilities being considerably more extensive) including the important area of raster operations; X defines resource management facilities for supporting multiple clients, whereas this type of capability was excluded from the CGI in attempt to limit its scope in order to progress in shorter timescales.

Without entering into a discourse on the merits or otherwise of each system it is perhaps worth noting that the CGI also provides a close match with the Computer Graphics Metafile standard for the generation and interpretation of metafiles, and a well-defined interface for supporting a range of GKS workstations. We suggest in this paper that all need not be lost for those with a requirement for a device independent virtual device interface standard, many of whom appear to be users rather than manufacturers. With relatively minor extensions to the CGI in the form of escape functions, a profile for the support of an X server implementation positioned on top of a CGI virtual device is certainly definable. This has great potential for a market place which includes both CGI devices and X workstations and terminals by increasing the coverage of those constituencies requiring device independent graphics and a widely adopted windowing system.

A CGI profile for an extension to an X server which gives a close match to the X graphics capabilities in a device independent way has also been shown to be definable. Such a profile could have been based on one of the GKS constituency profiles thus encouraging the porting of GKS systems developed for a range of CGI devices into an X environment without major software revision. As another option, a profile could be based on the CGM constituency profile for similar reasons and potential benefits. Finally, a CGI extension based on a combination of constituency profiles (e.g. GKS output and input, CGM , and CGI over X) should bring considerable benefits to developers of such products.

In deriving these profiles and examining their implications to both the underlying interpreter and the CGI client it is evident that there appear to be two distinct constituency profile classes, namely, generator profiles and interpreter profiles. Interpreter profiles correspond to the usual way of thinking about profiles, that is, they define a level of functionality that a client can expect to use successfully. Generator profiles however, constrain a CGI generator to a level of functionality that can be generated and successfully interpreted by the CGI virtual device. A profile for an X server on top of a CGI interface is an example of an interpreter profile, whereas a profile for a CGI extension to an X server is an example of a generator profile. This distinction is one that has not been made in the CGI document.

7 References

1. Reynolds G.J.: *Comparing the CGI and X - An Overview*, Interim report for the DTI and SERC, available as an internal report, School of Information Systems, University of East Anglia, January 1989
2. Reynolds G. J. and Arnold D. B.: *Mappings between CGI and X*, Eurographics '89, State of the Art technical report series. Also available as an AGOCG (UK Advisory Group on Computer Graphics) technical report no. 1.
3. ISO DIS 9636 (CGI) – Information Processing Systems – Computer Graphics – Interfacing techniques for dialogues with graphical devices - Functional Specification, October 1988.
4. Scheifler R.W.: *X Window System Protocol - X Version 11, Release 4* Laboratory of Computer Science, MIT.

5. Gettys J., Scheifler R.W., and Newman R.: *X Lib - C Language Interface - X Window System - X Version 11, Release 4,* MIT Project Athena.
6. McCormack J., Asente P., and Swick R. R.: *X Toolkit Intrinsics - C Language Interface - X Window System - X Version 11, Release 4,* MIT Project Athena.
7. ISO/IEC 7942, Information Processing Systems - Computer Graphics, Functional Specification for the Graphical Kernel System (GKS), ISO 7942, July 1985
8. ISO/IEC 8632, Information Processing Systems - Computer Graphics, Metafile for the Storage and Transfer of Picture Description Information (CGM), 1987
9. *PEX Protocol Specification*, document number ISO/IEC JTC 1/SC24/WG2/N2, 17 February 1988.
10. Powers T.: *Positioning CGI in a Managed Environment*, document number ANSI X3H33/87-70.
11. Powers T.: *Integrating CGI into X*, document number ANSI X3H33/87-71.
12. Hopgood F. R. A.: *A Graphics Standards View of Screen Management*, in Methodology of Window Management (Eds F.R.A.Hopgood, D.A.Duce, E.V.C. Fielding, K.Robinson and A.S.Williams), Eurographic Seminars Series, Springer-Verlag pp 87-95 (1986)
13. Vanderschel D. and Tucker C.:, document number ANSI X3H3/87-19.
14. ISO/IEC JTC1/SC24 Final Report of the Study Group for an Improved Graphical Text Model (Rapporteur - H.Stenzel), SC24/N363, August 1989.
15. Arnold D. B. and Reynolds G. J.:, Configuring Graphics System Components, Software Engineering Journal, November 88, pp248-256
16. ISO/IEC 9541, Information Processing Systems - Font and Character Interchange, ISO DIS 9541 [all parts]
17. ANSI X3H3/90-18 American National Standard for Information Systems – Computer Graphics – X Window System Data Stream Definition, Parts I, II, III, dpANS April 1990.

Chapter 20

Transporting CGMs Between Implementations. Some Practical Considerations

David B. Arnold, Stelios Th. Liapakis, Graham J. Reynolds, Nikos P. Vezirgiannis

1 Introduction

This paper describes some work which has been undertaken at the Univeristy of East Anglia, Norwich under the umbrella of the Esprit II Project 2463 (ARGOSI) [1]. The ARGOSI project is intended to improve the interworking of graphics and networking standards and impact on the direction of current and future standardisation efforts in these areas. One work package within the project is developing a demonstrator which will use CGM files to transport the definitions of pictures across Public Data Networks. For the demonstrator to provide a reasonable test bed for the current and proposed standards, it is thought to be important to use a heterogeneous environment with multiple hardware platforms and software environments.

As part of the testing of the accuracy and efficiency of interworking with different implementations of CGM generators and interpreters, experiments have been conducted in which metafiles generated on a number of different systems have been exchanged, to test:

(a) Accuracy and completeness of implementations. During this exercise it became apparent that, quite apart from considerations of the faithfulness of the implementations in implementing all the effects described in the standard, different implementors had adopted different error reaction philosophies.

(b) Efficiency (in terms of size) of generation of metafiles. For a system to provide the best response time achievable across a network it is important that the data transmitted should not be unnecessarily long winded in its description of any picture. A cross section of test metafiles was therefore examined to look for ways in which typical implementations might improve the efficiency of encoding metafiles.

2 A Brief Introduction to the CGM Standard

The reader is assumed to be reasonably familiar with the concepts of GKS [2]. The CGM standard [3] defines representations of graphics for storage and transfer between systems. These are fundamentally file format and file transfer encoding standards. Part 2 *et seq* of PHIGS [4] (which describes the PHIGS archive file) is also of this type.

The Computer Graphics Metafile for the storage and transfer of picture description information (CGM) [3,5-7] enables pictures to be recorded for long term storage, to be exchanged between graphics devices, systems and installations. Throughout this paper, CGM is used to refer to version 1 metafiles; other amendments of the CGM have not been considered here.

Pictures are described in CGM as a collection of elements of different kinds, representing, for example, primitives, attributes and control information. CGM is a multi-part standard. Part 1 defines the available elements, the structure of the metafile and the order in which elements may appear. Parts 2-4 of the standard define three representation schemes, or encodings, for the abstract syntax of the elements. Part 2 is a character encoding aimed at compactness and transferability across networks. Part 3 is a binary encoding aimed at minimizing the processor effort involved in generating and/or interpreting the metafile. Part 4 is a clear text encoding aimed at a metafile that can be read and edited by people.

A CGM is structured as a series of levels (figure 1)

(1) *Metafile*: A metafile consists of a metafile descriptor followed by a number of picture descriptions. The metafile descriptor contains information valid for the whole metafile, for example, the precision of real and integer quantities in the metafile. Picture descriptions are self-contained.

(2) *Picture*: Pictures are bounded by picture delimiters. A picture starts with a picture descriptor which contains information about how this particular picture is stored. This is followed by the picture body which contains the definition of the picture.

(3) *Picture body*: The elements at this level are essentially primitive and attribute elements describing the graphical content of the picture.

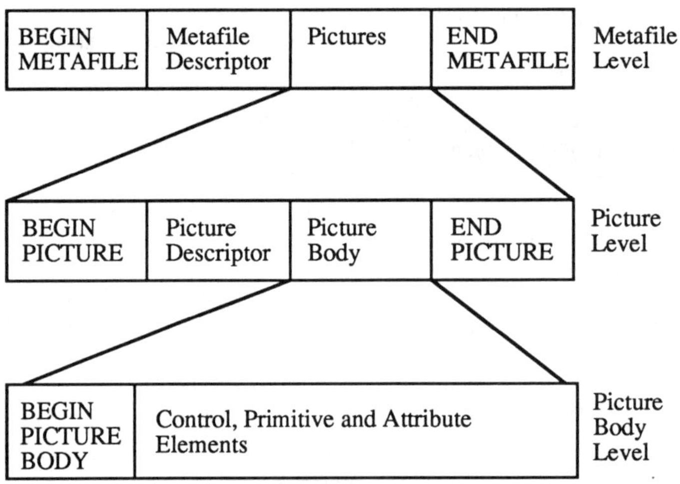

Figure 1. Structure of a CGM

CGM only allows 2D pictures to be described and provides a total of 19 graphical primitive elements; the main additions compared to GKS are polygon set, rectangle, circle, circular arcs, ellipse and elliptic arcs.

As will be seen below the encoding of colour information can be an important component in determining the efficiency (or otherwise) of an implementation's encoding strategy. Colour handling in CGM is an extension of the mechanism used in GKS. Colour in GKS is specified by indices into a colour table on each workstation. Two colour specification modes are provided in CGM, *indexed*, which is equivalent to the GKS mechanism, and *direct*. In direct mode, the parameters of the colour specification elements are RGB triples.

Similarly different modes are specified for the definition of line width, marker size and (polygon) edge width. These later modes correspond to a specification of the coordinate system in which the dimensions of the primitive are to interpreted.

3 Implementation Latitude

An important concept in many circumstances is that of *implementation latitude* in graphics standards implementations. There are many cases in which, for example, the actual rendering step may be constrained by the hardware on which a system is implemented – an obvious case being the issuing of requests for coloured graphics primitives to monochrome devices.

For this reason the standard itself relates to the definition of correct metafiles and, while containing the concept of metafile generators and interpreters, does not standardise their operation, merely providing guidance to implementors in a non-mandatory Annex. The definition of a CGM picture therefore relates to an idealised image.

In these circumstances when investigating the compatibility of the generators and interpreters provided by different implementations a number of aspects must be considered:

(a) Whether generators produce metafiles which not only conform to the standard, but also refrain from using optional facilities which the interpreters of other implementations do not support. This could be at the obvious level of complete encodings, but also at the level of different coordinate types or precisions. For example, the Binary Encoding's conformance section specifically mentions that "Interpreters are not required to respond correctly to the ISO 2022 controls for designating and invoking G-sets when those controls occur within text strings of a TEXT, RESTRICTED TEXT, APPEND TEXT or GDP element". In these circumstances it is clearly possible for a conforming metafile to be displayed without the original generator's visual intent through having selected particular features of the standard. Thus to guarantee succesful use in a heterogeneous environment generators should adopt a minimalist approach.

(b) Even when correctly interpreted, the sophistication of simulations of the effects requested may lead to unusable, but correct, output. For example a colour plot using filled areas may correctly be interpreted on a 1 bit/pixel device as white space, plus simulated colour for all other areas, where "simulated colour" is translated into black. Even on a device such as this much more useable interpretations are possible (for example using dithering techniques to generate grey scale simulations for filled areas). The Annex giving guidelines to implementors encourages interpreters to "do the best they can" in the face of errors in the metafile, but says of many more advanced features (e.g. transparency) that it is not expected to be implemented unless there is some direct hardware support. However for an interpreter to be most useable in a heterogeneous environment it is clear that a maximalist approach would lead to the most useful implementations.

The standards communities have long recognized that implementation latititude is a major stumbling block to the widespread interchange of graphics programs and images which use the standards unless there is also prior agreement as to the facilities, parameter values, etc which will be used. Such agreements are already being published by some groups of users (e.g. the CALS CGM Profile [8]).

4 Testing Metafile Transfer Between Implementations

A project [9] has recently been undertaken at the University of East Anglia in which a series of test metafiles, generated by a variety of systems, have been interpreted by two different implementations and the results compared.

The hardware used for this comparison was:

(i) Sun Workstations – a Sun 3/50 monochrome Workstation, and a Sun 3/110 colour Workstation, both running Unix;

(ii) Apple Macintosh II with a colour monitor running the Apple Finder;

(iii) Apple LaserWriter : printouts from both workstation types were taken from an Apple LaserWriter postscript laser printer.

All the above hardware is connected directly or indirectly to the School's Ethernet network (figure 2), which was used for the exchange of metafiles and printer access. The examples shown in section 5 of this paper were all produced as either screen dumps from the Sun workstations, or as PICT format files on the Macintosh. All were subsequently printed on a laser printer. The Sun colour screen dumps were converted to grey scale pictures prior to printing using a number of bitmap utilities. The PICT format files were printed as black and white images using the Apple provided laser printer software. With the exception of figure 12, the rest of the pictures shown in this paper were displayed and captured on colour workstations. Some testing was carried out on monochrome displays as well (see section 5.6).

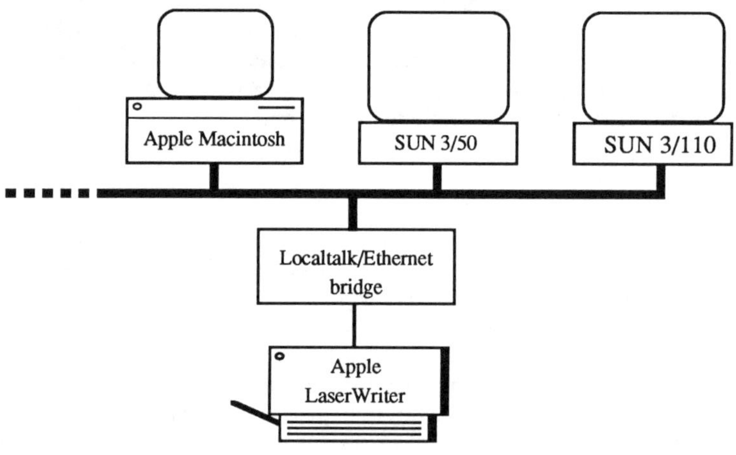

Figure 2. The heterogeneous environment

The following CGM implementations were used in the test:

(a) The Loughborough University CGM Toolkit (LUT-CGM Toolkit) [10]. The generator and the interpreter routines of the toolkit were used in the testing. Some Fortran 77 programs were written to generate simple test CGMs. To interpret CGMs, a program was written to call the toolkit routine which interprets a whole metafile. The interpreter used the GKS driver routine supplied with the toolkit to display the results. The GKS graphics package used was UNIRAS GKS [11].

(b) MetaPICT [12], which is a CGM interpreter for the Apple Macintosh developed by GSC Associates. It translates binary encoded CGMs to PICT or PICT2 file format as supported by most Macintosh graphics applications. Although MetaPICT is not intended to be a general-purpose CGM file viewer, the translated CGM file will be drawn on the screen, following a successful translation.

A third product, MetaCheck [14] was used to perform conformance analysis of the metafiles reported on in this paper. This product cannot be used to interpret and draw metafiles, but it does provide a form of clear text output for detailed checking of individual metafile elements.

The error philosophy taken by MetaPICT is worth noting here. MetaPICT only tests for and reports major state errors and tries to be forgiving of state errors and other types. In particular, it ignores the Metafile Elements List altogether and does not report discrepancies between the elements list and those actually encountered in the metafile.

Two sets of test metafiles were used. The first set was supplied by the Gesellschaft für Mathematik und Datenverarbeitung (GMD) and as such came from completely different hardware and software environments. These metafiles were known to contain some errors (whether for test purposes or unintentionally was never determined), but the presence of errors was seen as a useful part of testing the reactions of the implementations. Since these metafiles were supplied by a third party they are seen as a fair test of both systems.

The second test set came with the MetaPICT software from GSC Associates. As such, one would expect the MetaPICT software to interpret the metafiles to best advantage and the LUT-CGM Toolkit to be significantly disadvantaged. For this reason, but only partly compensating for it, some rather simple test metafiles were generated using the LUT-CGM Toolkit. As is to be expected these were reasonably interpreted by both systems.

5 Test Results

To illustrate the test results the following metafiles are selected from those tested:

GMD metafiles	**GSC Associates metafiles**
DONALD	BOEING
GPT0003	LOTUS123
KUGEL	
UNI0003	

Of these only KUGEL and LOTUS123 were reported by both systems as completely correct. In line with the Annex giving guidelines for intepreters MetaPICT interpreted and displayed something from all the metafiles, after reporting the errors it found. In contrast, the LUT-CGM Toolkit interpreter found significantly greater numbers of errors and was unable to display all the metafiles via the GKS interpreter and UNIRAS GKS. There were some obvious differences occuring in all tests. For example the two systems used different aspect ratios for the display area and the MetaPICT interpreter used a white background whereas UNIGKS used a black background. The other results are considered in more detail below.

Of the metafiles listed above, DONALD, KUGEL, BOEING, and LOTUS123, were reported as non-conforming by the conformance analyser, MetaCheck. The metafiles GPT0003 and UNI0003 were reported as conforming metafiles (but see section 5.4). Through experimentation, MetaCheck does not appear to look for descrepancies between the metafile elements list and elements actually used. Thus, in some cases MetaCheck reported less errors than the LUT-CGM toolkit.

5.1 Metafile : DONALD

This metafile was displayed only by MetaPICT on the Macintosh (see figure 3). The LUT-CGM/UNIRAS GKS combination aborted the interpretation, generating a Unix run-time error. By examining the interpreter code with the Unix source code level debugger (dbx), it was discovered that the interpreter aborted after decoding the GENERALIZED DRAWING PRIMITIVE element, and particularly when it called the GKS Generalized Drawing Primitive function (GGDP). Since there are no standardised GDPs, it is reasonable for UNIRAS GKS to be unable to plot the GDP requested. However, calling the GGDP function with an unsupported GDP identifier caused the run-time error, which should have been avoidable. This seems a UNIRAS rather than a LUT-CGM problem. With this particular metafile, the GDP identifier used was positive and , since the GDP could not be a registered GDP, the generator of the metafile is at fault.

Figure 3. DONALD displayed by MetaPICT on the Macintosh

Note that the CGM driver could inquire the list of supported GDP identifiers from the GKS system in order to avoid such catastrophic events. This assumes that the relevant inquiry is supported by the GKS system.

5.2 Metafile: GPT0003

Both MetaPICT and LUT-CGM displayed GPT0003. LUT-CGM reported the error "Invalid pattern index". Figures 4 and 5 show the resulting pictures from the two interpreters. Some information in the metafile has not been displayed by the LUT-CGM interpreter. In particular, the lines designating the wall boundaries. The picture stored in GPT0003 is defined in colour, and it is interesting to see the different handling of the colour simulation. The LUT-CGM/UNIRAS GKS combination used a simple black and white rendering method, with no attempt at greyscale simulation of colour values, e.g. using dithering techniques. MetaPICT produces a colour PICT output file which, when viewed on a monochrome display, can be dithered or thresholded by the display software. Colour simulation in both cases is performed by the graphics support routines and not by the CGM interpreters.

Figure 4. GPT0003 displayed by LUT-CGM on the Sun

The MetaPICT version appears to have exploited the available simulated greyscales provided by the underlying Apple Colour Quickdraw graphics system. Colour simulation may also have beeen applied by the LaserWriter printing engine. Control over these levels of simulation is usually not provided to the user.

5.3 Metafile: KUGEL

This metafile was interpreted and displayed by both MetaPICT and LUT-CGM. No CGM errors were reported by either interpreters. The results of the interpretation are shown in figures 6 and 7. Figure 6 illustrates an area of implementation latitude in the interpretation of the metafile by MetaPICT. The metafile includes a character orientation element that should skew the rendering of the text string, and a text precision element requesting STROKE precision. However, MetaPICT does not appear to have utilised all these text attributes, and has instead chosen a convenient axis-aligned font. This is a permitted fall-back behaviour defined in the CGM standard, i.e. if a STROKE precision font is unavailable, then a suitable font of less precision (either STRING or CHARACTER) may be used.

Figure 5. GPT0003 displayed by MetaPICT on the Macintosh

The LUT-CGM interpreter appears to have drawn the metafile correctly. However, on examination of the character orientation element (which sets the character up vector for the text to [(0.5, 1.0)] and character base vector for the text to [(1.0, 0.0)]), it is clear that complete support of the text attributes has also not been fulfilled.

5.4 Metafile: UNI0003

This metafile was displayed only be MetaPICT (see figure 8). LUT-CGM reported the following errors before it aborted interpretation:

VDC REAL PRECISION element not included in Metafile Element List;

TEXT PRECISION element not included in Metafile Element List;

COLOUR TABLE element not included in Metafile Element List.

LUT-CGM aborted the interpretation after decoding the COLOUR TABLE element, when it called the GSCR GKS function which sets the colour representation. Again it is unclear whether this is a LUT-CGM problem or a UNIRAS GKS problem, although it is clear that the LUT interpreter continued to attempt to interpret the faulty metafile after detecting the errrors listed. The problem appears to arise from the presence of a Metafile Defaults Replacement element that includes the above listed control and attribute elements. The metafile defaults replacement occurs before the metafile elements list, which declares that both DRAWING PLUS CONTROL SET elements are present. The CGM standard is unclear as to whether strict ordering of these elements is necessary, and consequently one would assume that either order of occurence was permitted.

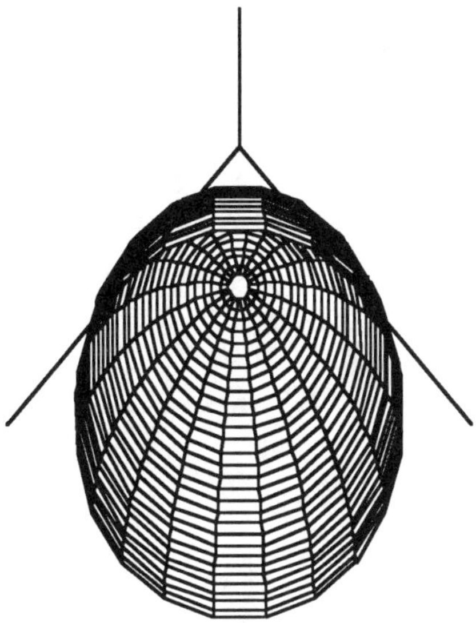

Figure 6. KUGEL displayed by MetaPICT on the Macintosh

5.5 Metafile: BOEING

This was one of the metafiles supplied by GSC Associates and one would therefore expect MetaPICT to interpret the metafile well. In fact both MetaPICT and LUT-CGM interpreted and displayed this metafile. They both reported errors. Presumably to demonstrate its error checking facilities, MetaPICT reported the following errors :

VDC INTEGER PRECISION element was encountered in state Picture Description, it is only valid in state Picture Open;

TRANSPARENCY element was encountered in state Picture Description, it is only valid in state Picture Open.

Rather more errors were reported by the LUT-CGM as follows:

COLOR MODE element not included in metafile element list;

VDC EXTENT element not included in metafile element list;

BACKGROUND COLOUR element not included in metafile element list;

VDC INTEGER PRECISION, CGM not in proper state. Should be in state Picture Open;

VDC INTEGER PRECISION element not included in metafile element list;

TRANSPARENCY, CGM not in proper state. Should be in state Picture Open or Partial Text;

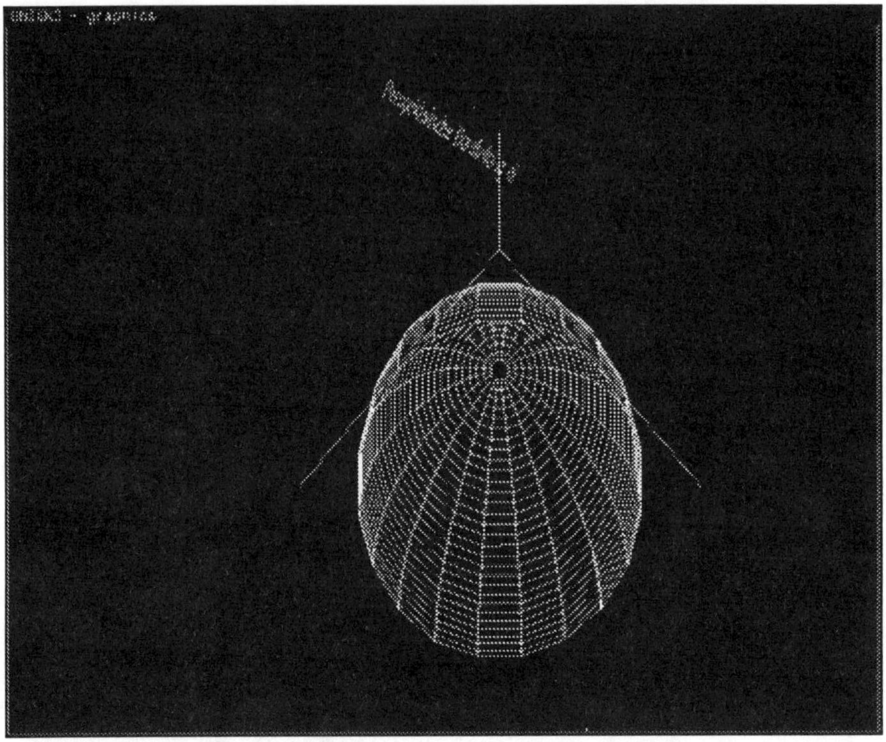

Figure 7. KUGEL displayed by LUT-CGM on the Sun

TRANSPARENCY element not included in metafile element list;
LINE TYPE, CGM not in proper state. Should be in state Picture Open;
LINE TYPE element not included in metafile element list;
COLOUR TABLE, CGM not in proper state. Should be in state Picture Open;
COLOUR TABLE element not included in metafile element list.

Figures 9 and 10 show the results of the metafile interpretation on both systems. There are a number of differences between the two images. It seems that LUT-CGM has displayed some of the line and text primitives at the wrong locations, and has not displayed some lines at all. These difficulties are almost certainly in response to the errors involving linetype and precisions reported above.

5.6 Metafile: LOTUS123

This metafile was displayed by both interpreters, without reporting any errors. Figures 11 and 12 show the results of the interpretation (figure 12 is the LUT-CGM results from a monochrome display). However, the conformance analysis using MetaCheck indicates two errors in the metafile concerned with extra data following the operands of Real Precision and Scaling Mode elements. When tested on a monochrome display the LUT-CGM/UNIRAS system reproduced the picture with grid lines and text. However, the total loss of colour information makes the graph virtually useless. In addition, some text attributes have not been used. The PICT file that is generated by MetaPICT actually includes the colour information and therefore can be displayed equally well on either colour or monochrome devices.

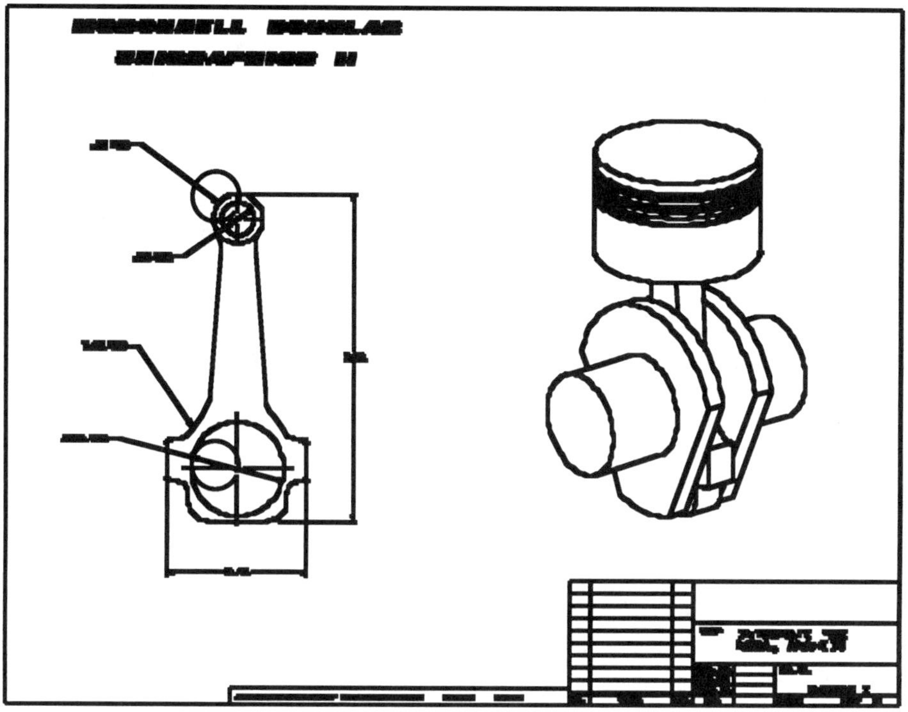

Figure 8. UNI0003 displayed by MetaPICT on the Macintosh

When tested on a colour display the LUT-CGM version fails to display any text, or the text is not visible, and that the loss of grid lines and some colour information renders the graph virtually useless. As noted above this is probably as much of a UNIRAS GKS problem.

5.7 Summary of Testing

Overall, there were some obvious differences occurring in all of the metafiles tested. For example, the two systems used different aspect ratios for the display area, and this can be attributed to the different underlying graphics systems that the two interpreters used. The MetaPICT interpreter used a white background, and ignored the metafile's background colour, whereas LUT-CGM used the metafiles background colour. On a monochrome workstation, LUT-CGM always used a black background.

A summary of other more metafile specific results is as follows:

- In some cases the LUT-CGM/UNIRAS GKS combination aborted the interpretation, generating a Unix run-time error, after decoding the GENERALIZED DRAWING PRIMITIVE element, and particularly when it called the GKS Generalized Drawing Primitive function (GGDP).

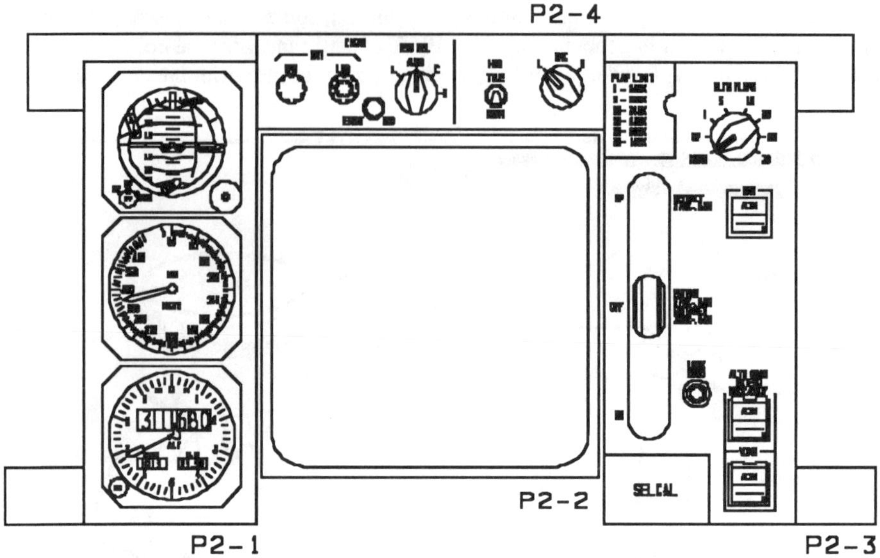

Figure 9. BOEING displayed by MetaPICT on the Macintosh

- In one case where the metafile was faulty, LUT-CGM aborted the interpretation after decoding the COLOUR TABLE element, when it called the GSCR GKS function which sets the colour representation. Again it is unclear whether this is a LUT-CGM problem or a UNIRAS GKS problem, although it is clear that the LUT interpreter continued to attempt to interpret the faulty metafile after detecting the other errors listed.
- The LUT-CGM/UNIRAS aborted interpretation of some of the test metafiles and exited with run-time error when it called the SET PATTERN SIZE GKS routine.
- An obvious shortcoming of the LUT-CGM/UNIRAS system is that in most cases the text attributes have not been used. As noted above this is probably as much of a UNIRAS GKS problem.
- In one metafile the picture displayed by MetaPICT does not appear to have used all the text attributes, but rather a convenient axis orientated font.
- MetaPICT simulated fonts which were not available in the system files, which in some cases resulted in illegible text.

5.8 Conclusions on the Interchange of Metafiles

The most obvious conclusion to be drawn from the above tests is that effects can only be guaranteed where there has been prior agreement between the generator and interpreter as to the range of facilities to be used. In addition the interpreter needs to be quite clever at simulating facilities not provided by the hardware if the resulting interpretation is to be useable on a variety of devices.

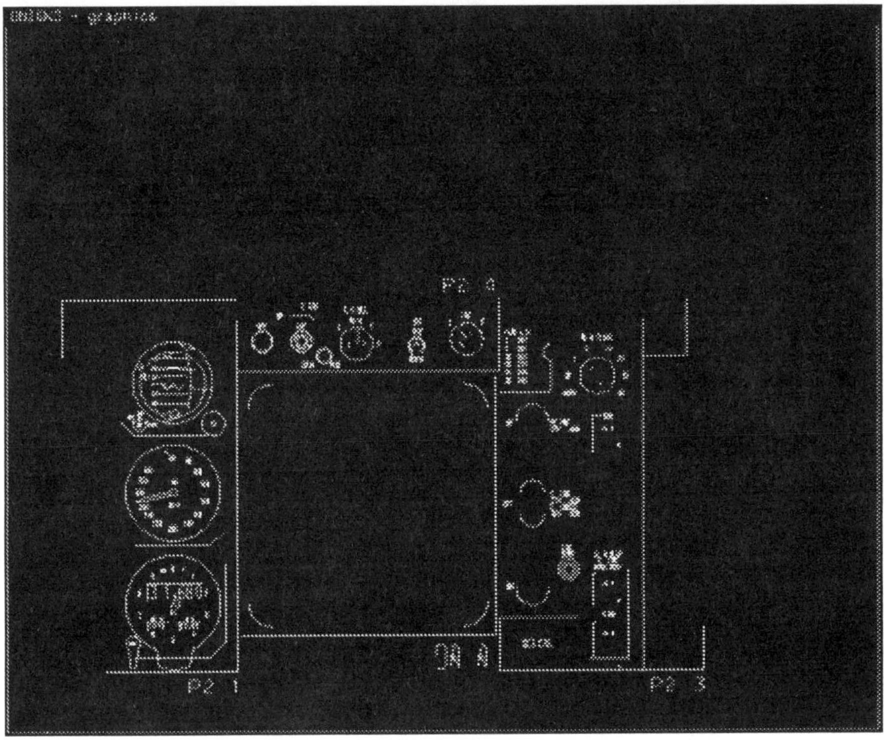

Figure 10. BOEING displayed by LUT-CGM on the Sun

Much play has been made in standards debates of the "restriction" placed by CGM that if supporting GKS with CGM metafiles there needs to be an assumption that the CGM was produced via a GKS metafile workstation. This appears to be no different to having an agreed profile for the functionality that will appear in a CGM.

The other conclusion is that the error diagnostic and capacity to display some visible effect even when the metafile contains errors is crucial to the user friendliness of the interpreter implementation in a heterogeneous environment.

6 Efficient Encoding of Metafiles for Transmission Over Networks

The second area of experimentation has been to examine the format of metafile encoding to see whether they could be compressed to produce more efficient (i.e. smaller) descriptions, which would be faster to move around networked systems. The experiments may be divided up between those operating at the function level (that is methods which seek to describe the same image with a more compact series of CGM elements) and those which operate at the encoding level (that is methods which encode a given sequence of CGM elements in fewer bytes).

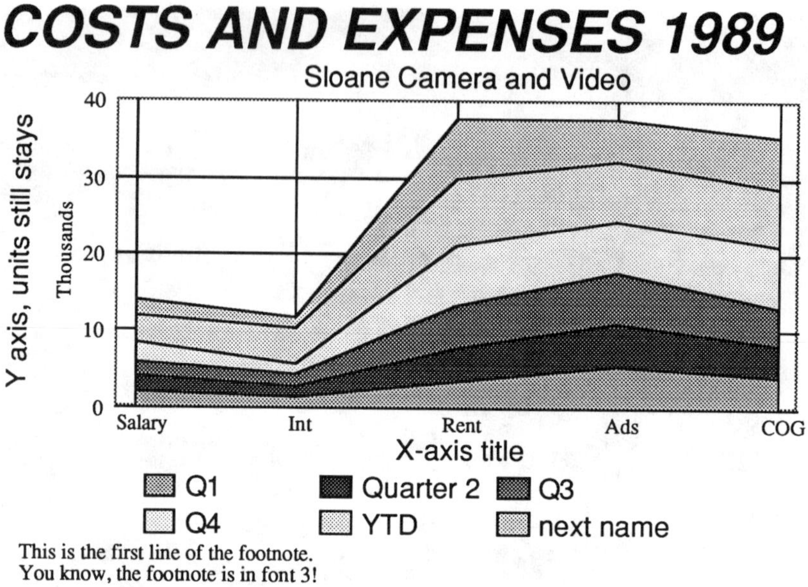

Figure 11. LOTUS 123 displayed by MetaPICT on the Macintosh

6.1 Functional Level Compression

Various options were considered for more efficient use of CGM elements in order to reduce the overall length of the metafile:

(a) Reordering the elements. One possibility might be for example to group all elements with the same attribute values such that attribute setting elements could be omitted. However the big disadvantage of this approach was that the CGM standard defines the metafile as "an ordered set of elements" which means that before reordering can be safely undertaken the compressor would have to be sure that no overlapping primitives were being switched in the ordering of the file. This operation could be very expensive to compute (being approximately the equivalent of a three dimensional sort) and it was felt that the gains in space would probably be small.

(b) A second, related technique is to delay the encoding of an attribute change until such time as a primitive element which uses the attribute is encountered. In this way for any attribute which is set more than once without being used the first occurance can be omitted from the metafile. Whilst simple to implement the expected compression is likely to be small, assumes that the CGM generator does not unnecessarily generate large numbers of attribute elements

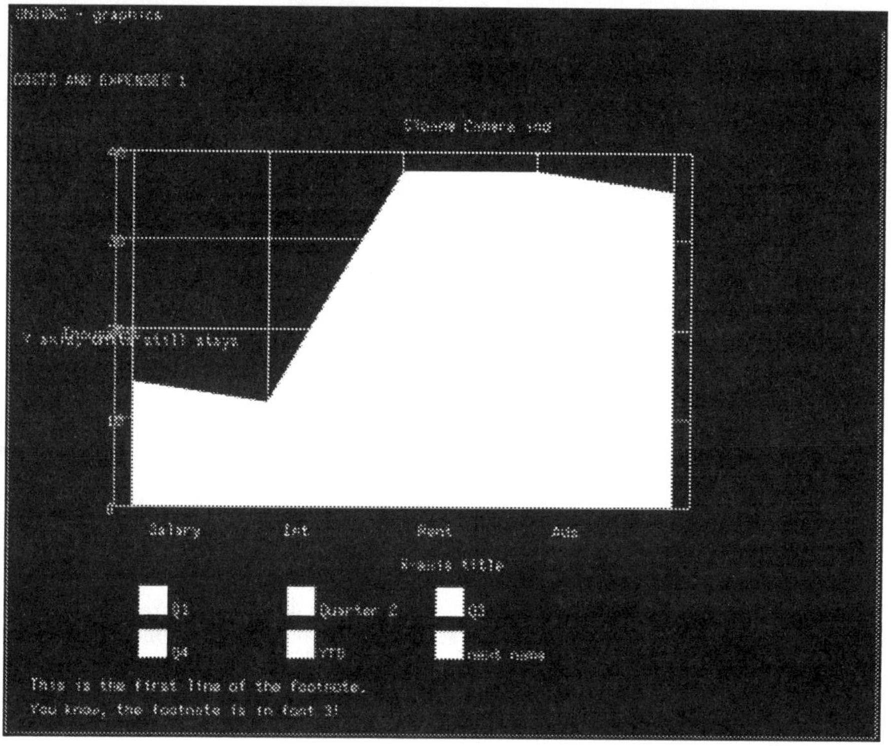

Figure 12. LOTUS123 displayed by LUT-CGM on the Sun

(c) A metafile element list is included in the header for any metafile to indicate the elements which an interpreter will encounter in the file. This element is required to contain all element types to be encountered, but not to be the minimum list of those used. In addition the standard defines a number of shorthands. A third compression investigated therefore was to use a catchall shorthand for the encoding of this element, by setting it to DRAWING PLUS CONTROL SET which effectively means everything. This method was found to save potentially hundreds of bytes of data. It is worth noting that the effectiveness of the metafile element list has been called in to question recently [5].

6.2 Encoding Specific Compression

Compression techniques have been considered for CGMs encoded in both the binary and character encodings. However only the techniques devised for the binary encoding have been implemented and tested. The techniques proposed for character encoded metafiles in [13] are therefore left as future work.

The following techniques were investigated:

(a) Removal of "No Operation" elements, which are only ever used for padding and are always redundant (unlike the padding bytes which are used to achieve word alignment at the start of each element).

(b) Encoding of Cell Array. The encoding of this element allows for the use of a colour precision which is local to the element. It is therefore possible to use the minimum size (1-32 bits in powers of two) on an element by element basis. This may seem to be of minor interest, but the element can be used to represent large amounts of data (e.g. screen dumps) where the local precision may be significantly lower than that required for general colour precision in a metafile.

    There are also two methods provided for encoding the colour list – packed mode or run length encoded mode. The local colour precision is more effective in compression of packed mode cell arrays (since they contain more colours and since the counts of run lengths are encoded as integers in a global integer precision). Using the choice between the two encoding modes as a further means to compressing the definition has not been investigated at the present time.

(c) Encoding of Pattern Array. This element also allows the use of a local colour precision.

(d) Encoding of data values. With the exception of the VDC datatype, the various datatypes used in the definition of a CGM can have the precision with which they are stored set in the Metafile Descriptor. Since the values apply to the whole metafile they can only be defined when all the values to be included are known. Thus compressing on this basis requires a 2-pass CGM generator (or a filter applied to existing CGMs).

    The VDC datatype's precision can be changed within a picture. This makes the decision as to whether or not to redefine the precision both more complex and potentially more beneficial. There is an overhead in changing precisions (and in changing back), but the technique is not constrained by the need to be able to encode all VDC values in the entire file, merely by there being a local advantage to changing to a new value.

    The other complications arise in ensuring that the range of values to be encoded are successfully detected for each type, recognising the needs of encoding fixed and floating point number, signed and unsigned, etc.

6.3 Results of Applying the Techniques

The above techniques were applied to a sample of 120 metafiles distributed with the three systems mentioned in section 4 (GMD CGM, LUT-CGM Toolkit and GSC MetaPICT). Over the complete sample an average of 9% of space was saved, but this figure hides a very wide range of results. Further analysis would be needed to establish the most commonly effective techniques, but the range of compressions achieved varied from zero to 80% compression, in one notable case where the metafile was predominantly Cell Array. For a great many files the compression achieved was minimal and the generator had obviously been operating efficiently. For example the technique of defering attribute changes described in section 6.1(b) is known to be implemented by the LUT-CGM Toolkit's generator. Over half of the test metafiles were compressed by less than 5%, 14% were compressed by between 5% and 10%, 13% by between 10% and 20%, and 9% by more than 20%.

7 Common Errors Found in Binary Encoded Metafiles

In addition to the results of applying the compression techniques some interesting observations were made as to the common errors found in binary encodings. It is possible that, since these were test metafiles, the errors were introduced deliberately in order to test interpreters. However, if this is the case the information about errors which CGM generator and interpreter implementors are expected to make may well still be interesting. The commonest errors found were:

(a) Exclusion of the bytes used to encode the integer recording the number of characters in a string, from the count of bytes used to encode the string. Even where there are no characters in a string the parameter list length needs to be recorded as 1 byte to hold the value of zero.

(b) Including the padding bytes used to ensure word alignment of the following element in the parameter list length of an element.

(c) Encoding Cell Array with local colour precisions other than 8, 16 or 32. With 1, 2, 4 or 24 bit precision padding is often required at the end of each row of the cell array. This padding should be included in the parameter list length. Note that this internal padding is not required in the Pattern Array encoding.

8 Future Directions for Work on Compression

The techniques described in section 6 have concentrated on binary encoded metafiles. Suggestions have been made [13] for different techniques to be applied to the metafiles using the character encoding. Techniques proposed include the examination of the choice between incremental and displacement mode in the encoding of point lists and the detection of optimal points at which to change modes. These suggestions would be likely to be particularly important to applications using long point lists (for example cartography).

In addition some further compression might be made if a compressor/decompressor system was developed. This would allow the restriction of only producing valid CGMs as a result of the compression to be lifted and other techniques to be employed. These might for example include removal of some of the state constraints on precision definitions, removal of the word alignment requirement and hence of padding bytes, removal of the restriction of precisions to certain specific values, etc.

9 References

1. Day R.A., Duce D.A., Ducrot A., Gallop J.R., Paolillo E., Maybury R., Reynolds G.J., and Sutcliffe D.C.: *ARGOSI – The Integration of Graphics and Networking*, in Proceedings of the Graphics and Interaction in Esprit Sessions, Eurographics 90 Conference, Montreux. Eurographics Technical Report Series.
2. ISO/IEC IS 7942 Information processing systems – Computer Graphics – Graphical Kernel System (GKS), ISO Central Secretariat, 1988
3. ISO/IEC IS 8632 Information processing systems – Computer Graphics Metafile for the storage and transfer of picture description information (GCM), Parts 1-4, ISO Central Secretariat,1987
4. ISO/IEC IS 9592 Information processing systems – Computer Graphics – Programmer's Hierarchical Interactive Graphics System (PHIGS), ISO Central Secretariat, 1988
5. Henderson L.R. and Mumford A.M.: *The Computer Graphics Metafile*, Butterworths, 409pp, May 1990
6. Arnold D.B. and Bono P.R., *CGM and CGI: Metafile and Interface Standards for Computer Graphics*, Springer-Verlag, Heidelberg New York ISBN 3-540-18950-5, 279pp, March 1988
7. Arnold D.B. and Duce D.A.: *ISO Standards for Computer Graphics: The First Generation*, Vol. 1 in Computer Graphics Standards Reference Series, Butterworth's Scientific. 273pp, March 1990

8. US Dept of Defence, *MIL-R-28003, Military Specification: Application Profile; Digital Representation for Communicationof Illustration*, 1988

9. Vezirgiannis N.P.: *Extending CGM in a Heterogeneous Environment*, Thesis submitted as part of the requirements for MSc, School of Information Systems, University of East Anglia, Norwich, 1990

10. Liddell A. and Mumford A.M.: *LUT-CGM Toolkit Guide*, Computer Centre, Loughborough University of Technology, 1989

11. *UNIRAS FGL/CGM User Guide and Reference Manual*, Version 6, IUCC, 1989

12. *MetaPICT User Manual*, GSC Associates, 1990

13. Liapakis S.Th.: *Compression/Compaction of CGM Metafiles*, Thesis submitted as part of the requirements for MSc, School of Information Systems, University of East Anglia, Norwich, 1990

14. *MetaCheck Version 1.13 – CGM Conformance analyser*, CGM Technology Software, 1989.

Chapter 21

The Graphics Standards PHIGS and GKS-3D in an X Window System Environment

Stefan J. Noll, Manfred G. Schendel

Abstract

After a short presentation of the two graphics standards and the X Window System, the impact of realizing PHIGS or GKS-3D in a Window environment is described. For output, a graphics workstation must use the X 2D graphics elements and an X window as display surface. For Input, the X event queue will be used and must be controlled by a separate process. The usage of the PHIGS PLUS extensions leads to three possible solutions for transferring data over the network: usage of pixel maps, usage of X 2D graphics or usage of X extensions. A comparison to the PEX (PHIGS PLUS Extension to X) protocol proposal will be made. The usage of X together with graphics standards leads to network-wide distributed graphics applications.

21.1 Introduction

For two reasons, an integration of 3D graphics in window systems is necessary:

- The window system should support 3D graphics applications
- PHIGS / PHIGS PLUS and GKS-3D should run efficiently in a window system environment

The main problem is, that both window systems and graphics systems control output and input devices.

21.2 Graphics Standards and Window Systems

21.2.1 GKS-3D

After definition of the two-dimensional graphics standard GKS (Graphical Kernel System, [3]) a 3D-extension was developed: GKS-3D, [4]. This is a fully upwards compatible system, that allows 2D-GKS programs to run in the 3D-environment. GKS-3D is an international standard already .

The main features added to GKS are:

- 3D primitives
- fill area set primitives
- edge aspects for fill areas
- 3D geometric aspects
- 3D transformation pipeline with viewing operations
- 3D input pipeline
- access to hidden-line/hidden-surface removal

GKS-3D extends each GKS primitive to three dimensions, and it adds one new primitive, fill area set. Fill area set allows to define a filled area with more than one polygon.

The same aspects for output primitives as in GKS are used in GKS-3D. Extensions are the edge control for fill area sets and the 3D geometric aspects for text and fill area/fill area set.

The workstation independent part of the transformation pipeline contains the normalization transformation (3D-window to 3D-viewport), the segment transformation (3×4 matrix) and the normalization clipping (rectangular parallelepiped oriented with edges parallel to the normalized device coordinate axes).

Viewing transformations are defined in a table at each workstation. In the first viewing stage objects are transformed by a 4×4 view orientation matrix. In the second stage the objects are transformed by a 4×4 view mapping matrix and clipped at a 3D volume. The projection type of the view mapping may be parallel or perspective.

After the viewing the workstation transformation maps from a 3D window to a 3D viewport in device coordinates.

The input devices are extended to three dimensions analogous to the output. The input coordinates are retransformed through the whole transformation pipeline applying all inverse transformations.

GKS-3D supports the use of workstation dependent hidden-line/hidden-surface removal which can be defined per output primitive.

21.2.2 PHIGS and PHIGS PLUS

The three-dimensional graphics standard PHIGS, [5], also defines a functional interface between an application and graphical devices.

PHIGS defines that the output primitives and their attributes generated at structure traversal time are identical to those of GKS-3D.

PHIGS addresses different needs using new functionality referring to GKS-3D. The concepts of hierarchical picture definition, and editing of data structures, as well as modelling of the objects are the major points of extended functionality (figure 1).

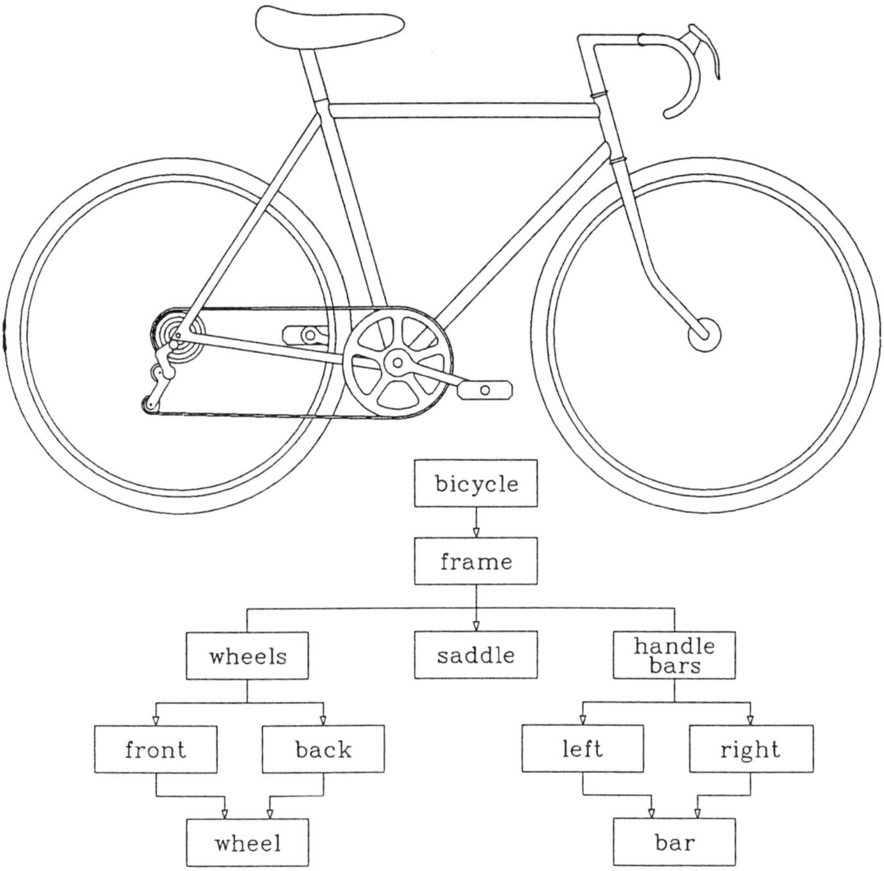

Figure 1: *Relationships between structures*

PHIGS supports the storage and manipulation of data in a centralized hierarchical structure store. The fundamental entity of data are structure elements and these are grouped together into units called structures, which are organized as networks. Structure elements contain the information for the definition of output primitives.

Each output primitive has associated with it a name set attribute defined at structure traversal time. This name set attribute defines the eligibility of the primitive for invisibility, highlighting and detectability. The workstation independent primitive attributes are specified modally and are bound to a primitive, when it is created at structure traversal time. Graphical output on a workstation is produced by traversing a posted (associated) structure to that workstation and interpreting the graphical structure elements (traversal time).

The workstation independent part of the transformation pipeline contains the modelling transformation (4×4 matrix) and the modelling clipping (set of half-spaces combined with Boolean operators defining the acceptance regions). The workstation dependent part of the transformation pipeline and the input model are identical to GKS-3D.

Besides the metafile interface to CGM, PHIGS defines a second way of saving, transferring and restoring graphical data: the archive file. The archive file allows random access to structure networks.

PHIGS PLUS (PHIGS Plus Lumiére Und Surfaces) is the extension of PHIGS for lighting, shading and general surfaces. PHIGS PLUS defines the Part IV of the PHIGS standard and is currently a standard proposal. PHIGS PLUS is upwards compatible to PHIGS, Part I-III, and specifies the following new functionality:

- output elements on a higher level
- lighting, shading, depth cueing
- direct colour specification (general colour)

The new output elements of PHIGS PLUS are: Polyline Set 3 With Data, Fill Area 3 With Data, Fill Area Set 3 With Data, Extended Cell Array, Triangle Strip 3 With Data, Quadrilateral Mesh 3 With Data, Non-Uniform B-Spline Curve, Parametric Polynomial Curve, Non-Uniform B-Spline Surface, Parametric Polynomial Surface

With the definition of a general colour the direct colour specification will be supported. General colour is defined by the parameters colour type and colour value. The colour type either indicates the colour model of the corresponding colour values or, that the corresponding colour value is an index into the colour table.

The light sources are defined independently to the graphics objects in world coordinates and have the following types: ambient, directional, positional and spot. Lighting calculations within PHIGS PLUS are applied on a primitive by primitive basis: no interactions between primitives are defined. Fore types of shading are defined: none (constant shading), colour (colour interpolation within segments), dot (dot products interpolation) and normal (colours and normals interpolation).

Lighting is applied only to area defining primitives, while shading also is applied to line defining primitives. The calculation of the depth cueing is done after the shading and applies to all primitives.

21.3 A Short Description of the Ideas of the X Window System

The X Window System has been developed at MIT. It is used as a basis for hardware independent development of graphical software for bitmap orientied workstations. The version 11, released in march of 1988, has gained worldwide usage. It is now available for nearly all workstations, beginning from a PC up to a superworkstation or mainframe. For further developments an X consortium was founded in January 1988. All important workstation developers are members of this consortium. Universities and software producers also take part, but they don't have a vote at decisions for the further development strategies for the X Window System.

The principal functionalisms of the X Window System is now described. To make the application programs completely hardware independent, the X Window System is devided into three different functional units:

Server: The server has to manage the hardware of the workstation. It receives demands over the network from the X clients. On the other hand, it generates events, when the user is handling a physical input device. Events are generated for side efects, resulting from window management or graphical output too.

Client: In the X Window System, all application programs are called clients. They are completely device independent. Without any changes, they could be compiled on all systems. Due binding the X library, named Xlib, they are able to communicate with all reachable X-servers on the network. The communication over the network can be done by the TCP/IP or DECNet protocol.

Window-manager: The window-manager is a special client. It has special privileges and a special task. None of the clients have full control over the size and position of their windows. They are just allowed to give hints of usable values. It is the freedom of the user to place the windows were he like it. He is able to change the window size and stacking order of overlapping windows. Windows could be iconified and deiconified to the full size by the user.

The hardware of an X workstation (X-display) can only be used by one user at the same time. As input devices exist a keyboard and a two dimensional pointing device. The pointing device is usually a mouse with three buttons. On output devices an X workstation must have at least one screen (X-screen) and a loudspeaker for acoustic information. A workstation can have null to thirtytwo signallamps. They are normally realized as LED's in the keyboard.

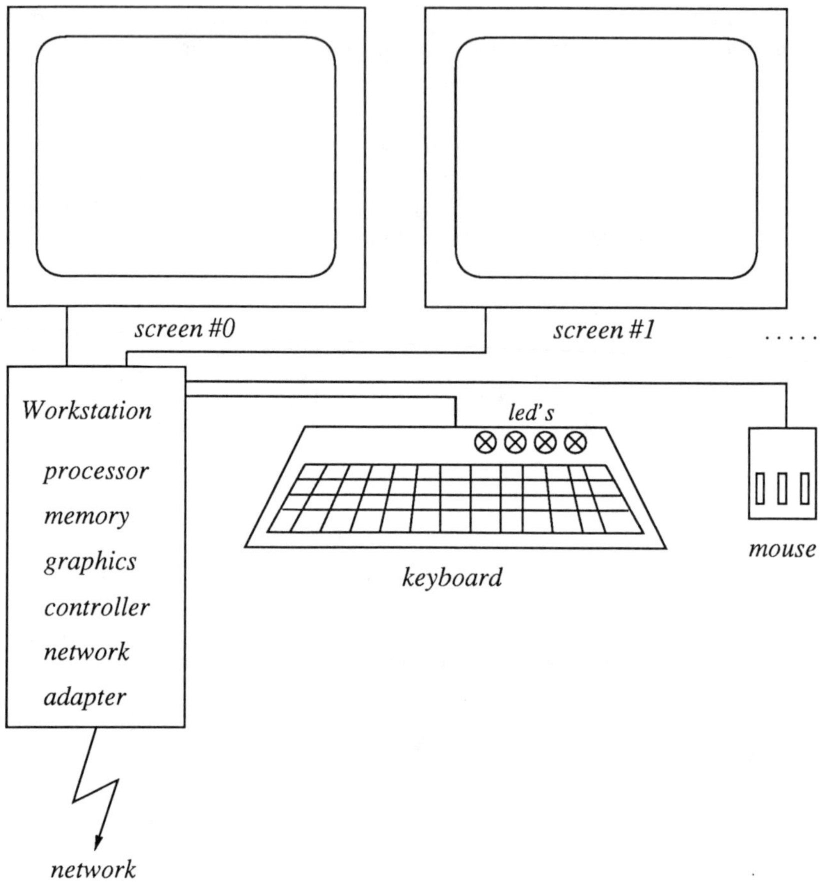

Figure 2: *The hardware of an X workstation (X display)*

Now we look at the window manager as it would be a normal client. The communication between the server and all clients is specified by the X protocol. The protocol consists basically of four different kinds of information:

request: All kind of information which is sent form a client to the server is named a request. An example is the request of drawing a line into the specified window. It is not necessary for a client to transmit a request at once. Normally all data are stored in a queue inside the client as long as possible. This strategy reduces the amount of network usage.

reply: Some of the functions of the Xlib inquires information from the server. The needed information could be about the specific hardware of the connected workstation or other data stored inside the server. All answers of the server according to calls by the client are named replies. The client waits for receiving the reply from the server.

event: A new concept of the X Window System is, that the application program does not advice an input, and then waiting for it. This is done in an other way. The client specifies the action about it will be informed. All action at the hardware of the workstation and the sideefects of window managing could advice the server to generate events. They are sent to all clients which want to know them. The events are grouped to classes. The clients allow or disallow sending of events from a whole class. One task of a client is for example the redrawing of the contents of a window after a part is visible again due changing of the stacking order or other changes. All events are queued inside the Xlib interface in the client. The storage order depends on the arrival time but the client can decide which event to be processed first.

error: All error conditions inside the server are solved by informing the client by a message. These messages are named error. There are two different types of errors. The first is just an information to the client of an error condition. The others are fatal errors. In this case, the client prints out a message on the device and stops running.

To reduce the amount of data transmitted between clients and the server, special data informations are stored inside the server. Using such an already stored information can be done just by sending its indentifier. All predefined objects are called X resources. Although there are user defined information types named properties. The properties are named by atoms. X resources are drawables, graphics contexts, fonts, cursors and colour maps.

Drawables are window and pixmap storages. Both are the basic elements on which it is possible to paint. The difference is only that it is possible to make windows directly viewable. Pixmaps must be copied into windows to make them viewable.

Inside the graphics context all information is stored about the way of drawing is done. It consists of information about linewidth, colour, dashing, fillstyle, textfont and so on.

Fonts and cursors are storages for textfonts and cursorfonts. Both are organized as bitmaps. One of the entry of the cursor font is the shape of the currently used cursor images to represent the position of the mouse pointer.

At least colour maps contains information about the used colour model as well information about the installed colour cells if an indirect colour model is used. The X Window System enables at least one of the following colour models for each workstation:

colourmap type	read/writeable	readable only
monochrome, gray	GrayScale	StaticGray
index for RGB	PseudoColor	StaticColor
one index for each RG&B	DirectColor	TrueColor

A server displays on each of its screens a rootwindow by itself. The size of the root window is identical with the physical dimensions of the screen. All client windows are subwindows of the rootwindow. It is possible for clients to have a hierarchy of own windows. A subwindow is always clipped by the border of its parent window. If the parent window is moved, the subwindows are moved with it.

Now have a look at the graphics primitives of the X Window System:

graphic primitive	Xlib function
pixel	XDrawPoint(s)
line	XDrawLine(s)
segment	XDrawSegments
regtangle	XDrawRegtangle(s)
filled regtangle	XFillRegtangle(s)
arc(segments)	XDrawArc(s)
filled arcs(segments)	XFillArc(s)
text	XDrawString
text with background fill	XDrawImageString
picture operations	XPutImage, XGetImage

To make the writing of application programs easier and to unify the appearance of the application programs in the last years a lot of shells about Xlib have been written. The shells are named toolkits. Lying above Xlib, they are device independent too. One of the most important topics of the toolkits is the availability of complex input devices like choices, scrollbars and buttons. The devices are simulated graphical on the screen. All drawing of prompts and echos, checking of validity, if possible, is done by the toolkits. The application program is only informed about completed input action.

Another possibility to extend the functionality of the X Window System is to extend the X protocol. This has been done for B-splines and Bézier curves, PostScript extensions and three dimensional graphic primitives yet. One of the most famous extension is PEX, the PHIGS+ extension to X.

21.3.1 PEX

For the X Window System, a 3D extension for efficient support of PHIGS PLUS is defined: PEX (PHIGS+ Extension to X). PEX is a protocol specification. Graphics libraries, which use the protocol, are GKS-3D or PHIGS/PHIGS PLUS. Supported functionality at client side is archive, logical input devices, workstations, state lists and structure store. Supported functionalities at server side are structure store, attribute lists, rendering pipeline, workstations and pick. Structures are supported on both sides of the protocol, therefore the realization of the centralized structure store of PHIGS is also possible on both sides.

21.4 The Integration of a Graphics Standard into the X Window System

First we want to describe here which changes are necessary for integrating a graphics standard into the X Window System. The advantages and disadvantages of different solutions are not discussed here. Here just the information is gathered at which we have to think at the integration. Possible ways of solutions are presented in the next sections followed by a description of one concrete solution, the XPHI-GKS project.

On the first view the most important difference between a traditional implementation of a graphics standard for one special workstation and the integration into the X Window System is, that these integration would be runable on all systems where an X server is running. This would work only, of course, if the integration is done in the normal way for X clients, that they are able to deal with different screen resolutions and different colour depths. But a "good" client is always written independent of special hardware features.

Now we will look at the special properties of the X Window System. They lead to the need of changing parts of the graphics standards.

21.4.1 Sharing of Resources

In the concept of the X Window System all input and output equipments have to be shared by the clients. The sharing of the output device screen is done by windows for example. On all common systems it is possible that the sum of the surfaces of all windows exceeds the physical screen surface. This means that not all windows can be seen completely at one time. Perhaps a part of the window is covered by an other window. But this is against the regulation of the graphics standard which says that it has the whole screen for its own usage. In the concept of the X Window System, if a former obscured part of the window is visible again, an information in form of an expose event is send to the concerned client. It has then to redraw the screen contents. This additional demand is not explicit handled in traditional implementations of a graphics standard.

The X Window System allows all clients to have their private colour table if the workstation hardware is able to switch between colour maps or to change their entries. This makes it possible for all windows of the clients to use full colour resolution. Since only one or a limited number of colour maps can be used simultaneously, not all windows, i. e. only one, could be shown in true colour at a time. Now the user has the opportunity to chose the window which he like to see in true colours. This task is done by using a window manager. It advices the X-server to install a private colour table of the active window. If one wishes to have all windows in its true colour, all clients have to share a single colour map. If only one client is a graphics standard and the other are clients which demands only a few number of colour cells like terminal emulations or clock, this is a proper way. This leads to a dynamic changing colour resolution in the view of the graphics standard. The application program should be able to choose between the two possible ways to match the users requirements.

21.4.2 Realization of Input Devices

The concept of graphical input of the X Window System does not meet the requirements of the input devices of the graphics standards. The input devices must be realized by software in a proper way. By the way we have to think about a mechanism to distinguish between logical input devices of two application programs using a graphics standard and having their output on the same screen. Confusion is possible if the realization is done by additional windows, in which the mouse actions of the user are prompted. With the window manager it is possible to move the windows on the screen. Windows for input have no visual connection to the output windows.

21.4.3 Mapping of Graphical Primitives

The graphical primitives of the X Window System are very simple two-dimensional primitives like pixels, rectangulars, lines, arcs and text. The rendering of three dimensional graphical data to these primitives must be done completely by the software of the graphics system. The text primitive of X Window System could only be used for annotation text. But the baseline of the text could not be chosen free.

21.4.4 Additional Functionality - Revised Standard?

The workspace viewport of the graphics standard is located in a window. This gives the possibility to define a lot of new operations on the workspace. It should be possible to access them not only by an user with his mouse, the application program has to be able to access them too. Therefore the graphics standards have to be extended and the relation to a window system has to be defined. Overlapping functionality in graphics standards and window systems should be avoided. This must be done in a way that all current graphics programs have not to be changed if running in an X Window System environment. The compatibility must be gained in both directions.

Another very important feature of the integration in the X Window System is the open door for networkwide usage of devices. The application program can use also other workstations in the network. This leads to dealing with workstation addresses inside the graphics standard like the X Window System does.

21.5 PHI-GKS, an Integration of Graphical Standards into X

There are two ways in principal of how to integrate a graphics standard into the X Window System. On one hand we can have both interfaces inside the application program, to the X Window System and to the graphics standard. The application program is using the graphics standard for all higher graphical input and output. But the manipulation of the windows or other pixmap operations are done by direct usage of the X interface. To realise this idea, at implementation time it is necessary to take care, that the application program does know all important identifiers of the X resources used by the graphics standard. Additionally the application program has to deal with occurring events generated by the X Window System. If a screen redraw has to be done, the application program has to call the proper functions of the graphics standard, in this case something like the update workstation function. This concept leads to a high freedom for the application programmer in decisions about the way of integration.

Another way of integration would be the following. All tasks occurring due the usage of the X Window System are resolved by the graphics standard implementation. In this way, it is possible to hide the usage of the X Window System to the application program. The interface between application program and graphics standard could be then exactly the same as by traditional implementations, only with some extensions, which will be discussed later. Here the application programmer has no influence on the way of integration.

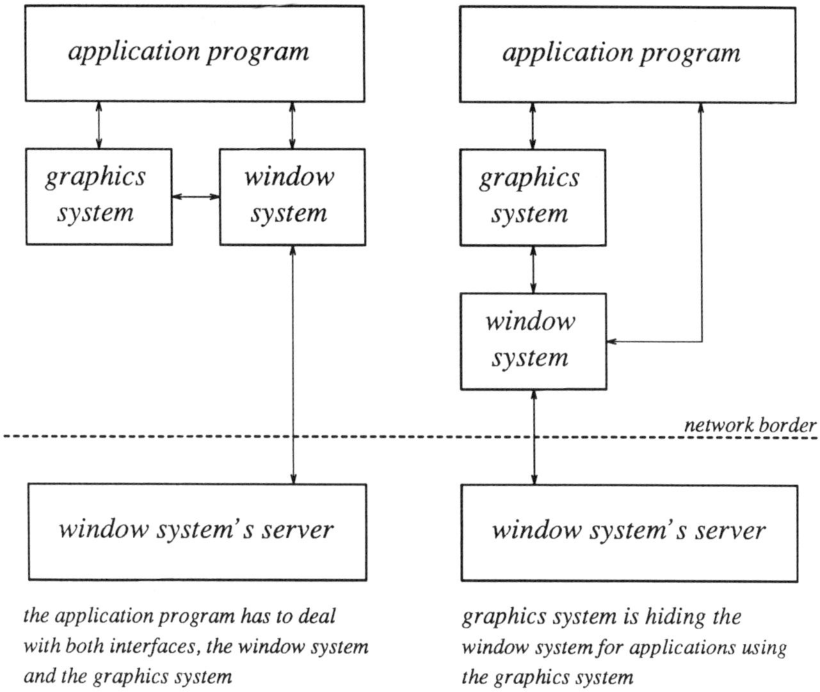

Figure 3: *Binding graphics standards into X*

The second solution, with small extensions (ESCAPE-function), is the better one. The interface for the application program to the graphics standard is the same as in traditional envirnment. So it is possible to run all applications, written for traditional graphics standard implementations, without any changes on the integrated graphics standard. The usage of both interfaces, the X Window System and the graphics standard by the application programmer is difficult. He has to think about the correlations between both systems each time he is using a function.

If the application process is not running on the same system as the graphics system process, it would be not easy to share the event queues and other resources of the X Window System. To make such a process distribution possible in the future, it is not good to allow the application any access to X resources used by the graphics system.

To make it possible for the application programmer to choose parameters of the appearance of windows for graphical input and output, we have to extent the interface to the graphics standard in some ways. The graphics standard offers for this case an ESCAPE-function with implementation dependent parameters. With this function it is possible for the application to inquire information about hardware properties of the workstation. On the other way it is possible to give hints of size, position and appearance of the input and output windows. The term "hints" in this context should mean that the parameters are only accepted if it is possible to realise what the application would like to do. All this facts would make the application program, using the integrated graphics standard, a full X client. Of course it is possible for the application program to use the X Window System for other tasks too.

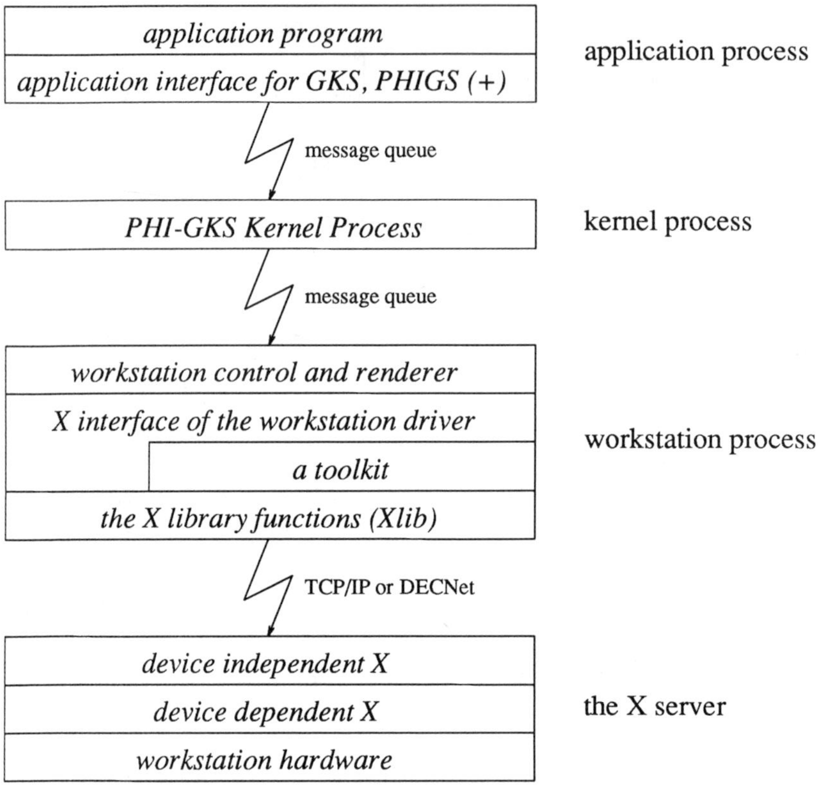

Figure 4: *Software layer hierarchy*

21.5.1 Distribution of Tasks

To solve all requirements of the X Window System, the integration of the graphics standard must be separated into functional parts. The parts are grouped by asynchronous running processes. To deal with messages, which are sent in form of events (implemented as UNIX System V messages queues, i. e.), from different sources the communication has to be asynchronous too.

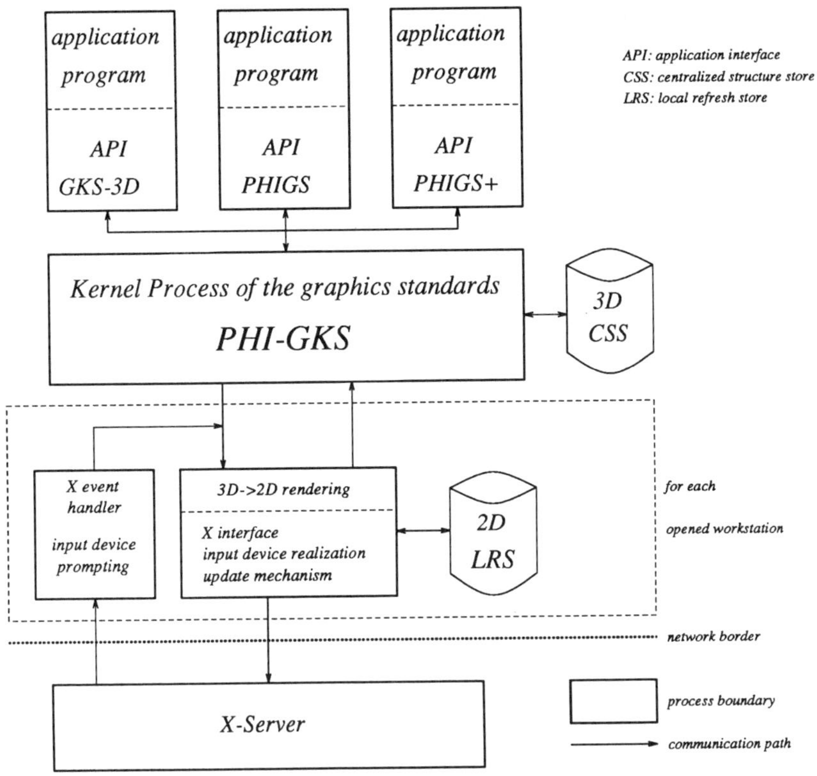

Figure 5: *Distribution of tasks, grouping of processes*

21.5.2 Multiple Interfaces to the Application Program

When grouping processes like shown in figure 4, it is possible to access a graphics standard like GKS3D, PHIGS/PHIGS+ with different interfaces between the kernel and the application program. The kernel must be able to solve the requirements of both graphics standards.

21.5.3 Localization of the Data Store

In graphics standards like PHIGS, all graphical data are stored in a hierarchical organized central structure store. All adding and changing to the objects are done by editing in the structure store. In dependence of the update mode which is set, the changes are displayed at once or later. The data could be shown on different workstations over the network. We have now to discuss the different methods about realization of the store, thinking at new refresh requests occurring due the integration into the X Window System. We can distinguish at least the following methods:

1. All data are stored in the central structure store only. This means, that the editing has to be done in this store only. Updating the workstation is done by sending all or the added graphical primitives. If the window must be refreshed in the X environment, the workstation sends a request to the kernel process. Doing this, there will be problems when the update mode is set to wait. Some changes to the segment store have been done but they should not be shown at that time. If now X requests an update it is not possible to send the unchanged data. To be conform to the graphics standard all data have to be stored twice.
2. All data are stored in the central structure store and the visible data for each workstation are stored locally at the workstation too. In this concept, all editing must be done in the central structure store and in all local workstation stores were the dismayed object is stored. All refresh requests from the X Window System can be solved without disturbing the kernel. Updating could be done correct, independent to the update mode.
3. In theory it is possible to have only local storages, but then we have again problems with the update mode wait. To be conform to the graphics standards we have to double the storage again.

Having more than one storage, results in the following problems. First there are at the moment only a few workstations, which are able to store primitives/segments of a graphics standard directly in hardware. This means, that the workstation hardware is able to store 3D objects. It should be able to do the rendering on the screen by hardware. In the most cases we have to realize the storage by software. If we now think about, i. e., three different views at one complex object, all views on different logical workstations of the graphics standard displayed on the same screen of the hardware workstation in three different windows of the X window system. We now have to hold the picture four times in a store. First in the central segment store, and then three times for each window local to the workstation at which the object is seen. This concept will cost much memory space. If we now allow pixmap primitives of the PHIGS+ graphics standard, it could be necessary to hold a 3 Mbyte picture three times additionaly to the structure store.

This is the reason for proposing storage concept number 1 with an addition. Like in a traditional implementation, we will have only one central structure store. The required redrawing of the window contents is done locally by the X interface of the workstation driver process. After rendering to 2D objects we have to send them to the X server. Not all (only a few) X servers have a full working backing store option, which saves the window contents inside the server. When the server requests the clients to a window redraw (by an expose event), the X interface has to send the picture again. The X interface has to store all 2D graphical data of its window (2D LRS, local refresh strore) for this reason. This could be done in two ways:

1. The X interface stores all 2D graphical primitives in a list before sending them to the X server. If an update request occurs, the data could be taken from this list instead of resending them from the kernel.

2. The X interface stores the whole image of its window. This can be realized by drawing each element on the window and on a pixmap (X resource) of the X Window System.

Possibility number 2 is better for PHIGS+ and number 1 for the graphics standards of simpler 3D graphical primitives. The advantages of 1 are the less memory space which is necessary for line based pictures. It is easier to store the endpoints of a line and its attributes than the image of a line. The memory usage depends on the complexity of the images. In concept number 2, the required memory storage size depends only on the window size. But a window of 1024 by 1024 pixel on a true colour system with 24 bit/pixel needs 3 MByte of memory. The mechanism for updating is then very easy because only the image has to be copied to the window.

21.5.4 Integration of Workspace Surface into Windows

Using windows, there is no absolute limit in display size. According to the graphics standards, the workspace viewport has the size of the physical screen. To have the possibility to see the whole picture in its true dimension, we have chosen the maximum display size to the size of the X screen. This is the size of the physical screen too. But an application program can specify a smaller workspace size. According to the concept of hiding the X integration to the application program, the size of the workspace is fixed with this attribute settings. Using more than one logical workstation on a X screen, it is necessary to specify the position and size of the workstations window too. The new feature is now, that the user is able to change the size and position of the window that represents the workspace of a logical workstation of the graphics standard. He is able to change these attributes by a window manager using a mouse and due to the extented application interface too. This leads to dynamic changes to the window size. How can be the relationship between the workspace and the window size? There are three posibilities:

1. The user can change the window size as he likes. This would mean that the aspect ratio could be changed too. The workspace mapping is scaled exactly to the window size.

2. The same as above, but only changes of size are allowed which does not change the aspect ratio. This could be done by giving a window size by the user. Then the X interface is extracting the window width and calculating the proper window height followed by a resizing of the window to the correct height.

3. Changes to the size of a window would not change the scale of the mapping. Only the visible part of the window could be enlarged or reduced. The user is equipped with a mechanism like scrollbars to specify the region he wants to see. By this way he can choose the viewable part of the workspace and its size.

Following item three, there are now three reasons of obscuring part or all of the workspace. The new one is that the user is able to hide parts of the workspace. The other two are, the window of the workspace is obscured by another window or the window is clipped by the root window.

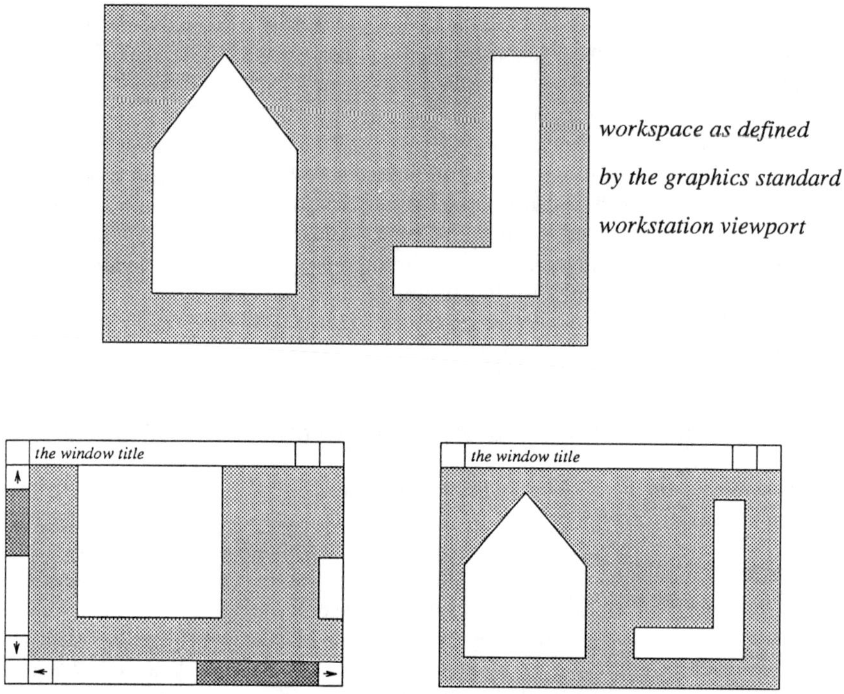

region of workspace is displayed

the region is selectable by scrollbars

workstation viewport unchanged

workstation viewport changed

to window size

Figure 6: *Workspace mapping*

We prefer a combination of number two and three. Then the user can change the window size and specify the way of mapping the workspace to its window. It is important that the aspect ratio could not be changed.

21.5.5 How to Manage the Colour Maps

Having a true colour system or unchangeable colour maps there is no question about managing the colour map. But the most used X workstations have the pseudo colour model. Here two solutions are possible.

1. All workstation windows have their private colour map. Each application program could use the full colour resolution by this way for its graphics. On the used X screen a window manager has to run which is able to install colour maps. The user has now the ability to specify the window which should be displayed in its true colours. By using private colour maps, all other windows are shown in random colours.

2. The other possibility is to share the default colour map. This concept is used by all common X clients. But if more than one logical workstation is used at the same

time on the same screen, the application programs have to divide the colour map. All colour cells used by the application program have to be changeable. This is a request by the graphics standards. Running a lot of clients on the same screen which are using a large number of colour cells can result in a condition that no free colour cells are allocateable. Under this condition, the new logical workstation is running like on a X workstation with a few number of colour cells. If no colour cell is allocateable, then the workstation is running like on a monochrome bitmap device. In this case the X colour cells BlackPixelOfScreen and WhitePixelOfScreen are to be used. These colour cells are not changeable.

An implementation of a graphics standard should run on a workstation with a lot of colour cells. But in either case, the user of the application program should be able to choose between displaying all logical workstations in true colours but with a few number off different colours for each workstation, or to have the full colour resolution for each window in which the workspace of the logical workstation is mapped. Before opening the workstation, the application program could specify which rule of colour cell allocation is to be used. By default a shared colour map for all X clients is used.

21.5.6 Extension of the Interface to the Graphics Standard

In the last paragraphs we have been talking about a lot of the information which the application program can give to the integration of the graphics standard into the X Window System. Now we have to talk about the way this can be done. For special interfaces the graphics standard like PHIGS offers an ESCAPE-function. The data records of this function are implementation depended. The information in it could be extented to the requirements of the integration into the X Window System. We have extented the language binding of the graphical standard to get the following information about special X display and screen attributes:

- X screen size and resolution
- colour resolution

The following information could be sent to the graphics standard:

- window size
- window position
- window inconify state
- changes on stacking order (window push/pop)
- window and icon title
- private or shared colour map
- number of colour cells to be used
- workspace to window mapping rule, scaling or scrollbar usage

21.5.7 Realization of Graphical Input Devices

In our concept of task distribution shown in figure 4, it is shown that the workstation process does the rendering from 3D to 2D primitives. At this abstraction level the mapping from 3D to 2D input devices should be done too. We won't accept 3D input devices in a 2D X environment. For the common 2D input devices of class locator, stroke, pick, choice, string and valuator the devices are realized by software. The way of realization is done according to the prompt and echo types defined in the graphics standards. For the input classes choice, valuator and string additional windows are created with unique titles. All input devices at the X interface and below are event based. The drawings of prompts and echoes are done by the event handler process. Only complicated actions like refreshing the window or search the pick path for a pick are done by the workstation process. This makes it possible to do all prompting without disturbing the kernel process. Even the window refreshing and prompting to input devices could be done at the same time by the two different processes.

The workstation process above the X interface level has to map all 3D input devices to a number of 2D input devices. A 3D locator, i. e., could be realized by a 2D locator with an additional valuator for the z axis component. The workstation process waits for both triggers of the 2D locator and the valuator input device. After combining them together, the result is sent to the input queue of the kernel process.

It is not allowed by the graphics standards to have three different views of an object for 3D input. The graphics standards defines the usage of real existing 3D input devices. Calculation of 3D prompts would be very slow on X workstations which does not support 3D operations by hardware. To make an interactive use possible, we think that the above decripted method is the best way of implementation for 3D input devices.

A special feature must be added for pick input. We don't like to disturb the kernel process for calculations of the pick path for a pick input. To do this, in the 2D local refresh storage (2D LRS), the structure hierarchy pathes are to be added for getting information about the pick pathes. A pick it done by calculating the nearest 2D primitive. At 3D pick, a z axis component is given by an additional valuator. For the nearest primitive, the pick path is taken from the 2D LRS (accepting to lose the z axis information) and sent to the kernel process after input processing is completed.

21.6 Bibliography

1. S.S. Abi-Ezzi, A.J. Bunshaft: An Implementer's View of PHIGS. In: IEEE Computer Graphics & Applications, Februar 1986, pp. 13-23.

2. A. Burkert, L. Froböse, S. Noll, J. Poller, J. Rix: GEX GKS/GKS-3D Extension for X. Darmstadt, 1988.

3. ISO/IEC Information Processing Systems - Computer Graphics -Graphical Kernel System (GKS), Functional Description, ISO/IEC 7942 und DIN 66252, 1985

4. ISO/IEC Information Processing Systems - Computer Graphics - Graphical Kernel System for Three Dimensions (GKS-3D), Functional Description, ISO/IEC 8805, 1988

5. ISO/IEC Information Processing Systems - Computer Graphics - Programmer's Hierarchical Interactive Graphics System (PHIGS) ISO/IEC 9592 Part I, II, III, 1989

6. ISO/IEC Information Processing Systems - Computer Graphics - PHIGS PLUS, PHIGS plus Lumiére und Surfaces. ISO/IEC JTC1/SC24 N223, 1989

7. S. Noll, J. Poller, J. Rix: Approach to solving the compatibility problem between GKS and PHIGS. Computer Aided Design, Vol. 19, Nr. 8, October 1987, pp. 456-464.

8. S. Noll, J. Poller: PHI-GKS: An implementation to support GKS-3D and PHIGS. In: Computer&Graphics, 2/88.

9. S. Noll, J. Poller et al: Graphische Standards. ACGA Austrian Computer Graphics Accociation, 1989.

10. PEX PHIGS Extension for X. Version 3.0, MIT Massachussetts Institute of Technology, 1987.

11. M. Plaehn: PHIGS: Programmer's Hierarchical Interactive Graphics Standard. In: Byte, McGraw- Hill, Vol. 12, No. 13, November 1987, pp. 275- 286.

12. R.F. Puk, J.I. McConnel: GKS-3D: A Three- Dimensional Extension to the Graphical Kernel System. In: IEEE Computer Graphics & Applications, August 1986, pp. 42-49.

13. R.J. Rost, J.D. Friedberg, P.L. Nishimito: PEX: A Network-Transparent 3D Graphics System. In: IEEE Computer Graphics and Applications, July 1989, pp. 14-25.

14. R.W. Scheifler, J. Gettys: The X Window System. ACM Trans. Graphics, Vol. 5, No. 2, April 1986, pp. 79-109.

15. H. L. Stern: Comparison of Window Systems. In: Byte, McGraw-Hill, Vol. 12, No. 13, November 1987, pp. 265-272.

16. X Window System, X11 Version 3.0. MIT Massachussetts Institute of Technology, 1989.

Chapter 22

The Image Model and the Image Interchange Format

Georg Rainer Hofmann, Christof Blum

0 Abstract and Remark

This report deals with the image data model and the Image Interchange Format (IIF) for the first International Image Processing and Interchange Standard (IPI), which is under elaboration by ISO/IEC JTC1/SC24 - i. e. ``information processing"/``computer graphics" - committee work. The authors are contributors and co-workers within the ISO/IEC committee and the DIN German Institute for Standardization (DIN Deutsches Institut für Normung). The paper focuses on the image data model which describes image data structures and image attributes. Finally, the paper reports on the prospective design of an Image Interchange Format (IIF) which will be one part of the IPI standard and, thus, will be based on the common image data model.

Parts of this report are included in the paper *``Requirements and Basic Concepts for the first International Imaging Standard"* by *Blum*, *Hofmann*, and *Krömker*, which has been submitted to the journal ``IEEE Computer Graphics & Applications" for publication.

1 Introduction

In May 1990, ISO/IEC JTC1/SC24 approved the proposal for a new work item on ``Imaging". The need of such a standard and the imaging market requirements have been outlined in the ``New Work Item Proposal" document [14].

Due to the New Work Item Proposal, the IPI standard will consist of three parts:

1. the Common Imaging Architecture,
2. the Application Programming Interface (API), and
3. the Image Interchange Format (IIF).

The most important contributions of Germany's DIN to the ISO/IEC work have been the ``Ikonisches Kernsystem" [10] and the FTCRP, [8] and [9]. These contributions concentrate on Parts 1 and 3 of the IPI standard.

2 History and Background of Work

Prior to the IIF efforts, there has been the FTCRP. FTCRP stands for *File for the Transfer of Coloured Raster Pictures*. This file format has been developed by the authors at the Fraunhofer Computer Graphics Research Group (FhG-AGD) in Darmstadt, in order to meet the need for a file format of very high functionality and flexibility for a large variety of computer graphics and imaging applications.

During the last time, AGD has been putting much effort in the development and conception of the FTCRP. The version 0 of FTCRP has been published within a GI symposium in Berlin in 1987; the version 1 of FTCRP has been published within SPIE/SPSE Electronic Imaging in Los Angeles in 1989; see [6] and [7]. AGD brought the concepts of FTCRP into discussion of the imaging study group within the DIN German Institute for standardization. These activities lead directly to the attendance of AGD at the ISO/IEC development of an Image Interchange Format IIF.

Since 1987, for the FTCRP and IIF, both FhG-AGD's concept development and FhG-AGD's ISO/IEC work have been funded and sponsored by the Berlin Communication System BERKOM. The BERKOM project puts special emphasis on the positive correlation of conceptual and standardization efforts in the whole area of multimedia communication and data structuring, including concepts and data structures for digital image communication.

3 Overall View of the IIF Architecture

For the design of the IIF Architecture, FhG-AGD assumes that distributed environments for imaging will play a major role in the near future.

As shown in Figure 1, the environment consists of several components, which are imaging applications as well as image sources and sinks. All these components are linked together by communication means of local area networks LAN, or by telecommunication networks. These networks form the physical basis for the image interchange. Within the IIF project, one will neither develop networking technology nor channel codings for communication via networks.

Components of the distributed imaging environment may be:

- Image sources, devices such as cameras, scanners, image rendering systems, any kind of optical sensors.
- Image sinks, devices such as monitors, hardcopy devices, slide, film or video recorders.
- Image storage and archiving media, such as tapes, magnetic and optical discs, image data banks, realtime discs for the storage of motion pictures.
- Image processing workstations or graphics workstations equipped with an application programmers interface API of the IPI. By means of the API, IIF images may be imported and exported, meanwhile these may be enhanced and processed via API functions in an application-dependent manner.
- For telecommunication purposes, all components may be implemented as data terminals, connected to PSTN, ISDN, and B-ISDN, respectively.

According to the environment - shown in Figure 1 -, the design rules of the IIF architecture may be listed as follows:

a) IIF needs to cover all known functionality of the popular de-facto standards for the interchange of all common types of images in use by applications, such as bitonal document images, static greyscale images, static tri-colour images, static multiband images, static volumetric images, time sequences of images, tiled images, etc., with or without compression schemes as appropriate.

b) The IIF will support all the various combinations of the parameters of the dimensionality, organization and compression. The IIF must be able to express relationships between individual images, such as tiling, time sequences, spectral sequences, image records, image sets, stereo pairs, etc.

c) The IIF must provide a reference mechanism, whereby associated non-image data (text, graphics, voice, ...) may be exchanged.

d) The IIF will apply equally to storage and communication applications and will be independent of physical network or storage media.

e) The IPI standard will only make use of image compression and coding schemes standardized by other national standardization bodies (i. e., via this proposed IIF project, no new compression and coding schemes will be developed or proposed).

f) IIF will make use of the ASN.1 (Abstract Syntax Notation One; refer to CCITT Rec. X.208 and X.209) syntax notation and coding mechanism for channel coding and data transfer.

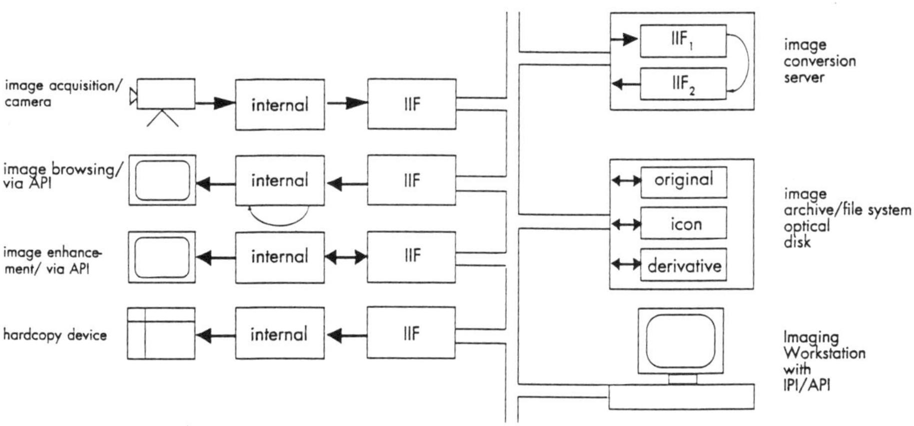

Figure 1 - Distributed environment for imaging

A necessary condition for the development of an International Standard is matured and stabilized technical work in the related area. Although image processing is a discipline which has been around for a long time, it is only recently that the influence of the developing hardware has given the opportunity and the confidence that consensus on an Imaging Standard can be achieved. One measure of this consensus is that the similarities of the different imaging systems around do exceed their differences.

4 The Image Data Model

The image data model shall give definitions and form the mathematical basis for the notation of image data on storage or interchange media (via the IIF). The model is intended to be as broad and flexible as possible in order not to be limited to certain applications. Therefore a mechanism to *constructively* and *dynamically* define image data types is proposed. Constructive descriptions can be found, e. g., in the CSG method (constructive solid modelling) for computer graphics applications, or in the recently submitted ISO TC130 proposals for a constructive prepress data interchange standard [15].

Within the IPI, digital images are *discrete* representations of pictorial information. They are discrete in space and time. Digital images are *compound* objects of a hierarchical structure. The structure is application-dependent. The image data model must be able to describe any kind of application-specific image structure. In addition to its structural composition, images and its components need to be attached with *attributes* in order to express semantics of both the image components and its composition. As an example, an RGB image consists of three colour separations. For accurate colour presentation, each separation needs to be attached with the corresponding colour primary. The composition of the three colour separations to one digital colour image is done via the colour mixing model, e. g. ``additive".

In the following, some basic data types are introduced in order to construct complex image data types upon these basic data types. For the purpose of the IPI standard, two categories of basic data types exist: elementary data types, and compound data types. Compound data types are constructed from elementary data types via construction mechanisms. Other data types such as image data types and non-image data types shall refer to basic data types.

4.1 Basic Data Types

Basic Data Types are either ``elementary data types" or ``compound data types".

Elementary data types are:

bits, characters, integer numbers, real numbers, and **enumeration types**.

These elementary data types are common to most of the well-known programming languages. A large variety of integer formats is currently needed in different application areas depending on the sensors and signal processing hardware used. Common formats are 8 bit, 12 bit, 16 bit, 32 bit, etc. signed or unsigned integer numbers. A similar situation applies to real numbers. Thus, the detailed presentation and precision are left open. The definition of elementary data types, as mentioned above, may lead to the following problems:

- The portability of programmes built upon this standard can be limited.
- It does not allow for open IIF communication.
- The complete conference testing of an implementation of this international standard will be impossible.
- The portability of implementations of this international standard will be limited.

These problems are inherent to all standardized programming languages, and, thus, apply to future language bindings of the IPI standard as well. Language bindings or data protocols may make the above data type definitions more precise.

A **compound data type** is a data type constructed by the following construction mechanisms from basic data types:

- **(N_1 x ... x N_n) arrays** of components of identical data types. Individual components are accessed by their indices (i_1,...,i_n).
- **Sets** are collections of elements of identical data types. The elements cannot be accessed individually. It can only be checked whether an element belongs to a set or not.
- **Lists** are ordered sets. Individual elements can only be accessed via successor/predecessor relations.
- **Records** are collections of individually named data types. The attributes may be of different type and can be accessed via their names.

Compound data types of this kind are provided by most of the modern programming languages, some of which have been standardized or are in the process of standardization, e. g. PASCAL, C, ADA. They proved to be useful for structuring large scale non-imaging applications and, thus, should be part of any Imaging Standard.

4.2 Non-Image Data Types

The following types are considered to be non-image data types:

- **text data types,**
- **graphics data types**, and
- **audio data types.**

It is not intended to define their internal structure within the IPI standard, but to give a reference to an appropriate text, graphics, or audio standard. For text standards, refer to ISO IS-8613, ISO IS-7942, ISO IS-8632, etc.; for graphics standards, refer to ISO IS-7942 etc.

It is the intent of these broad categories of non-image data types to provide a flexible interface to other non-imaging standards. These data types can be integrated into image data types to allow for textual, auditory, and graphical descriptions of the image content, according to some application-specific requirements.

Examples for image-related data types are colour look-up tables, histograms, feature lists, or the regions of interest, etc. Examples for text data types are textual descriptions of images or sets of images, e. g., descriptions of sensor types, recording conditions, patients data, etc., which have to be stored and manipulated in conjunction with the image data. Examples for graphical data types are structures for describing contours, region boundaries, drawings, etc., which have to be stored and manipulated in conjunction with the image data, e. g., for the manipulation as graphical overlays for display purposes. Examples for auditory data types are the audio tracks for motion pictures, or the digitized voice protocols of medical diagnosis procedures.

4.3 Image Data Types

Image data types are either ``elementary image data types" or ``compound image data types".

4.3.1 Elementary Image Data Types

Image data types may be constructed using the following **primitives**:

- arrays of picture elements with picture elements (``pixels") being of any basic data type (see Section 4.1)
- non-image data types (see Section 4.2)

The following **image data attributes** may be attached either to image primitives, or to compound images (for compound images see Section 4.3.2):

- identifier
- metric description
- channel description
- colour description
- free-form description

These five attributes (or better: attribute classes) are described in more detail below. The image data attributes carry information on how to correctly interpret the associated image data. Thus, the image data attributes are relevant for API functions, and for the image interchange via IIF as well. Attributes, which are not attached to pixel rasters but to higher-level structures of compound images, are effective for all lower-level components (i. e. hierarchical attribute inheritance). It is possible to overwrite inherited attributes. Most attributes listed below are defined to be attached to pixel rasters, but not to single pixels. Nevertheless, the specification of attributes has to refer to the internal pixel structure of the actual raster they are attached to, in order to unambiguously describe how to interpret the pixel structure.

Identifier

The identifier is a list of characters according to ISO 646, serving as an unambiguous reference to instanciations of basic image data type .

Metric Description

The metric description consists of the following entities:

- Specification of the **coordinate system**, which is isomorph to the R^n. The coordinate system serves as the system of reference for all further metric data. It provides the spatial framework for the positioning, placement, or transformation of any other image primitive or compound image object.
- Specification of the **region of interest (ROI)**. The ROI allows to specify intervals in any dimension of the coordinate system. Thus, points or windows can be described.

- Specification of the **orientation and scaling** of an image raster with respect to the coordinate frame. Reference is given to physical measurements in space and time. The specification of an orientation in terms of ``left", ``right", ``up", and ``down" is only meaningful with respect to a viewing system, e. g., a human observer, or a camera.
- Specification of **metric transformations** to be applied to the image raster before accessing picture elements in the image raster. The transformation shall be defined either as a mathematical expression, or by means of tables, or by mapping a list of points geometrically onto another list of points. Metric transformations may also be applied to single pixels in order to achieve irregular gridding.

The metric description may provide general information about the geometry of the raster associated with the picture elements, e. g., regular rectangular grid, regular hexagonal grid, orientation of the raster with respect to some reference system. The metric description may provide the information of the actual size of the image, i. e., the number of rows and columns in the raster, parameters of an affine distortion of the grid, etc.

Channel Description

The channel description consists of one or more of the following entities:

- an unambiguous **naming** of the channel (e. g., ``grey", ``red", ``green", ``saturation", ``hue", ``thermal infrared", etc.);
- specification of the **response function** of the sensor used to acquire the data of a channel being either defined as a mathematical expression or by means of tables. The response function is used to specify the spectral sensitivity of the sensor, e. g., bandwidth, or noise characteristics;
- the **quantization depths** of the signals stemming from a channel;
- specification of **transfer functions** being either defined as a mathematical expression, or by means of tables and interpolation rules;
- specification of a **primary chromaticity**, given in x,y-coordinates of the CIE1931-(Y,x,y) colour space;
- a **transparency mask** which gives the percentage of the transparency of a channel, sub-pixel information, etc.

The transfer function can be used in several ways. It defines a homomorphism from one (colour-) value to another. It serves for the expression of gamma-correction and linearization, as well as for the manipulation of histograms. This may be, e. g., brightness control or contrast enhancement, as applied for the display of images without biasing the original amplitudinal values of the image. Also, transfer functions are used for the modelling of channel morphisms in images, commonly referred to as ``look-up tables".

Since parts of an image may spatially overlap other parts while being geometrically transformed, the transparency value can control the visibility of ``underlying" parts; among other useful features.

In case of additive colour mixing, the specification of a primary chromaticity is needed to achieve an accurate colour reproduction. All specifications dealing with the mixing of multiple channels for colour reproduction are given in the ``colour description" below.

Colour Description

The colour description encompasses all entities dealing with the mixing of amplitude values of multiple channels in order to achieve an accurate colour reproduction:

- specification of the **colour mixture model**;
- specification of a **white point**, given in x,y-coordinates of the CIE1931-(Y,x,y) colour space;
- specification of one or more **test colours** with respect to a region of interest (ROI). The test colours shall be described in x,y-coordinates of the CIE1931-(Y,x,y) colour space.

In case of an additive colour mixing based on an RGB colour space, the following specifications have to be made for accurate colour reproduction:

- primary chromaticities for each channel,
- a white point describing the luminance relation between the tree channels, and
- a transfer function for each channel.

In case of subtractive colour mixing for print media, it is hardly possible to give an unambiguous and complete specification for the colour reproduction process. Therefore, the test colours are provided. They allow to decide whether the colour reproduction process is performed accurately on the level of the human observer. Colour attributes are required in two different cases: On the one hand, they are needed to specify the meaning of amplitude values which represent some ``visible information", and, on the other hand, they are needed to attach colour to channels which do not consist of ``visible information" for visualization purposes. The latter case may also be covered separately by ``visualization attributes".

All aspects of channel and colour description may be subsumed as shown in figure 2.

Free-form Description

The internal structure and syntax of the free-form description attribute is not specified within this standard. It is application-dependent. The free-form descriptor is provided to allow highly application-specific descriptive information to be included. It is left to the application to decide on the actual way of storing and manipulating this information. No API function will be provided to care about the content of the free-form description. The processing of this description has to be performed by the application programme. The use of the free-form description attribute for transmitting image-related semantics within IIF communication must be based on a transmitter/receiver agreement. Otherwise this image-related semantics will be lost for the receiver.

An example for a free-form description which is defined in detail by an application-specific standard, is the header information as defined by the ACR-NEMA standard for medical applications

[1]. It provides specific formats for describing the nature of the image, orientation of the image with respect to the human body, patient data, etc.

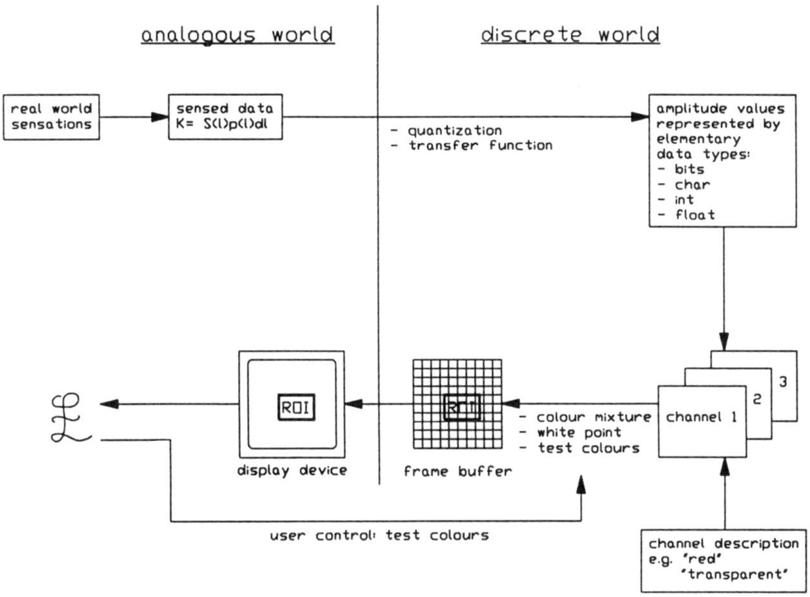

Figure 2 - Channel and colour description architecture

4.3.2 Compound Image Data Types

A compound image data type is a data type constructed by one of the following construction mechanisms from elementary image data types, or compound image data types:

- **(N_1 x...x N_n) image arrays** are arrays of images of identical types which can be accessed individually by their indices (i_1,...,i_n).
- **Image Sets** are collections of images of identical types. The images cannot be accessed individually. It can only be checked whether an image belongs to a set or not.
- **Image Lists** are ordered image sets. Individual images can only be accessed via successor/predecessor relations.
- **Image Records** are collections of individually named data types or image data types. The attributes may be of different type and can be accessed via their names.

The central idea behind images as defined in this standard is the integration of raw image data and related information into one compact data type.

The **compound image data types** deliberately provide more than only one way for structuring the same amount of data to optimally meet the demands of the final application. Depending on the access mechanisms needed by the application or the properties of the sensors, multi-spectral images can be represented either as:

- an elementary image, whose picture elements are 1-dimensional arrays of integers representing the intensities of the respective frequency channels,
- or as a 1-dimensional array of elementary images whose picture elements are integers representing the intensities in one of the frequency channels, if regularly spaced frequency channels have to be accessed randomly,
- or as a list of elementary images whose picture elements are integers representing the intensities in one of the frequency channels, if irregularly spaced frequency channels have to be accessed sequentially,
- or as a record of elementary images whose picture elements are integers representing the intensities in one of the frequency channels, if the frequency channels are of different spatial resolution or have to be accessed by name.

An example for a **record of images** is a set of images of exactly the same object, which has been imaged with different sensors at different spatial, temporal, or frequency resolution, e. g., images of increasing spatial resolution forming a picture pyramid, multi-spectral images describing the same object using infra-red, visible and radar signals, or combinations of ultra-sound, X-ray, computer tomography and magnetic resonance images of one and the same patient, etc.

Pixels - i. e., picture elements - are of arbitrary complexity, i. e., they can be elementary data types for storing scalar amplitude information of the original sensors, but they can also be compound data types for associating more comprehensive and structured information with every picture element.

5 The Image Interchange Format

A variety of image interchange formats is being used today. Most of them have been designed according to the needs of a certain application or user requirements group. In addition to the pure image data, they cover some information about the application-specific context, e. g., the page number and position of an image within a document. Some formats contain a description of the acquisition process, describing technical characteristics of sensors, or the time and location of image acquisition [13]. Other formats are combined with the specifications of lower protocol levels. The ACR/NEMA format [1], which has been designed to meet the image communication requirements of the medical imaging community, covers patient information, software commands, and a physical connector description.

Many image formats require the assumption of implicitly agreed parameters for a correct interpretation of image data outside of the usual application area. All ``programmer's RGB formats'', which do not refer to primary chromaticities or pixel aspect ratios, are typical examples. A few formats are ISO standards or national standards, but most of the formats currently being used are industrial standards (de-facto standards). Although this is not the place for a comprehensive analysis of standards (which is described elsewhere [3]), the following two commonly used image formats should be described, since they may be considered as the most comprehensive current formats:

- **Tag Image File Format (TIFF):**
  This de-facto standard has been developed for desktop publishing purposes. The list of image attributes (tags) has been extended to a comprehensive attribute set, supporting bi-level, grey-scale, RGB full colour, and so-called palette colour images. The specification of colour response curves and primary chromaticities according to the CIE-1931-(Y,x,y)-system [4] allows an accurate colour reproduction. Multiple ways of periodicity organization and several compression schemes (CCITT Group 3, among others) are supported [16].

- **User Exchange Format (UEF):**
  The ANSI standard IT8.1 contains a User Exchange Format (UEF00) for the exchange of colour picture data between electronic pre-press systems via magnetic tape (DDES00). To meet the requirements of print media, the UEF format supports the CMYK colour space and user-definable colour spaces in addition to RGB and LUV colour spaces. The attributes for colour definition also include one tag for the specification of the percentage of dot size for minimal and maximal amplitude, i. e., the percentage of paper covered with ink or dye. In addition to the UEF00 colour picture format, standardized within IT8.1, the IT8.X series contains extensions for the exchange of geometric art (i. e., the IGES data format subset) [11].

The design of the IIF format, being a part of the IPI standard, has been influenced by research activities at FhG-AGD which started in 1987 with the development of a prototype general purpose image format called ``File for the Transfer of Coloured Raster Pictures (FTCRP)" [6], [7], [8], [9].

During the development of the FTCRP, which gradually becomes now the IIF, the following design principles have been applied in order to improve the capabilities of the preliminary prototypes:

- The syntax of the interchange format shall support any kind of colour representation and raster geometry.
- The description of colourmetric and geometric properties of the image data shall be complete in order to make an error-free image reproduction possible.
- The syntax shall facilitate a flexible (hierarchical) structuring of multiple images within a single IIF file.
- The encoding of the image data shall be separated from the syntax of the file format. It shall be specified in a hardware-independent way.
- The encoding of image data shall be separated from algorithms for data compression. Thus, the format may enforce the introduction of new data compression algorithms.

The FTCRP has been encoded in the ``Abstract Syntax Notation One (ASN.1)" [5], which is an ISO standard [2] and guarantees a hardware-independent encoding. Data compression methods are optional. AGD's FTCRP referred to international compression standards which are under development by ISO/IEC JTC2/WG8 [12], [17]. Due to positive former experiences, the same facts about coding and compression shall hold for the IIF as well.

The syntax of the IIF format shall result from an unambiguous mapping of the image data structures defined within the image data model of the IPI onto a sequential order. Thus, the image data model of the IPI describes the structuring capabilities of the IIF in terms of guide-lines for the construction of application-specific image data types. This guarantees a maximum flexibility for the interchange of images via IIF. The image data model has been described in section 4.

The use of an Image Interchange Format, which is designed to define a superset of existing special purpose formats, is only the first step in enhancing image communication among different applications. It solves the problem of syntactical understanding without the limitations of a ``hard" application-dependent image format. Nevertheless, the problem of image type conversion remains a major topic to be solved for frictionless image communication. In this context, the term ``image type" does not stand for syntactical but for structural image attributes. For this reason, it is appropriate to combine the development of a standardized IIF with imaging functionalities as standardized by the API.

6 The IIF Software Tools

Due to these design goals - which have already been identified by the ISO/IEC JTC1 SC24 WG1 study group on imaging - the IIF will be set up during the next time. In any case, one may identify several tools (i. e., software products) to be developed within this proposed project. These tools accompanying the IIF may be listed as follows:

1) IIF Generator: An IIF Generator produces a file or a data stream which is conform to the ISO/IEC IIF standard syntax. It scans the application format or the device format of the image source which shall be converted to the IIF, identifies the IIF attributes which are needed, and produces an IIF file with these attributes. This IIF file needs to pass the stage of image compression algorithms (e. g., ADCT, run-length, Lempel-Ziv, etc.), as well as the stage of channel coding via the ASN.1 mechanism. IIF attributes which correspond to the device format are identified by a table-driven mechanism. Within an IIF generator, only a minimum of computation is necessary.

   1a) IIF Generator for IPI/API: An IIF Generator for the *export* function of the API of the IPI. The export function is able to convert the API-internal image data structure to IIF.

   1b) IIF Generators for the converting of other de-facto image file formats, such as TIFF, GIF, Fax Group 3, ACR/NEMA, into a IIF file: Therefore, these IIF generators allow the direct access to established applications and markets.

2) IIF Parser and Decoder: For the processing of received IIF images, every application needs a tool for the transformation of the image's IIF representation into the internal application-specific representation. A table-driven IIF parser will solve this problem. It decodes the ASN.1-channel-coded file and decompresses the image data. After that, it generates a syntax tree of the input image and identifies all image attributes. It then decodes the pixel data due to the coding method specified within the IIF file. Since the application usually does not support the whole set of IIF attributes, the set of attributes which accompanies the internal image data structure is reduced by constraints. These constraints are specified in the table - mentioned above - driving the parser programme. The table has somehow the functionality of a device or system description table.

2a) IIF Parser for IPI/API: A IIF Parser for the *import* function of the API of the IPI. The import function is able to receive an IIF file and convert the contained image into the API internal image data structure. However, if the IIF image is accompanied by other data - e. g., text, graphics - this data needs to be handled via API functions by appropiate user programmes in an application-specific manner.

2b) IIF Parsers for the converting of IIF into other de-facto image file formats, such as TIFF, GIF, Fax Group 3, ACR/NEMA. These IIF parsers work vice-versa as the generators of 1b), and allow also the direct access to etablished applications and markets.

3) IIF Image Conversion Server on top of API: IIF generators produce syntactically correct IIF files, nevertheless these files contain different subsets of IIF attributes. For example, IIF images have different geometric resolutions, or may employ different colour models. To convert from one set of IIF attributes to another, the IIF image conversion server provides image-to-image conversion tools. These tools are required for conversion tasks as, e. g., geometric resampling, colour calibration, or colour space transformation such as RGB to CMYK, full colour to look-up table, CIE1931 Yxy to RGB. The IIF image conversion server is the most important tool within the IIF environment. It ensures that all application-dependent instantiations of images may be computationally reached by the IIF. On the other hand, the IIF image conversion server needs to run on an appropiate machine, since resampling tasks require some computational power.

For the implementation of the IIF Image Conversion Server, the API of the IPI will be employed, thus keeping the programme hardware-independent.

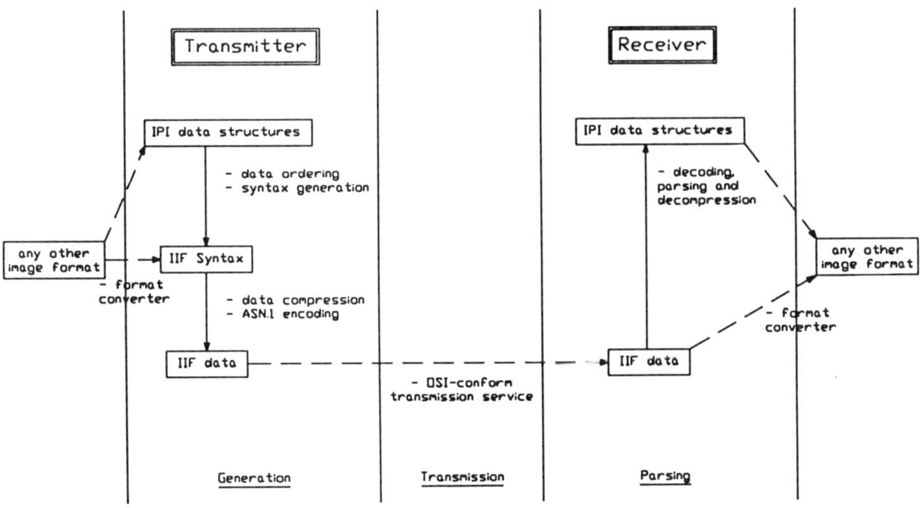

Figure 3 - The IIF communication process in detail

4) IIF Syntax Checker and Debugger: The IIF syntax checker and debugger is an interactive software tool for the testing and the correction of received IIF image files. The tool scans the IIF file, finds errors of the syntax - if there are some errors in the IIF file at all. Via interactive user input, the error may be corrected in a way that the received IIF file becomes meaningful.

The role of some of the diverse IIF software tools and the relationship of the IIF to the API and to the compression and coding algorithms is subsumed in the diagram shown in Figure 3.

7 Time Schedule for the Development of the IPI

During the Summer 1990 Ottawa meeting of SC24 WG1, the Study Group on Imaging approved a time schedule, which is as follows:

1991, Jan. 1: New Work Item Proposal (NP) approved by JTC1

1991, Apr. 15: Part I frozen

1991, Oct. 10: Part II and Part III frozen; trial use may begin

1992, Jan. 1: 1st Committee Draft (CD) circulation

1992, Apr. 30: 1st Committee Draft (CD) closing date for voting.

1993, Jan. 1: Trial use standard until this date

1993, Apr. 1: 2nd Committee Draft (CD) circulation

1993, Jul. 31: 2nd Committee Draft (CD) closing date for voting

1993, Oct. 15: Draft International Standard (DIS) prepared

1994, Jul. 31: Draft International Standard (DIS) closing date for voting

1994, Oct. 31: International Standard (IS) text prepared

This time schedule takes into account that there is much demand from the industry for a timely ISO/IEC-official international standard in Imaging.

8 Acknowledgements

The authors would like to thank their committee colleagues in DIN, ISO/IEC, and other related committees, for many helpful suggestions and fruitful discussions in a real good and open-minded atmosphere. Detlef Krömker, who is the rapporteur of ISO/IEC JTC1 SC24 Study Group Imaging, has made essential contributions to this report.

9 References

1. American College of Radiology (ACR) and National Electrical Manufacturers Association (NEMA), Standard Publication Nr. 300, ``Digital Imaging and Communications", 1985.

2. ``Abstract Syntax Notation One", Recommendation of the CCITT, No. X.208, X.209, and ISO standards No. IS 8824 and 8825.

3. BERKOM Reference Model II, ``Application-Oriented Recommendations", Version 2.0, DETECON, Berlin, 1990.

4. Deutsche Industrie-Norm, Nr. 5033, ``Farbmessung", Berlin, 1979.

5. Miguel Encarnacao, ``ASN.1-Codierung für FTCRP", Studienarbeit, Technische Hochschule Darmstadt, 1990.

6. G. R. Hofmann, ``FTCRP - Format for the Transfer of Colored Raster Pictures",Version 0, GI 4.1.4 Fachgespräch, Berlin, 1987.

7. G. R. Hofmann, D. Krömker, ``FTCRP - File for the Transfer of Colored Raster Pictures", Version 1, SPIE/SPS's Conference on Electronic Imaging, Los Angeles, 1989.

8. ``FTCRP - Implementation Manual and Report, Vol.1: Concepts and Syntax; User Options", Version 1.1, G.R. Hofmann (ed.), Bericht Nr. FAGD-89s003, Fraunhofer-Arbeitsgruppe für Graphische Datenverarbeitung, Darmstadt, 1989.

9. ``FTCRP - Implementation Manual and Report, Vol.2: Compression and Codings", Version 1.1, G.R. Hofmann (ed.), Bericht Nr. FAGD-89s004, Fraunhofer-Arbeitsgruppe für Graphische Datenverarbeitung, Darmstadt, 1989.

10. ``Ikonisches Kernsystem", FGAN-Fachgruppe Mustererkennung, Ettlingen, 1989.

11. The National Printing Equipment and Supply Association, ``User Exchange Format (UEF00) for the Exchange of Color Picture Data between Electronic Prepress Systems via Magnetic Tape (DDES00)", Reston, Virginia: NPES, 1988, (ANSI IT8.1).

12. ISO/IEC JTC1/SC2/WG8 and CCITT SGVIII Joint Photographic Experts Group, Document No. JPEG-8-R5, ``JPEG Technical Specification, Revision 5", 1990.

13. ``Computer Compatible Tape (CCT) format for raw or system-corrected Landsat Thematic Mapper (TM) imagery data acquired from Landsat 4 and 5 satellites", Revision 2, P. Gilles (ed.), DFVLR, Oberpfaffenhofen, 1987.

14. ISO/IEC JTC1/SC24/WG1 document N138, ``New Work Item Proposal on Imaging".

15. J. Schönhut et. al., ``Constructive Page Description"; technical contribution submitted to ISO TC 130.

16. ``Tag Image File Format Specification", Revision 5.0, Aldus and Microsoft Corporation, Seattle, 1988.

17. Hiroshi Yasuda, ``Standardization Activities on Multimedia Coding in ISO", Signal Processing: Image Communication, Volume 1, No. 1, 1989.

Chapter 23

Integration of X Applications with Open Systems Standards: Panacea or Pariah?

Rita E. Brennan

1 Introduction

The past several years popularity of X™ has led to it being used in almost all technical areas relying on heterogeneous end-user computer support. Now that open systems protocols are considered the best strategy for networked distributed applications and computing, there is a natural interest in the advantage offered by the open distributed nature of X to provide a windowed and graphical front-end to open systems applications.

However, the strategic direction of X applications coupled with open systems standards (both for information processing and telecommunications) is dependent on several critical factors:

- new control, resource resource, data structures and interfaces necessary for multi-media applications employing a distributed window system are evolving. To date, no formal models for any of the above have been widely adopted. (For this paper, multimedia will be any networked application employing two or more forms of information (i.e., text, graphics, image, video, sound) in a spatial and/or temporal form from one or more remote sources to one sink point in a network. This paper also assumes that open systems standards development will encompass multi-media applications.)
- the stability of communications architectures such as OSI, ATM/SONET and even metropolitan area standards such as Distributed Queue Dual Bus (DQDB) and Fiber Distributed Data Interface (FDDI). (The Asynchronous Transfer Mode (ATM) and Synchronous Optical Network (SONET) standards make up the core part of Broadband ISDN (BISDN). The Synchronous Digital Hierarchy (SDH) is the European/Asian equivalent to SONET.)
- the convergence of traditional terminal media such as text and 2D graphics with multimedia and hypermedia. De jure standards for multi-media and hypermedia are under development but are currently unstable.

This chapter explores each of these factors, offering examples of how they can be harmonized to provide sophisticated networked multi-media applications.

2 The X Networking Model Revisited

While the X model is probably the best known for being networked and extensible, by studying window functionality available in the industry today, one can conclude that the X model needs to include more robust:

- scheduling mechanisms,
- input and area management and
- control

to adequately support multi-media applications. Figure 1 shows the X networking model revisited. (This diagram is an adaptation of X applied to a window management system model developed by Jonathan Steinhart for his ACM SIGGRAPH 90 Course Notes "Introduction to Window Management".)

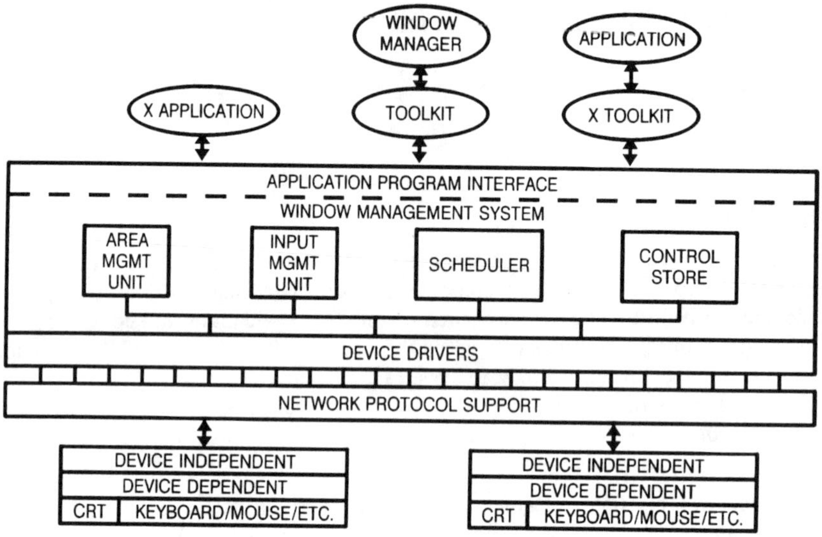

X Networking Model Revisited

Fig. 1

By examining Figure 1, we can break down the components of the window management system to see where X offers strong support for multi-media and where it does not.

Area management in X is a core component of the window system, mapping bits in the frame buffer onto the actual server screen. The management of this mapping in X is accomplished via a hierarchy of regions of parent and children. For some applications such as those involving multi-user window sharing, mapped windows may be arbitrarily clipped on some stations, but not others. This is an issue because X does not give control over windows to manipulate them as objects within other windows. The X tree (of windows) is also one of graphical containment. Hence, related pop-up windows cannot be sub-windows, but rather peer windows. This hinders communication between them. ICCCM conventions, if implemented efficiently, may alleviate this problem somewhat.

Input management can be a complex process involving the operating system kernel, an external policy application and a user application itself. In X, the input process is managed outside the operating system kernel by a window management application that is treated as any other application by X. This can cause performance problems for certain time constrained applications such as interactive videoconferencing. Additionally, applications may have different requirements of policy functions. Due to the diversity of multi-media applications, no single style of input management can be chosen. In many cases this is a strength of X. However, input management for X (and other future window systems) still needs to be rethought. Currently X only supports input events known to the active implementation. This is sometimes called non-autonomous state (Patterson 1990). For some applications, especially those for multi-users, it may be advantageous to allow users to call upon an autonomous change of state so that they can control network resources and perhaps even other user inputs.

The scheduling requirements of multi-media applications are complex. There is scheduling of application data transmission, of input events, for resource sharing, etc. X applies a simple scheduling mechanism for applications whereby each system call operates until completion before another one begins. For graphics intensive applications and temporally constrained ones, this *single-threaded* approach is not acceptable. However, work on X is progressing for a multi-threaded server (Brezak, et al, 1990). However this introduces new issues of control that need to be resolved; especially for multi-media conferencing applications. Care needs to be taken to insure that processes are synchronized and do not interfere with one another, but work together. This is an issue being worked by many and is a topic for an in-depth future study by the author.

''All window systems include a control store.'' (Steinhart, 1990). Control stores may be readable and writable or read only. X is read only and requires extensions to the state machine which must be compiled and linked within the window system kernel (the server implementation) to support application specific control mechanisms.

All the above concepts of a generic model for X can be extrapolated to include the issues underlying multi-media communications. Hence there is an analogy between evolving window systems development and multi-media applications. In later sections of this chapter, some of the common issues between the two are examined and potential solutions for window systems to adequately support multi-media are offered.

3 Future of X Applications

As window system applications mature, increased sophistication supporting more than traditional text or graphics based applications will be evident. For instance, resources traditionally available only to advanced programmers (e.g., Unix™ system call libraries) for development, control and maintenance, will be available to users desiring to configure network entities from remote databases to network connection and monitoring. The next three sections describe:

- potential X applications possible for multi-media applications,
- X as a ''front-end'' to sophisticated OSI applications, and
- the role of X in telecommunications applications.

Many of these application scenarios are based on existing prototypes.

3.1 In Multimedia

X has played quite an impressive role in setting the groundwork for distributed windowing applications, and has led to the increased proliferation of raster bitmapped displays. If one were to assemble a multi-media ''toolkit'', the nuts and bolts of such a toolkit would probably be a sound window management system. In fact, when viewing X as just an often used tool in a multi-media environment, it is obvious that it is being used as a model for new distributed application components such as VOX, (Hedges, et al., 1988), a project for audio windows, and other video related projects for managing distributed video resources (Ludwig, 1987). X has also played a role in impacting the modelling work of new standards (PIK, 1990). Figure 2 shows a high-level example of how the X model has been extended to encompass other types of ''window'' systems.

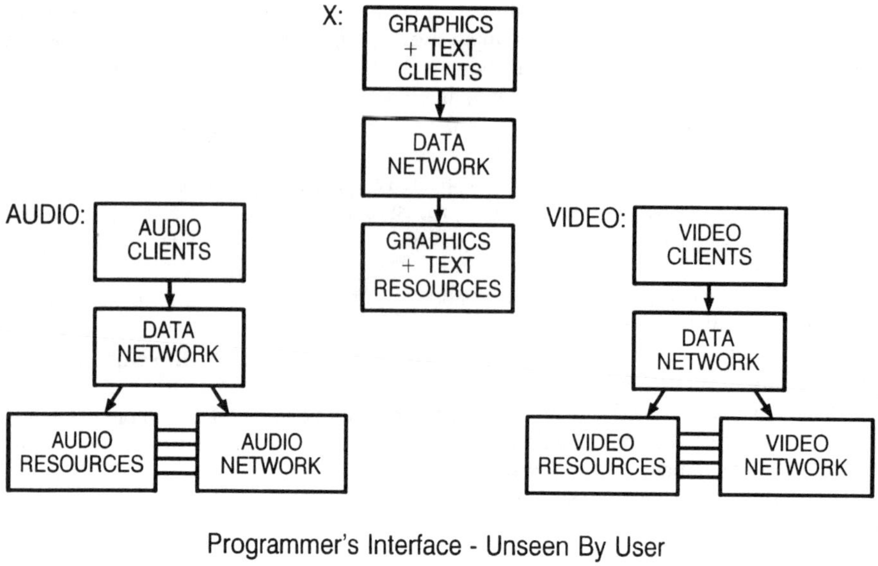

Borrowing X's Resource Management Model

Fig. 2

3.2 Front-ends for OSI Applications

X applications have also impacted the development of OSI Applications. A new project to integrate X into the OSI communications suite is underway in ANSI under X3H3.6 (Part IV: OSI Mapping, 1990). Why use a standard window system? Some answers might be:

- it makes harmonization simpler across applications,
- it facilitates the use of a window manager for OSI users, and
- encourages new end-user customization and creativity.

There has also been considerable interest shown in using the distributed window and user interface properties of X as a front-end for OSI applications. This approach has been fostered by certain product suppliers who implement a graphical user interface that is easy to use and intuitive as a way to sell more products. End-user organizations looking to make their OSI migration less painful and more attractive believe X/OSI is a way to convert their existing X users and simplify the learning curve for new users. Developers of OSI applications are also interested in developing their software as X clients. Graphical and event driven user interface development is a trend amongst developers as the next growth wave in application design. Already we have seen an X interface to directory services with a planned extension to X.500 (Rose, 1990). Others developing OSI applications such as message handling and management are planning X interfaces to their services. In addition, an Office Document Architecture (ODA) and Remote Open Document Editing (RODE) work effort at KDD Telematics Laboratory in Japan (Yamada, 1990) includes the use of X as their interface to the document system.

There is more to X and OSI than just simply providing an attractive front end to OSI applications. In some circumstances, the design philosophy of OSI can be applied to X application development and vice versa. Bellcore is currently prototyping a groupware application based on X that employs a CMISE architecture for modelling the conference manager. The heart of the system is deliberately modelled after the agent/manager concept in CMISE (Bellcore, 1990).

3.3 In Telecommunications

When simple visualization of network data is necessary and a window system is convenient, X has potential as a tool for graphical layout in telecommmunications. X has been used as a platform independent, distributed interface for network monitoring and trouble ticketing (Flood, 90). This could be considered a low-level form of ''telecommunications visualization'', displaying bandwidth allocation gauging and flow control and latency visualization. For the most part however, X does not provide the kind of sophisticated graphics that these applications require. Figure 3 depicts a screen from a telecommunications application for network monitoring developed using X at Bellcore.

X also has potential over low bandwidth ISDN links, particularly for non-graphics intensive applications. There are projects that use compressed video over 64Kbps ISDN links with X (in particular, see D. Lewis' chapter in this book, Chapter 9, for more details).

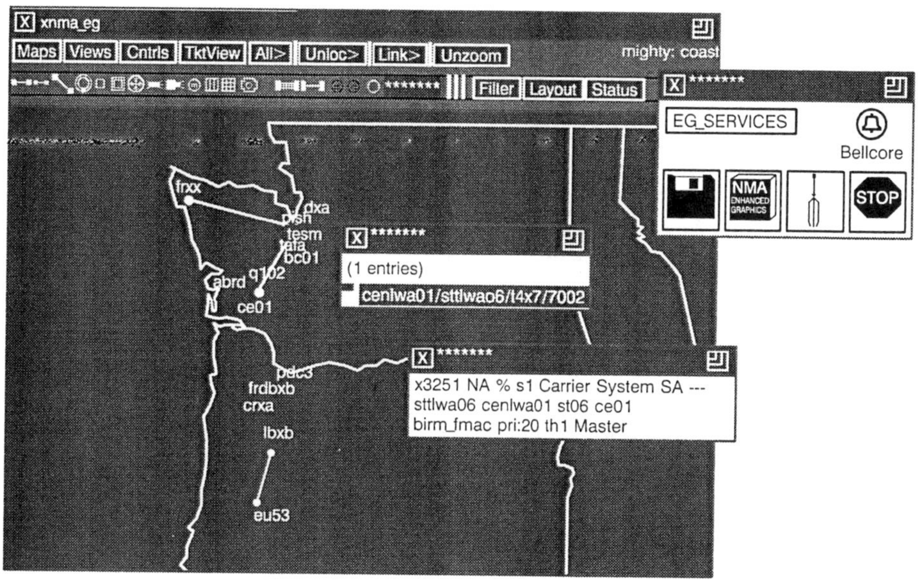

Bellcore's Network Monitoring Analysis Project (Cont.)

Fig. 3

4 Application Scenarios

Many different application scenarios lend themselves well to future X applications, whether they are multi-media or open systems related. The ones of most interest from a research perspective making their way into mainstream computer based applications are:

- computer support cooperative work (or groupware)
- networked video (e.g. videoconferencing)
- high performance graphics/imaging applications

Let's take a closer look at the characteristics of each.

4.1 Cooperative Work

These multi-user applications involve precisely synchronized control and scheduling on multicast networks. They generally involve multiple users interacting with a program or multimedia/hypermedia document over a network. Usually, precise coordination of multiple media resources for graphics, images, even animation combined with audio or voice is required. Sometimes special pointers and overlays are used, which complicate the user synchronization even more. Overlays of graphics or images over video or other computer image sources is achieved through genlocking. Genlocking is a function supported by hardware vendors for many platforms (e.g., PCs, Macintoshes, Unix workstations, etc.) that synchronize two different types of video output to the display. For instance, one can synchronize the 30 frames per second or (approximately) 30Hz interlaced scan rate of NTSC video with 60Hz non-interlaced RGB signals by using a genlocking board and an external key function.

The requirements from the network perspective have been solved mainly in the local area network world, but not in the wide area domain. The reason for this may be the widespread use of multicast datagram packets for application transport in the LAN arena. There are many new high speed protocol specifications being designed (Interop, 1990) that will provide the type of transport shared applications over a wide area network need. However, no one has yet adequately addressed the demands of shared resources and shared data structures these applications require to be robust. Some examples of shared resources are:

- conference bridges
- media editors
- compression/decompression boards
- multi-media data bases
- media conversion utilities
- shareable CPU cycles

What goes into building a cooperative work environment? Some of the enabling technologies found to be useful are;

- window systems
- adequately proportioned bandwidth
- videographics boards
- other special purpose video and graphics utilities such as chroma, alpha and external keys

X's generality and extensibility make it better suited to shared applications than other window systems. Other distributed systems like NeWS from Sun Microsystems, are difficult to use because they usually require the downloading functionality of PostScript routines. The limitations of having to download PostScript prevent NeWS from being implemented in a centralized architecture (which is the simplest to develop).

To date, there are two known architectures for window sharing, replicated and centralized (Lantz et al., 1990). Figure 4 shows both. In the replicated architecture, each user has a copy of the application that has to be synchronized with the copy of the user in control "at the moment". In the centralized architecture, a single application located on a bridge in control is multicast to each user. Often, a local database holds a copy of the data that requires updating.

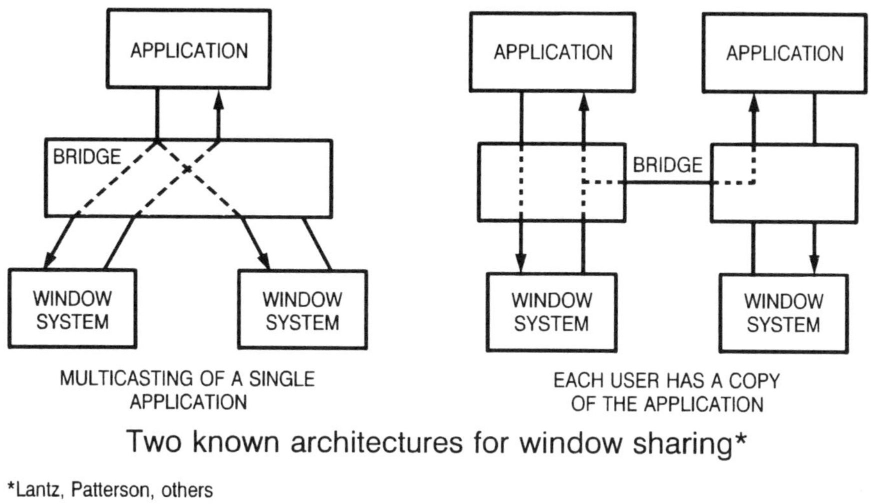

CSCW Sometimes Means Using "Shared Windows"

Fig. 4

4.2 Networked Video

While this section does not include an exhaustive analysis of the future (or even the present standing) of networked video, an overview of some of the requirements of video at different bandwidths will be explored. The video bandwidth possibilities can be divided into three categories:

- full motion requirements:

  need at least DS3 bandwidth, generally more (i.e., at least 50 Mbps). One source claims full-bandwidth video including audio and ancillary data support requires a 140 Mbps throughput rate (Paulson, 90).

- ''minimalist's'' video:

  compressed for IEEE 802 architecture (e.g., ethernet, token ring) type throughput

- non-real time compressed video:

  over 64Kbps links

  over X.25

  not sure of usefulness

Within X, there are request messages and events to control video synchronization and control from the server, but no actual support for transport of video signals through the X connection. It is possible then, from a telecommunications perspective to think of video in X as ''out-of-band'' control. The video source itself (whether it be NTSC, PAL or SECAM) is ''piped'' direct to a video decoder where data is digitized onto a dedicated bus into a raster frame buffer. Live video has one or two more constraints placed on it than still video, like a state for loss-of-sync. This is not necessarily an error for still video as the sync portion has already been achieved.

In general, one can think of extensions to X as employing either in-band control (such as in the generation of a structure store in PEX) or out-of-band control (as in the video sync controls in VEX). A new extension for imaging emerging from X Consortium work is IEX, which will be primarily in-band for most imaging operations (IEX, 1990). However, add the capability for overlays and stereo optics for X and it will probably be addressed via out-of-band mechanisms. For example, consider a simulation of a distributed process where shared applications and users interact to build a simulated environment. This simulated environment might contain specialized applications for graphics design, animation, scientific visualization; all geared toward making the simulated environment as realistic as possible. It may be necessary to introduce new input sources such as a new 3D input device or a glove, which is not supported in X. However, it can be interfaced to one of the applications that is part of the shared X environment. It would not be difficult to add an extension to X to send signals to that application on how to interpret and control the new input device.

4.3 Imaging Applications

With imaging, a greater range of bandwidths and end system processing speeds are possible. Anything from 10Kbps to 1Gpbs transport may be adequate depending on the size of the image and how quickly you need to get it to its destination for rendering. Some burgeoning application areas such as scientific visualization and image processing rely heavily on supercomputers for processing, and high-end workstations for modelling. It is hoped that new standards, such as the one proposed in SC24 for imaging (PIK, 1990) will provide network hooks for indicating bandwidth requirements. Today, network standards of choice for scientific visualization and image processing are ethernet, Hyperchannel, FDDI, DS3 and those services built on top of it.

5 Future Network Requirements

To best determine what type of network support best applies to new media applications, we should attempt to classify application media types, resources and bandwidth requirements. Future networks must be capable of coordinated multiple media types such as:

- audio
- animations
- graphics
- images
- overlays
- text/titling
- video

Specialized shared resources of the following type will also be expected:

- mail/message systems
- conference bridges
- document editors
- databases

- special purpose graphics/animation systems
- image processors
- high-performance CPUs
- media conversion
- remote file systems

Depending on the application, network utilization will vary significantly. For example, a simple 2D X graphics application may utilize approximately 40% of an ethernet LAN (DEC, 1990), but a video based mail system may require on the order of 80% utilization of a Hyperchannel based network.

What will future network standards require to properly support X applications? Depending on the sophistication of the end users and the information content to be conveyed, a balance must be achieved between transparency of the application (and its users to the network) and an awareness of the network protocol to the application. This is necessary so that the program can dynamically control the bandwidth allocation and control schemes. This may involve providing transparency on the system to the user sector and a complex open interface on the application to system sector.

Also, instead of layering and separating processing unconditionally, it may prove fruitful to layer and separate data (Tufte, 1990). Then depending on the context of the layers, a system can map the level of abstraction and its representation to the best available communications support. Thus the generality is not rigid from either the communications or the applications perspective.

Another idea might be to allow data and processing to be atomic with the object communicated as an atomic unit. This is an extrapolation of a fairly common concept in object oriented system design.

Also, application standards must no longer restrict "application" communication to synchronous/asynchronous and/or connection-oriented/connectionless communication. These should be left to the underlying network operations. Imposing such restrictions on the upper layer protocols may hinder their usability.

Not to be ignored are the constraints placed on modern day wide area communications by gateways, both at the network layer and the application layer. Very often, transport requirements for distributed multi-media information are impacted by gateways. Application gateways may be necessary (at least temporarily) between support applications such as information servers. Network gateways have to be accommodated and will continue to prevail. Most of these gateways come with sophisticated translation mechanisms.

5.1 Media Support Issues

When thinking about what comprises a multi-media architecture, three general concerns come to mind:

- what sort of data structures apply?
- what are the synchronization issues?
- who allocates and controls data resources?

Let's examine each in turn.

5.1.1 Data structures

Data structures need to consider the infrastructure, display structure, manipulation and applications environments of the supporting system. As display presentation has changed over the past several years, so has application design, authoring styles and composition of the data being manipulated. Multimedia objects need a common storage abstraction encapsulated by a shared communication and operations system that aids authoring systems, query systems and end users themselves. As the process of media object/systems harmonization becomes more familiar to systems designers, a form of ''composition bypass'' should be possible allowing users to specify what they need for a service or application. This could be accomplished without the need to specify the media format, distribution path and location of the data themselves. This could be viewed as another form of run-time composition.

Traditional system data flow concepts may change, reducing the overhead of distributed processes (from synchronization and retrieval procedures) by making processes independent instead of dependent on an overall controlling process. The relationship between display and data structures should be a dynamic run-time type where an instance of a display structure collects and organizes the actual display objects. Direct manipulation studies (Hutchins, et al., 1986) have shown that responsiveness can be improved by supporting such things as fast picking, shared display data structures, and rapid screen refresh/redraw.

Figure 5 shows a possible data structure/operations system infrastructure for data organization and access. This is just one example of the rethinking necessary in systems design to support future applications. To support multi-media applications adequately, traditional operating system libraries need to be extended to support things like an abstract and global media indexing service. This is denoted in Figure 5 by the arrow entering the *virtual composition* box. This media indexing service, referred to as *metamedia addressing,* requires that operating system libraries be extended to support simple abstract constructs analogous to file descriptors that call upon multi-media data services without needing to know the data format(s) of the objects the programmer or user wants. The virtual composition entry then simply performs the media translation if necessary for the system and for storage.

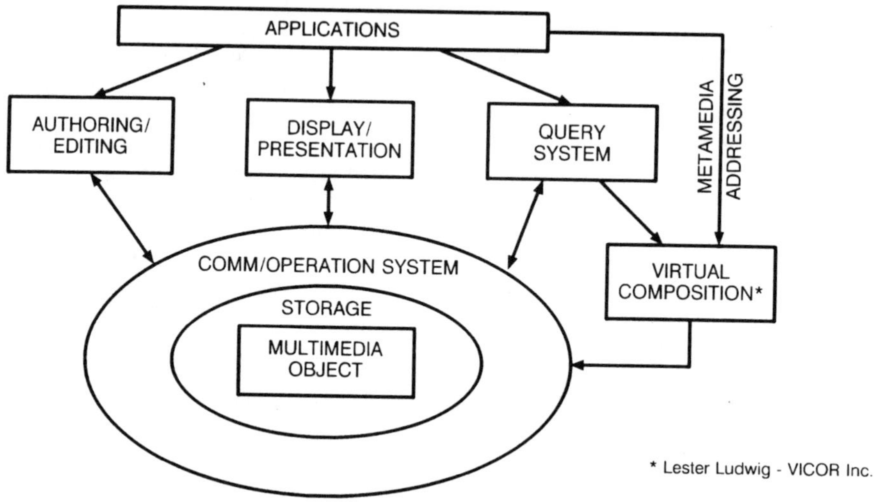

Fitting multimedia into their infrastructure, display, manipulation and applications environments

Data Structures

Fig. 5

5.1.2 Multimedia synchronization

Multimedia synchronization is still quite nascent. Many papers are emerging, but a model of how best to achieve a "well-synchronized" output is still quite far off. This is due to the large number of data types in the multi-media world that require synchronization. Not only must you synchronize the different contents of a point-to-point multi-media connection, you need to consider media components coming from different distributed databases and proceses. So there is synchronization of a single dialogue from multiple sources, multiple dialogues from multiple sources, time synchronization (one proposal in CCITT and ISO considers the Internet community's Network Time Protocol for a general time synchronization service), process synchronization and event synchronization: not to mention ordinary synchronization of media with a window manager like X. Some processes are temporally constrained and some are not. For instance, if you simply want to annotate a graphic, or audio/video tape with text being displayed in a window, either use a titling package to overlay the text (a separate hardware based form of synchronization) or open another window to display the text that goes along with the graphic. For still images, this is really quite simple and just takes the form of a hypermedia document. However, you may require synchronization primitives to take effect when inputting the text into the window displaying the clip at some sync points.

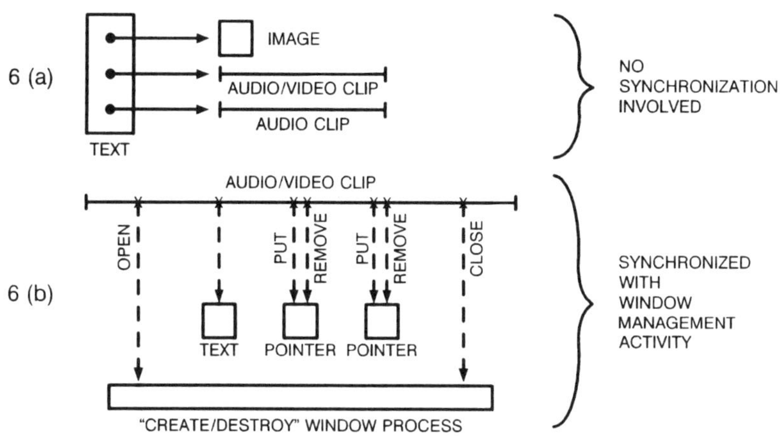

Various constructions of multimedia objects.
For convenience, dots denote a trigger dialog box utility.
Solid arrowed lines denote points; dashed lines denote sync primitives, and "X's" denote sync points

Synchronization Of Media With A Window Manager

Fig. 6

Figure 6 shows a representation of this. Figure 6(a) depicts a situation where no sync primitives are necessary for alignment with a window process, whereas in Figure 6(b), sync primitives are used to indicate when to send data while the window process is active.

5.1.3 Allocation and Control of Data Resources

If you design a new model for resource allocation with an *allocation mediator* as the heart of your model, you will soon find that your allocation mediator is dependent on several critical factors:

- the resources themselves,
- who has control over those resources and who has them statically available,
- what is the nature of the transport mechanisms (i.e., is multi-channel support provided?), and
- what is the interworking between the above.

Figure 7 depicts a new model for protocol support designed with new control capabilities for resources and transport capabilities with allocation as the key component for each, including control. Today, no standard specification languages adequately address allocation. Consider an example of an audio/video mixer on a standalone system. The control processes for the mixer must be capable of mixing application specific parameters, switching configurations on demand, performing certain features such as titling, communicating with a master process, etc. If you extrapolate this concept and look at communications, you will find that the same sort of heterogeneous mix of capabilities is necessary for sophisticated distributed multi-media. We need to architect a model with a network(s) knowledge of these features when necessary. Dynamic extensibility is the key here.

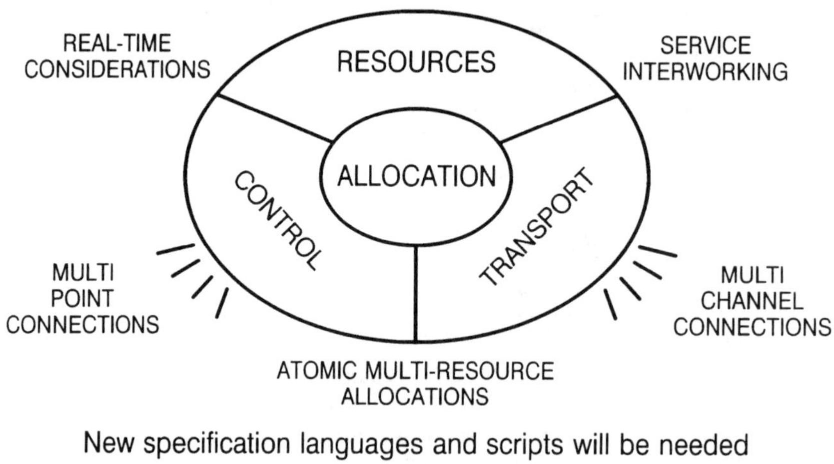

Network Protocol Support Will Require New Control Capabilities

Fig. 7

5.2 The Broadband Holy Grail

Recent developments in high bandwidth, high speed networks make the use of distributed multi-media objects possible and even practical. However, broadband research appears to be motivated by the data communications sector interested in higher network speeds and by the telecommunications sector motivated by the desire to distribute multi-media services (mostly video). However, with little investigation it becomes quite apparent that these groups are coming from different perspectives, and neither is wholely solving all the problems, particularly those problems related to latency, error control, flow control and synchronization. Consider that the telecommunications industry is developing standards based on small (53 byte) fixed length packets called ''cells'' and the data communications industry in general is providing high speed protocols with variable length packets that can be quite large (e.g. in the Mbyte range). The rationale behind cells is that they require less ''composition'' and checking time, hence latency is reduced. The cells will then be able to support isochronous services such as video. The potentially large variable length *packets* of high speed data communications will promulgate large steady streams of data (e.g., non-real time image transmission) with no real concern over latency. Another factor is that while most isochronous services can tolerate some amount of degradation and error, most basic data services, such as file transfer operations, cannot.

Let's relate this to future X Window applications. Assume a window has been opened to support a 10 minute video clip with accompanying audio track and a genlocked titling function. The audio track is coming from a channel multiplexer/demultiplexer directly onto a bus supporting digital audio. The video is coming from an outside source, being digitized and then dumped into a frame buffer, and a graphics engine with a genlocking board is generating the titling software on the same graphics bus as the video rasterizer. In real time, using a real-time operating system, a high speed network could be used to move the graphics from a remote site to the local workstation, store it locally to be synchronized with the audio/graphics portion of the window, retrieve the audio from a basic analogue connection over a circuit-switched connection and digitize it, take the digitized video from the frame

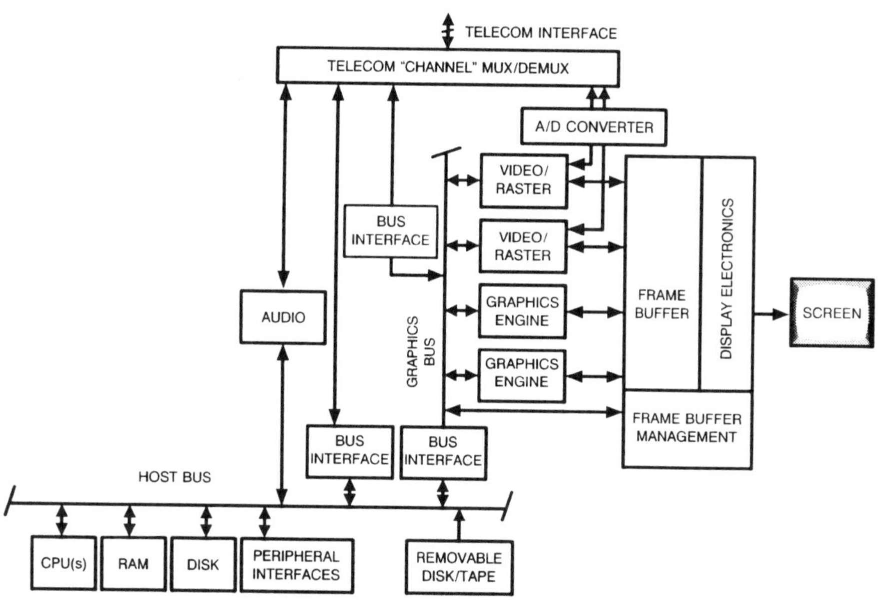

A Typical Multi-Media Workstation

Fig. 8

buffer and coordinate all of these in a way that the user is not aware they have all just been "gathered" and dynamically synchronized.

Figure 8 shows an example model of such a communications path to and within a multimedia workstation. A much cleaner way would be to have the various remote media types used within an X window be transported through one intelligent pipe capable of handling both the connection-less data stream style data of traditional X applications and the isochronous data services of next generation telecom applications integrated in a data independent manner.

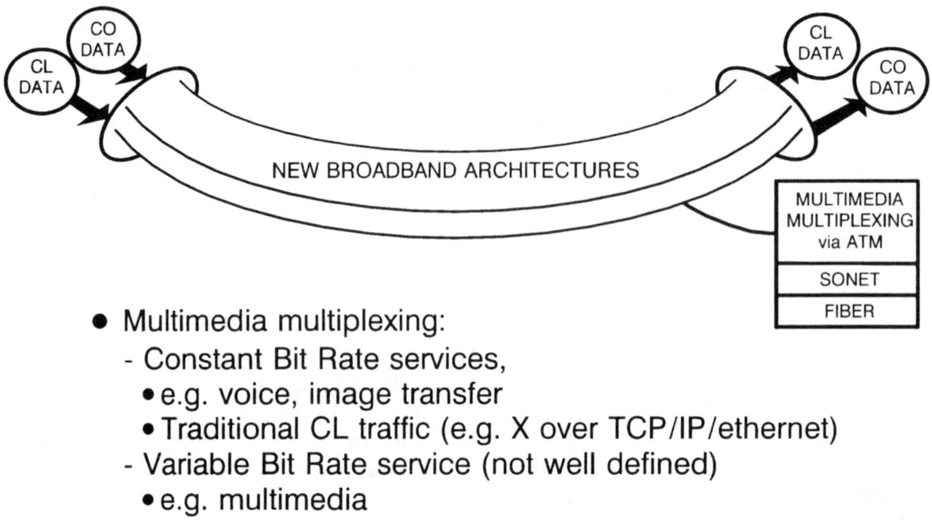

X's Relationship To Broadband ISDN

Fig. 9

In Figure 9, the concept of a *great white pipe* for any kind of data transport appears overly simplistic, but remains desirable. Such a model using new broadband architectures is possible, provided that cells be available when necessary for time-constrained services requiring synchronization with another source. Furthermore, it should not be too difficult to introduce an extension mechanism to the still nascent telecommunications standards that will allow for a stream oriented mode of data transfer. A stream protocol may require a unique setup phase prior to data transfer. This setup phase would then be used instead of the ATM cell bandwidth negotiation phase. Hence, all that is needed is a simple "switch" at connection time between ATM and the stream supporting transport. Note, however, that the Asynchronous Transfer Mode (ATM, 90) Standard from CCITT defines a constant bit rate (CBR) service as being able to support traditional data such as today's ethernet LANs over DS1 and DS3 services. This will work well if you allocate the average bit rate of your channel to be the peak rate of the offered traffic (assuming no buffering) and disregard the clocking signals on a Variable Bit Rate (VBR) service that may support a well managed stream-oriented transport within the ATM Adaptation Layer. Details of how this will work have not yet been specified. While ATM appears to be open-ended in its attempt to support several protocols within its Adaptation Layer (i.e., a CBR stream service, a datagram protocol, a VBR service), it may be interesting to look at what the underlying fiber protocols have to offer and how extensible they might be to different data services.

SONET can also support streams through what are known as Virtual Tributaries (VTs). VTs are used to primarily handle DS1 streams (i.e., VT1.5) which can be multiplexed with other streams. VT1.5 is a synchronous transfer mode signal that is a constant, not variable data rate. Groups of VT1.5 signals can then be multiplexed into the payload of a SONET frame. For instance, a number of VT1.5 signals can be multiplexed into the payload of a STS-1 signal (approximately 50 Mbps). (SONET frame header information is used to identify the position of each VT in the SONET frame.) These STS-1 signals can be byte interleaved into an STS-3, if higher layer capacity throughput is necessary. The STS signals are subsequently converted into an optical signal (known as an optical carrier - OC) for transmission on the fiber. This will probably be one of the first SONET services to be widely deployed.

Broadband research integrated from both a telecommunications and a data world perspective *is* the next Holy Grail of computer communications research. How soon before we will see truly robust applications from this union is not known.

6 What Lies Ahead?

New reference models for distributed multi-media communications are evolving. ISO is working on one, known as the Terminal Management Model (TM, 1990). The future of this work effort is unclear. Without adequate resources and prototyping experiences, its future is questionable. Other groups, such as the multi-media/hypermedia experts group (MHEG) in ISO/IEC JTC1/SC2/WG 12 and the broadband multi-media group in CCITT SG VIII are developing hypermedia/multimedia models, but from different perspectives. The MHEG group is focusing on application based media interchange formats and the broadband ISDN groups on new control and call models for BISDN multimedia. There is, however, some consensus on separating display and configuration variables from control and communications. Separating and layering functionality is now common practice; but how to separate and remap information to best support functionality is still relatively unexplored in the communications fields.

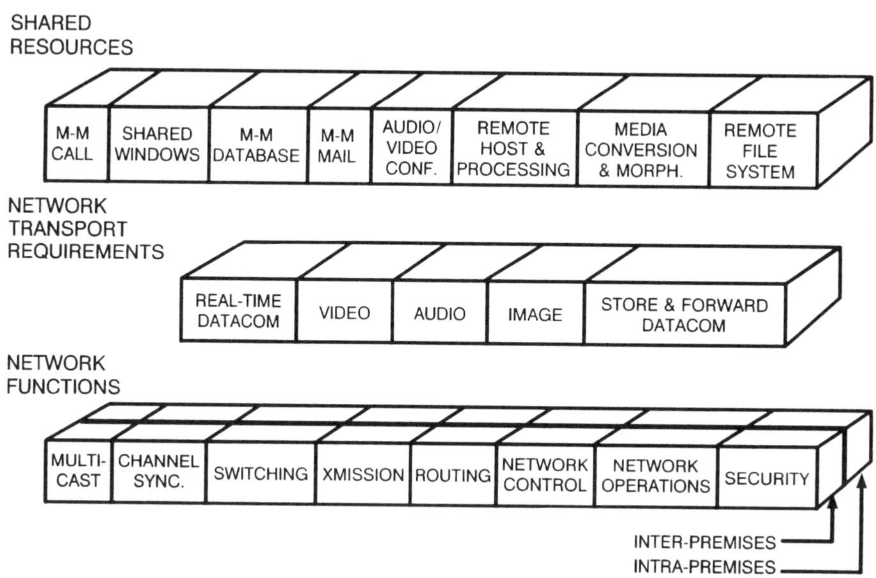

An Organization For Multi-Media Communications

Fig. 10

Figure 10 depicts an organization model for multi-media communications. The first *block* stratifies shared resources, the second network transport functions, and the third low level network functions. With a comprehensive organization of these functions, it should not be too difficult to use a building block approach to satisfy application requirements.

So far, studies of future service issues have resulted in the following:

- users want more control over their environments, but they want to start out from a high level of abstraction from where they can gently work their way into more detailed control. We have to offer users options to satisfy requirements.
- at the lower levels, we need
  - sophisticated pipes for input/output
  - splicing of dialogues to merge one into another
  - pre-emptive scheduling of applications
  - different types of synchronization primitives
    - parallel ordering
    - support for independent and isochronous data
    - time ''tags''
    - event and process synchronization
    - an interactivity ''metric'' that is monitored at all times

Future window managers should be capable of:

- intuitive graphical interfaces (that do not require a command-line ''kick-off''),
- multi-threaded operations and shared libraries,
- inter-application standardized communication (e.g., strong IPC and RPC),
- full recoverability from errors and tight security,
- device independence through abstraction granularities,
- intrinsic knowledge of device independent metafile mechanisms, (e.g., of text, graphics, videodiscs, etc.),
- providing a scripting mechanism for user defined extensions to the protocol.

From the perspective of user interface architecture, we need to provide the necessary ''plug-and-play'' interface components that users can choose to build their own customizable interfaces. This may determine which window manager is used. However, the window manager should be augmentable by ancillary services such as extensible font services, graphics libraries, non-standard input/output devices and special interfaces (e.g., MIDI - Musical Instrument Digital Interface).

7 Acknowledgements

Over the past 2 years, my interest in multi-media window systems has been enriched by many. I would especially like to thank Richard Gero of Intel and Jonathan Steinhart for introducing me to the world of window systems, and Lester Ludwig of VICOR for his many exciting forward thinking ideas about multi-media while contributing to multi-media communications prototypes at Bellcore. Lester Ludwig in particular is responsible for initiating Figures 2, 5,6 and 10.

Many individuals at Bellcore have contributed to multi-media and conferencing based applications. In particular, I would like to thank Ronnie Potter for introducing me to end-user architectures in general, Randy Jackson and Stan Switzerfor their ideas on the role X can play in OSI and vice versa, and Richard Flood and others in his group for their ideas and experiments with network visualization using X. I would also like to thank John Patterson for helping me to understand conferencing applications based on the X Window System; Greg Brenner and Phiroz Madden for their BISDN thoughts. Last but not least, I would like to thank my patient and inspiring managers, Tim Bauman, Jean Zolnowski, Tricia Deering and David Kessell for allowing me the time and freedom to explore multi-media and other diverse areas outside the scope of my general assignment.

8 References

Patterson, J. (1989) The Implications of Window Sharing for a Virtual Terminal Protocol, Position Paper for a groupware workshop, Bellcore Technical Memorandum TM-ARH-013897, New Jersey

Brezak, J., Elliot, I., Meyers, N. (1989) A Multi-Threaded Server for X and PEX, Presented at the 1990 X Technical Seminar, Boston, Massachusetts

Steinhart, J. (1990) SIGGRAPH 90 Course Notes, Introduction to Window Management, Association for Computing Machinery, New York

Arons, B., Binding, C., Lantz, K. Schmandt, C. (1988) The VOX Audio Server, joint project between M.I.T. and Olivetti Research

Ludwig, L. (1989) Real-time Multi-media Teleconferencing: Integrating New Technology, MCC Groupware Technology Implementor's Workshop, Palo Alto, California

Paulson, B. (1990) Light up your dark fiber roots, Telephony, August 13, 1990 Issue

ANSI X3H3.8 – Imaging Applications Programmer Interface Task Group (1990) Programmer's Imaging Kernel (PIK) Strawman V7, American National Standards Institute, New York

ANSI X3H3.6 – Window Systems Task Group (1990) X3196-199x, X Window System Data Stream Definition – Part IV: OSI Mapping, American National Standards Institute, New York

Rose, M. (1990) An X Window System Interface to the White Pages, Performance Systems International, Inc. PSI Technical report #90-04-01-1

Yamada, M. (1990) KDD ODA/DTAM X Windows Project, *Personal Communication*

Huleatt, S., Desai, S. (1990) The Distributed Concurrent Design Application, Bellcore Internal Technical Memorandum, New Jersey

Flood, R. (1990) The Network Monitoring and Analysis project, *Personal Communication*

Partridge, C. (1990) INTEROP 90 Tutorial on High Speed Protocols, Interop, Inc., San Jose, California

Lauwers, J.C., Joseph, T.A., Lantz, K., Romanow, A.L. (1990) Replicated Architectures for Shared Window Systems: A Critique, COIS'90 Conference on Office Information Systems, Menlo Park, California

Mirchandani, D., Biswas, P. (1990) Ethernet Performance of Remote DECwindows Applications, Summer 1990, Vol. 2, No. 3, Digital Technical Journal

Tufte, E.R. (199) Envisioning Information, Graphics Press, Cheshire, Connecticut

Hutchins, E.L., Hollan, J.D., Norman, D.A. (1986) Direct Manipulation Interfaces, Lawrence Erelbaum Associates, Hillsdale, New Jersey

CCITT SG VIII (1990) BISDN ATM Protocol Characteristics, Draft Recommendations I.150

ISO/IEC JTC1 Subcommittee 21 Working Group 5 (1990) Terminal Management Model, Committee Draft

List of Participants and Authors

D.B. Arnold, School of Information Systems, University of East Anglia, Norwich NR4 7TJ, UK

R. Brennan, Bellcore, 331 Newman Springs Rd., Post Office Box 7020, Red Bank, NJ 07701-7020, USA

G.S. Carson, GSC Associates Inc., 2304 Artesia Bld #201, Redondo Beach, CA 90208-3114, USA

R.A. Day, Informatics Department, Rutherford Appleton Laboratory, Chilton, Didcot, Oxon OX11 0QX, UK

F. Dilonardo, TECSIEL, Via S. Maria 19, I-56100 Pisa, Italy

D.A. Duce, Informatics Department, Rutherford Appleton Laboratory, Chilton, Didcot, Oxon OX11 0QX, UK

A. Ducrot, INRIA, BP 105, F-78153 Le Chesnay Cedex, France

P. Egloff, GMD FOKUS, Hardenbergplatz 2, W-1000 Berlin 12, Germany

D.W. Fellner, Memorial University, Department of Computer Science, St. John's, Newfoundland, Canada A1C 5S7

C. Fuhrhop, GMD FOKUS, Hardenbergplatz 2, W-1000 Berlin 12, Germany

J.R. Gallop, Informatics Department, Rutherford Appleton Laboratory, Chilton, Didcot, Oxon OX11 0QX, UK

G.R. Hofmann, Fraunhofer-Arbeitsgruppe fuer Graphische Datenverarbeitung, Wilhelminenstrasse 7, W-6100 Darmstadt, Germany

F. Kappe, Technical University Graz IICM, Schiessstattgasse 4A, A-8010 Graz, Austria

K. Klement, Fraunhofer-Arbeitsgruppe fuer Graphische Datenverarbeitung, Wilhelminenstrasse 7, W-6100 Darmstadt, Germany

P. Kokkinidis HITEC, 18 Poseidonos Str., GR-17674 Kallithea, Athens, Greece

S. Liapakis, School of Information Systems, University of East Anglia, Norwich NR4 7TJ, UK

D.E. Lewis, RT 4321, British Telecom Research Labs., Martlesham, Ipswich IP5 7RE, UK

R. Maybury, Informatics Department, Rutherford Appleton Laboratory, Chilton, Didcot, Oxon OX11 0QX, UK

J.F. Mortelmans, University of Leuven, Celestijnenlaan 200A, B-3030 Leuven, Belgium

A.M. Mumford, Computer Centre, Loughborough University, Loughborough LE11 3TU, UK

S.J. Noll, Fraunhofer-Arbeitsgruppe fuer Graphische Datenverarbeitung, Wilhelminenstrasse 7, W-6100 Darmstadt, Germany

E. Pelucchi, COSI, Via Varahini 29/3, I-20127 Milano, Italy

M. Planes, INRIA, BP 105, F-78153 Le Chesnay Cedex, France

M. Ramart, Thomson CSF, 160 Bld de Valmy, F-92704 Colombes Cedex, France

M. Re, TECSIEL, Via S. Maria 19, I-56100 Pisa, Italy

P.J. Robinson, ICL, Loverace Road, Bracknell, Berks RG12 4SN, UK

D.C. Sutcliffe, Informatics Department, Rutherford Appleton Laboratory, Chilton, Didcot, Oxon OX11 0QX, UK

P. Tabastot, Thomson CSF, 160 Bld de Valmy, F-92704 Colombes Cedex, France

N. Vezirgiannis, 22 Ypsilantou st., N. Psychiko, GR-15451 Athens, Greece

The following authors were unable to be present at the Workshop.

P. Artico, TECSIEL, Via S. Maria 19, I-56100 Pisa, Italy

C. Blum, Fraunhofer-Arbeitsgruppe fuer Graphische Datenverarbeitung, Wilhelminenstrasse 7, W-6100 Darmstadt, Germany

J. Dyer, Joint Network Team, Rutherford Appleton Laboratory, Chilton, Didcot, Oxon OX11 0QX, UK

C.T. Little, Meterological Office, London Road, Bracknell, Berks, RS12 2SZ, UK

G.J. Reynolds, School of Information Systems, University of East Anglia, Norwich NR4 7TJ, UK

M.G. Schendel, Fraunhofer-Arbeitsgruppe fuer Graphische Datenverarbeitung, Wilhelminenstrasse 7, W-6100 Darmstadt, Germany

EurographicSeminars

Tutorials and Perspectives in Computer Graphics

Eurographics Tutorials '83. Edited by P. J. W. ten Hagen.
XI, 425 pages, 164 figs., 1984

User Interface Management Systems. Edited by G. E. Pfaff.
XII, 224 pages, 65 figs., 1985

Methodology of Window Management. Edited by F. R. A. Hopgood, D. A. Duce, E. V. C. Fielding, K. Robinson, A. S. Williams.
XV, 250 pages, 41 figs., 1985

Data Structures for Raster Graphics. Edited by L. R. A. Kessener, F. J. Peters, M. L.P. van Lierop. VII, 201 pages, 80 figs., 1986

Advances in Computer Graphics I. Edited by G. Enderle, M. Grave, F. Lillehagen.
XII, 512 pages, 168 figs., 1986

Advances in Computer Graphics II. Edited by F. R. A. Hopgood, R. J. Hubbold, D. A. Duce. X, 186 pages, 96 figs., 1986

Advances in Computer Graphics Hardware I. Edited by W. Straßer.
X, 147 pages, 76 figs., 1987

GKS Theory and Practice. Edited by P. R. Bono, I. Herman.
X, 316 pages, 92 figs., 1987

Intelligent CAD Systems I. Theoretical and Methodological Aspects.
Edited by P. J. W. ten Hagen, T. Tomiyama. XIV, 360 pages, 119 figs., 1987

Advances in Computer Graphics III. Edited by M. M. de Ruiter.
IX, 323 pages, 247 figs., 1988

Advances in Computer Graphics Hardware II. Edited by A. A. M. Kuijk, W. Straßer.
VIII, 258 pages, 99 figs., 1988

CGM in the Real World. Edited by A. M. Mumford, M. W. Skall.
VIII, 288 pages, 23 figs., 1988

Intelligent CAD Systems II. Implementational Issues. Edited by V. Akman, P. J. W. ten Hagen, P. J. Veerkamp. X, 324 pages, 114 figs., 1989

Advances in Computer Graphics IV. Edited by W. T. Hewitt, M. Grave, M. Roch.
XVI, 248 pages, 138 figs., 1991

Advances in Computer Graphics V. Edited by W. Purgathofer, J. Schönhut.
VIII, 223 pages, 101 figs., 1989

User Interface Management and Design. Edited by D. A. Duce, M. R. Gomes, F. R. A. Hopgood, J. R. Lee. VIII, 324 pages, 117 figs., 1991

Advances in Computer Graphics Hardware III. Edited by A. A. M. Kuijk. VIII, 214 pages, 88 figs., 1991

Advances in Object-Oriented Graphics I. Edited by E. H. Blake, P. Wisskirchen. X, 218 pages, 74 figs., 1991

Advances in Computer Graphics Hardware IV. Edited by R. L. Grimsdale, W. Straßer. VIII, 276 pages, 124 figs., 1991

Advances in Computer Graphics VI. Synthesis, Analysis and Interaction. Edited by G. Garcia, I. Herman. IX, 449 pages, 186 figs., 1991

Intelligent CAD Systems III. Practical Experience and Evaluation. Edited by P. J. W. ten Hagen, P. J. Veerkamp. X, 270 pages, 116 figs., 1991

Graphics and Communications. Edited by D. B. Arnold et al. VIII, 274 pages, 84 figs., 1991

In preparation:

Photorealism in Computer Graphics. Edited by K. Bouatouch, C. Bouville. Approx. 250 pages, 1991

Advances in Computer Graphics Hardware V. Rendering, Ray Tracing and Visualization Systems. Edited by R. L. Grimsdale, A. Kaufman. Approx. 200 pages, 1991